china
IN THE YEAR
2001

chIna
IN THE YEAR
2001

HAN SUYIN

BASIC BOOKS, INC., PUBLISHERS

New York

Published in Great Britain by
C. A. Watts & Co. Ltd. in "The New Thinker's Library,"
General Editor: Raymond Williams

Library of Congress Catalog Card Number: 67-27150
Printed in the United States of America

PREFACE

THIS book is the result of a decade of visits, eleven in all varying from two weeks to three months, to China, and the collection of data over a wide area in cities and rural districts.

The tremendous pace of change in China, especially since the Cultural Revolution of 1966, tends to leave every study of events out of date. These chapters are meant as an introduction to the non-initiate, as well as a point of reference for those who are interested in Chinese developments, and within this limitation may be of some usefulness.

A good many studies made abroad have suffered from the fact that standards of measurement and deductive logic derived from Western and Russian developments have been applied to the Chinese progress, and perhaps these premises should be questioned more thoroughly than they have been so far.

Since the writer is not a Marxist, the interpretation of some events, and their motivation, the attempt to explain the Chinese way of grappling with their own situation and problems, may be faulted by a theoretician. In view of the fact that the Chinese point of view has so far been refused its proper validity, though it is the most essential element in the present situation in China, and also in the world at large, a book which tries to fill this gap may prove to stimulate more thought on the subject by those who are interested in present-day developments.

March, 1967   HAN SUYIN

ACKNOWLEDGEMENTS

My profound gratitude goes to respected personalities and friends in the People's Republic of China for granting me interviews and arranging visits which permitted me to collect the material present in this book.

I am also indebted to friends in Hong Kong and in other places for reading the material and making suggestions of great value.

Care has been taken to collate and evaluate only the essential features, disregarding the temporary and the detail; the encouragement of such friends as were good enough to interest themselves in this work is most appreciated, as has been their criticism. But it must be emphasized that the interpretation is the author's, and does not reflect the views or opinions of anyone else.

CONTENTS

There's no Jade Emperor in heaven,
No Dragon King on earth.
I am the Jade Emperor,
I am the Dragon King.
I order the three mountains and five peaks:
"Make way! Here I come!"

(Popular song in 1958)

as in
    A. L. STRONG *The Rise of the Chinese Peoples' Communes—and Six Years After*

Peking   New World Press, 1964

china

IN THE YEAR

2001

I

PERSPECTIVES FROM THE PAST, OR HISTORY REAPPRAISED

"But China obscures" you say, I reply: "China obscures, but there is clearness to be found; look for it."

PASCAL, *Pensées*

"WHERE China is concerned", writes Dick Wilson,[1] "we have in the past, formed the habit of ignoring her, ignoring what she really thought and felt. We preferred our own build-up, our own fanciful images."

Only twenty years ago, as anyone who lived in China may remember, many assumptions, redolent of racial superiority, were current about the Chinese people. That they were effeminate, cowardly, superstitious, incapable of organization, corrupt and untrustworthy was accepted as fact. Today "the Chinese have changed" and the change shocks, because it was unexpected. Nations and classes, which for a time have lorded it over others, come to accept their superiority as natural and feel threatened when the cycle of change overtakes them, and overthrows their domination. Yet the mischief of history, as it is taught today in the West, is that it was written yesterday, in the full flush of nineteenth-century Europocentrism; that the changes which have occurred since have therefore been obscured by an overlay of past attitudes; and that the young, in school, are moulded to a world which has stopped existing.

China's emergence and her importance in the world,

[1] DICK WILSON, *A Quarter of Mankind* (Weidenfeld & Nicolson, London, 1966).

I

influence the immediate future and preoccupy every government; but they are still regarded as something untoward, therefore frightening, to be exorcised or pulverized out of existence.

During the last two decades China has not ceased to prove every pronouncement, uttered about her, false; the pace of her development, the rapidity of her growth, outdate any book written about her. "To know China, one must first recognize her", says Robert Guillain,[1] an aphorism which applies not only to diplomatic recognition of China as a full sovereign power to be treated as an equal, but which should bear the added connotation of recognizing a Chinese point of view, world outlook, ethos, policy, international role, uncluttered by traditional concepts. For China comprises a fourth of mankind, an educated, knowledgeable, highly aware quarter, with a great and fervent Marxist faith, an intense consciousness of its responsibility towards humanity. The rediscovery of China by the West is of paramount importance; for as we accord respect to the pronouncements and views of the governments of the United States, Russia, France or England, in the same way we shall have to learn to listen to what the Chinese say, without automatically discounting, warping or insulting their statements, or ascribing their desire to be heard to imperial arrogance. The complaint that China "cannot be understood", that it is her complexity, her self-imposed isolation, which stand in the way, must be denounced, for it is not her doing but the wilful refusal of the West to accept her as she is, which obscures our understanding. China is not isolated, except by the exertions of others to isolate her; and there is nothing complex about her, which cannot also be ascribed to many another nation; but there are many built-in, conditioned complexes in those who slander her, which must be overcome.

Today, seventeen years after the Revolution of 1949,

[1] ROBERT GUILLAIN, *Dans Trente Ans la Chine* (Gallimard, 1965).

China is kept out of the United Nations; her territory of Formosa is still the seat of the ousted Chiang Kai-shek, and a base of the USA; an outspoken policy of containment against her is the declared aim of both the USA and her ally Great Britain. No self-respecting nation could accept this treatment as "normal". Yet China is expected to accept it, and her protests are regarded as "arrogance". The USA does its best to isolate China, and then maintains that China "is isolated". It is hard to visualize *any* government so unfairly treated not voicing its sense of injustice.

Past depredations have conditioned many in the West to consider China as "object", the passive, natural recipient of the actions of Western powers, and like all victims, unable to decide for herself. Like all colonies, her revolts against foreign oppression were treated as "rebellion" against a God-made order.

This "object" has now changed into an active, independent Great Power; yet the study of China continues to be directed by the interests of Western powers in Asia, with the ultimate aim of justifying these interests—past or present—rather than to be undertaken from the standpoint of the Chinese nation, its emergence into the modern age, and its own interests and values.

When the fixed pattern of political forces, *as accepted*, is challenged by new, rising political forces, in other areas of the world, there is a lag in understanding and in bridging the transition period between one epoch and another. This lag leads to a perpetuation (often disastrous) of ideas and reflexes, a hankering for a return to *status quo ante*, already illusory but which we have been conditioned to expect as the "normal" state of things. In the case of China, this lag is reinforced by an unwillingness to accept the evidence of today's reality. For that evidence would destroy the easy assumption that the West still has a right to interfere, either in the name of balance of power, or containment of communism, in an Asia where the liberation of China by her own forces marks the real end of colonialism. Instead, courses of action are chosen, such as the "containment" of China, which are only an attempt to reinstate a world order already doomed when policies concerning China were made in London or Washington, and Western military and financial domination on the Asian mainland was regarded as a natural state of affairs.

Fifty years ago, even twenty years ago, Asian destinies were decided in Europe, in the USA. Today, the emergence of China, and, because of that emergence, the increasing momentum of change in India, Indonesia, Africa, Latin America (areas of the world where wants and needs become more vast and the clamour of revolt more strident by the hour) mark this epoch as that of a universal upheaval—the epoch of world revolution. With the development of China, the first non-white power to grow strong on her own resources and through her own efforts, and today the self-proclaimed vanguard and leader of revolutionary change, a new pattern is reshaping the world, as old alliances, commitments and ruling powers decline and disintegrate. Not recognizing the pace and scope of this change will not prevent the future from coming into being; but will only keep the many deluded a little longer, sleep-walkers pacing the corridors of yesterday's dreams.

In the nineteenth century missionaries, traders and civil servants wrote "histories" of China and thus became scholars in an age when the exotic was prized and the wars of colonial conquest extolled as crusades of enlightenment. China attracted them, as did the dead civilizations of Egypt or Assyria; their studies sought to perpetuate in translation her classic traditions, but they were not interested in the changes in which she travailed, nor could they perceive the profound transformation which their nations' misdemeanours would make upon her. The wars of aggression, the opium traffic,

gunboat diplomacy, the unequal treaties and the heavy
indemnities which ruined China were then transmogrified
into a civilizing mission.

When the Communist Revolution of 1949 (called Liberation in China) achieved its headlong triumph, the shock
to a world of historians was considerable, for the downfall
of Chiang Kai-shek came very swiftly, much more swiftly
than expected by US military men.[1] Transformation began
at such a swift pace that the old formulas and assumptions
about Chinese tradition, character, culture, backwardness,
lack of organization, etc., had to be jettisoned one by one.
This sudden rending of the fabrications of history stimulated
a spate of books, essentially justificatory, attempting to explain
the "failure" of the West—and by that time the West was
synonymous with the United States of America—in China.
For the last seventeen years an avalanche of such studies, which
provide much data, even if their evaluation is based on wishful
thinking rather than on percipient observation, has poured
from universities and study centres. However, in the hectic
speed of advance which is the characteristic of Chinese
progress, most of these short-range works have either become
outdated or been replaced by equally authoritative works in
flat contradiction to their arguments. The basic flaw in most
of these studies is a preoccupation with *immobility* in China
as the ideal they seek, rather than a realistic appraisal of the
accelerated advance which China is achieving.

The main trend of world events is in the opposite direction
to the ambitions of domination of Asia by the West. A new
pattern is taking shape, whose most conspicuous trait is the
new prominence of socialist China, unmistakably advancing
towards the status of a world power.[2]

[1] GENERAL G. MARSHALL's report: *U.S. Relation with China*, p. 383.
[2] G. BARRACLOUGH, *Introduction to Contemporary History* (London, C. A.
Watts & Co. Ltd. 1964, 1966).

We must consider how much Western reactions to China's reality are still conditioned by the premise that a "vacuum of power" exists wherever a corner of the globe is not occupied by a Western presence, for it is this assumption, namely that such a presence outside the boundaries of Europe or the USA is the *normal* feature of a normal world, that is abnormal.

Among the subjects never taught adequately to a colonized people is its own history. In many "independent" African countries today, culture still begins with Europe's entry into Africa.[1] Chinese intellectuals escaped total mental subservience because of their own long, and resistant, tradition of written history, the most extensive and the oldest in the world. History, in the Chinese sense, has always implied *continuity* rather than merely a study of bygone days; past, present and future form a single time entity, and this notion of historical time as a human dimension is fundamental to the Chinese cultural concept. This view of time, as an ingredient of human history, affects decision making; it promotes today, in the era of Mao Tse-tung, the same sense of the continuity of the process of revolution through the education of generations to come, as it promoted in the days of the great philosophers (500 B.C.) the sense of ethical continuity. The Cultural Revolution of 1966 which is directed towards the next generations, is in this historical tradition. The accumulation of revolutionary knowledge, through decades of fighting, the Red bases, the Sino-Japanese War, the application of Marxist theory and concrete practice to the Chinese revolution, can be studied by all the peoples who want to liberate themselves. It is in

[1] Though many new States are trying to reinterpret their own history in their search for a past which will re-identify them with their national ethos. Author.

this sense that the revolution of China, as lived and fought in the last fifty years, forms the groundwork of historical experience, which can now be passed on to others as guiding principles to their own revolution-making, and today makes the history of China an integral part of world history.

Since 1949 new perspectives for the study of history in China have unfolded. Thousands of institutes, at all levels, have been organized, to collect, assess and undertake research into historical problems. Publications concerning many events of the nineteenth century, the Taiping, the Niens, the Boxers, the reformers of 1898, the revolution of 1911, have been accepted by conscientious scholars everywhere. History museums have been erected in every main and provincial city; local as well as provincial chronicles have been studied and reprinted. To fill the gap of the turbulent pre-liberation years, 1919 to 1949, a nation-wide collection of personal memoirs is being made; the collection now runs into millions, an immense primary source of historical data.

The study of historical development is no longer the prerogative of scholarly authorities, but a conscious function of the entire Chinese people;[1] by making the people aware that they are intimately involved in this vast historical process, that they can even create and guide it, the Chinese Communist Party seeks to abolish the lag in understanding which, because of the pace of material change, leaves the mind, attitude and behaviour still fettered to a previous epoch. To create understanding of the historical forces at work in the world, is in itself to accelerate historical processes, since the mental reluctance to change is diminished. "History is all inclusive. The development of social productive forces, class struggle, oppression by the rulers and resistance by the masses of the

[1] Almost the whole population of China able to read is reading Mao Tse-tung's works, which consist of a series of documents of historical importance, covering the last forty years of revolution.

people—all are closely interwoven.... The masses will ... master their own historical destiny."[1]

The very study of history thus becomes a force shaping the future; arousing a greater awareness of events, "to help people to free themselves from mental enslavement, to emancipate their minds".

It is this role of history-study as history-maker, actively involving every single person within the perspective of his time, either as critic of the past or creator of the future, which is in action today in China, where "700 million critics, 700 million statesmen, 700 million students of the thought of Mao Tse-tung" are being trained to see themselves in the historical forces and to participate in them, to hasten the process taking place. In this conscious push to the wheel of time, the legend of a world forever dominated by a superior Western "civilization", the notions of inferiority and servility inculcated by the technical achievements of the West, are more than challenged, they are actively attacked. Mao proclaims "The East Wind vanquishes the West Wind" and "Imperialism is a paper tiger", indicating how America's renewed attempts to dominate the Asian continent are doomed, even in the matter of holding on to a few comparatively minor enclaves upon the ocean shores of Asia.

The history of Asia must be reappraised and events re-interpreted by Asians themselves within the context of their own independence movements. The record of colonial exploitation, as well as the present reiterated attempt at domination by military means, must be seen in its proper sequence. The great waves of resistance to colonialism, which turned Asia in the nineteenth century into the most intensive battlefield ever known, must be studied anew, especially the pattern of peasant uprisings.

[1] *Peking Review*, 5th November, 1965, "How to Appraise the History of Asia".

In the middle of the nineteenth century peasant uprisings all over Asia had an interlinked effect, coalescing in their timing. The Taiping and Nien in China (1851–67), the Indian uprisings (1857–9), Persia (1844–52) formed one "wave" of revolt; at the end of the nineteenth century a second upsurge of such "national-liberation struggles" took place, in Persia (1890–1), in Assam and Manipur (1891), Tilak in India (1895–7), in Vietnam (1891–8), in Korea (1893–5), in Turkey and the Philippines (1896–8), and in China (1899–1900[1]). The abortive Russian Revolution of 1905 was followed by a third series of Asian revolts: in China the 1911 bourgeois-democratic Revolution of Sun Yat-sen, the All-India National Congress (1905–8), Persia (1905–11), Turkey (1908–9). The October Revolution in Russia of 1917 heralded yet another series of upsurges: in China (1925–7), in Europe, in Vietnam, in India. The triumph of the Communist Revolution in China, in 1949, occurred in the midst of another such series of risings, in Malaya, Burma, Indonesia, Vietnam, the Philippines, Africa. At no time since 1945 has the world been free from war, unrest and upsurges, and these have increased. Today Asia has become a focal point of revolutionary change in the world, the acuteness of the crises between the old order of exploitation and the new national movements being concentrated in Vietnam; tomorrow in India, in Indonesia, in the Philippines, renewed or greater, even more violent upheavals are in the offing; and though revolutionary parties may be defeated, yet the world upheaval goes on; the bush fires are never really extinguished. China, having completed her own revolution, is now consciously entering the arena as the vanguard and guide of all the revolutionary movements in the despised two-thirds of the world, the so-called "undeveloped" Africa, Latin America and the rest of Asia.

[1] The Righteous First Uprising, also known as the Boxers.

The national-liberation movements of the first half of the twentieth century coincided with another force, the socialist revolution, which began with the October Revolution of 1917 in Russia. These two forces, nationalist and socialist-communist, form the major historical currents of the present-day world, dominating, either in conjunction or with a gap in time, the historical processes in each country. A bourgeois-democratic revolution, giving rise to a capitalist structure, is simply not possible in the "undeveloped" countries today. According to Mao Tse-tung, the formidable monopoly capital strength of Western imperialism will never brook any serious competition from a strong capitalist power in Asia or in Africa; it will subjugate, sabotage, or buy off any independent capitalism in any other country, as it did in China. Inevitably, therefore, the struggle for independence (which means political and economic independence) can only be achieved through a socialist structure, or else it becomes a sham, undermined by continuing economic and cultural slavery under cover of a nominal independence— a state of affairs prevalent among many so-called independent States today.

China's accumulation of experience in the various stages of combat for national liberation and for the construction of a socialist State now forms a body of knowledge at the disposal of all revolutionary parties in the world, as a guide to action. This body of experience is called the "summit of Marxism-Leninism in our time", or "the thought of Mao Tse-tung". According to the Chinese appraisal of the historical situation, the next thirty years will see an increase in number, depth and amplitude of armed uprisings, for these are inevitable as hunger, poverty, and exploitation continue to increase the seed-beds of revolt; China's experience, positive moral support, and the assistance she can render to such movements will help to shorten the period of struggle and diminish the losses.[1] China herself expects the continual and incessant *cordon sanitaire* of threat and provocation of the last seventeen years, culminating in the American presence in Vietnam, on her doorstep, with half a million troops and an armada out of proportion to local requirements, to be the prelude to an attack upon herself. She has accepted the challenge.

It is precisely this Great Revolt of the Third World, which the focusing of land, sea and air forces of the USA upon Asia and the destruction wrought by these weapons in selected areas such as Vietnam are designed to dissuade. Military measures are accompanied by promises that once "peace" is restored and "communism" destroyed or checked, a new era of plenty and happiness will dawn for the hungry millions of Asia. But few in Asia still believe these specious promises; the example of India, the largest "aid-receiver" in the world, is too stark. The humiliations endured by Asians seeking better terms of trade or aid are bitter; and though the ruling *élites* are servile, their own peoples are becoming more violent. The outcome will be decided, say the Chinese, not by the massive accumulation of weapons, however genocidal, but by the local and historical consciousness of the masses, the peoples involved and determined to resist with violence, to defend themselves with weapons in hand in an implacable contest.

In such a struggle, a politically conscious, educated people, led by a dedicated, revolutionary party will win in the end; for *ideas* and *men* are stronger than weapons, however

[1] But "revolution cannot be exported nor imported". Each nation or country must work its own way and fight its own liberation, relying on its own people. This very clear distinction, with the proviso that China will never send soldiers beyond her borders to fight someone else's revolution, has been repeated often by Peking. (*See* LIN PIAO's article: "Long Live the Victory of Peoples War!" 3rd September, 1965.)

fearsome. This is the essence of the Chinese view on the historical processes in the next decades.

The awakening and arousing of the Asian masses to their historic role, to their responsibility, the recognition of their right to become masters of their own future, assume imperative significance in this contest. A new and unsurvey-able phase of world history (to paraphrase Barraclough), is beginning. China's power, her people, her social system and her historical perspective, are bound to play a very important role, in the shaping of this phase.

The Feudal Past and its Peasant Uprisings

An essential element in Chinese history, is the role of peasant uprisings, similar to those of medieval Europe. Agricultural masses eking out a subsistence with inefficient tools, living under antiquated exploitation systems, continue in India, Indonesia, South Vietnam, Iran, and Latin America. In China a similar state of affairs lasted 2,500 years until 1949. Even today, its emotional fetters and thought processes are still in evidence, though the actual system has gone. The same kind of exploitation is the basis of India's stagnant rural economy, and its consequent famines; it is the cause of re-peated Huk uprisings in the Philippines. The Chinese call this system Feng Chien, or feudalism. Some historians reserve the word "feudal" for the period 841 B.C.–221 B.C., and speak of "the disappearance of feudalism" with the unification of the Chinese State (Han dynasty, third century B.C.). But if we define the feudal system by its modes of production and their relationships, as Marxist historians do, whether an aristocracy or another class wields authority, we must agree that eighty-five per cent of an agricultural population, living under a system of land tenure, land rent and corvée, essentially the same as that of the feudal ages of Europe, does constitute feudalism.

Dr. C. P. Fitzgerald[1] writes that the "feudal aristocracy had been destroyed in the third century, but they *transmitted their ideals and political outlook* to a new class, the scholars and officials, i.e. the administrative bureaucracy of the centralized empire". Ownership of agricultural production by an *aristocratic* hereditary nobility was superseded by a landlord class, out of which grew an aristocracy by education, a *literocracy*, which manned the administrative services of the Chinese Empire.

The significance of this long tenure of power by the Divine Right of Education is that today in China, in spite of a communist revolution, in spite of seventeen years of socialized education, one can still find attempts at the resurgence (even if disguised by Marxist labels) of a feudal bureaucratism, so deeply entrenched in the mind, habits and tradition of a whole nation that it seems at times almost inexpugnable. Its roots are in the very language, the ideograms (many of which are based on feudal concepts) the system of education, the (still very active) notions of "face" and many other attitudes. Two millennia of government by the Divine Right of Reading are not easily abolished in less than two decades; the Cultural Revolution of 1966 is attempting once more to uproot the strong deep stalks of this oligarchic mentality, for unless it is uprooted feudal processes of thought and affects will remain.

Landowner families produced the bulk of the literocracy, the civil servant class. This class had many privileges. No "scholar" could be forced to do manual labour, nor beaten; contempt for manual labour was a natural concomitant of being educated. This alone, it seems, would be an inhibiting factor, precluding the rise of scientific experimentation, which requires manual manipulation, in China.

While China was evolving this feudal bureaucracy, Greece

[1] *See* Bibliography.

had built its restricted "democracy" on extensive helotism: the Roman Empire operated slavery as its social system, we might also recall, to get our time scale in perspective, the resurgence of slavery as a source of profit after the sixteenth century, when nascent European capitalism accumulated wealth from the importation into America of African slaves. The American Southern States were slave States on the Roman model and remained so until past the middle of the nineteenth century.

The Chinese peasant was not a slave, but there were many aspects of serfdom in his condition. The right of corvée (unpaid labour for landlord or for the State) was practised in Szechuan province as late as 1948. Exorbitant land rent in kind (up to fifty to seventy per cent of the crop in certain areas) was the instrument by which the exploitation of the peasantry was continuous. Since rent was paid in *kind* throughout the period of bureaucratic feudalism (2,500 years), little money circulated among the peasantry; commerce and exchange of goods were stunted by the smallness of the monetarized economy. Landowners maintained private armed bands and employed physical violence towards refractory peasants. In decades of prosperity a tendency to the expansion of city handicrafts and trade, leading to guilds, larger workshops, intensified commerce and capital accumulation, was manifested. This might have given rise to a mercantile, capitalist bourgeoisie; but the administrative bureaucracy, based on the landowning class, and the State power were averse to the growth of such a powerful class in the cities; strict control of industry and commerce, government monopoly of essential goods, a bureaucratic rigidity, reinforced by a Confucian moralist outlook in a non-competitive society, contributed to fetter nascent capitalism. The stability of this system was ensured by the large and fertile land base, sound irrigation works and agricultural surpluses, dispite the uneconomic means of production; however, in times of mis-management, drought or floods, this self-sufficient economy broke down.

Vast peasant uprisings, of which eighteen large and several hundred small ones are recorded, occurred during those two millennia. No Renaissance took place as in England or France, where the capital accumulation of the mercantile middle classes in the cities allowed them to destroy or neutralize the feudal kingly power, and replace it with their own bourgeois democracy. When capitalism came to China, it was foreign capitalism, not Chinese.

The long tenure of a codified system of administration achieved cultural cohesion; the stability of the twin, anti-thetic classes, the peasantry, the landlord bureaucrat, seemed perpetually renewed. Cultural unity was achieved by the ideogram; the recruitment of scholars for the administration drained talent out of any other form of endeavour and in-hibited innovation and experimentation. The central power early recognized the importance of economic as well as cultural unification, and achieved it by State control of com-munications, salt and iron: salt essential to life, iron for tools and military weapons.

Control of iron tools enabled irrigation and transport canals to be cut, and manpower to be mobilized on a national scale for such projects; China acquired a system of inland communi-cation by water, as well as roads; key economic areas were thus linked to sustain strategic zones of political power and defence.

The mobilization of millions of peasants for vast public works—the Grand Canal, Great Wall—left in China a tradition of collective work among the peasantry. Millions of hands, millions of baskets, millions of peasants building dams, canals and dykes, terracing mountains and detouring rivers is the labour-intensive way to prosperity in countries deprived of machinery; the new aspirations integrate well today with this collective tradition of labour.

The earliest documented peasant uprising in China occurred in 209 B.C.; the last (before the contemporary epoch) were the enormous Taiping and Nien uprisings of the nineteenth century. The Communist Revolution itself has its roots in the agrarian revolts of the Taiping, and the first revolution, of 1925–7, was spoken of as the Great or the Agrarian Revolution. The first uprising Mao Tse-tung led in person as a military commander was the Autumn Harvest Peasant Uprising in 1927.[1] Mao Tse-tung affirms that these peasant uprisings were the motivating force of historical development and that this holds true today, for the world revolution in the making will be made by "the peasantry" of the "undeveloped" world of Asia, Africa, and Latin America against the "cities" or affluent metropolises of the West.

The literocracy was sensitive to peasant revolts, analysed its causes and sought to prevent, by judicious reformist concessions, the downfall of existing imperial houses. Remission of taxes, pardons from corvée, land-reform enactments were urged by the magistrate-scholars to placate the peasantry. Land rent, in particular, was reduced in time of drought or flood on the advice of "good officials". But these palliatives did not correct the fundamental abuses of the landowning class, the stunting oppression of the feudal system. "In A.D. 17 a year of terrible drought, two peasants, Wang Kuang and Wang Feng, set up an army and attacked the landlord estates; in A.D. 184, a massive peasant uprising called the Yellow Turbans shook the Eastern Han régime, and it fell." Thus write the chronicles. In A.D. 617 peasant revolts broke out under the emperor Yang Ti because he "forced the people to build many giant projects". These

---

[1] Previous to that Mao had led strikes among the Anyuen coal miners.

works took away millions of labour hands from agriculture during harvest time, "even women were conscripted". Taxes were collected ten years ahead, a custom repeated by militarists up to 1949, when in Szechuan province taxes were levied from the peasantry seventy years in advance.

The Tang dynasty consolidated bureaucratic feudalism; recruitment for the government administrative service by official recommendation as under the Hans was abolished and replaced by competitive examinations.[1] Theoretically, almost anyone, son of emperor or son of peasant (with the exception of actors, prostitutes and boatmen) could become officials, but in practice only the sons of the wealthy could indulge in the long classical studies needed for the final degrees. With practically no change at all, this competitive examination, with its various grades, rituals, solemnities, the classic themes set, the style of writing imposed, continued till 1901; and the state of mind this system developed and the ruling class complex it created have endured until today. This explains the suspicion of the intellectual, and especially of the classical scholar, entertained by the Chinese Communist Party. "All intellectuals want to become officials with power and influence and an easy life" said one of them to me. It is only in 1966 that the system of competitive examinations has been abolished at last, after a long 1,332 years.[2]

After the occupation of China by the Mongol (Yuan dynasty) agriculture was reduced by the conversion of hundreds of thousands of cultivated hectares in North China into horse pastures, and the eviction of millions of peasants.

[1] First used actually, in the preceding Sui dynasty, but systematized under the Tangs.

[2] Actually the imperial examinations were suspended in 1901, after the Boxer uprising, by order of the European powers; this facilitated the entry of Western learning into China. The new Chinese universities created thereafter followed a system of examination for degrees, copied from the Western model.

This has contributed to an increasing dust bowl and desert formation in the North-West and all along the upper reaches of the Yellow River, threatening to turn this whole area into a sandy waste before the year 2000. By A.D. 1368 the Mongol power was shattered by vast popular resistance movements; a poor peasant monk became the founder of the great Ming dynasty. He encouraged the peasants to return to their homes and to reclaim waste land; he exempted them from taxation or service for some years, constructed water-conservancy works and reduced corvée labour to twenty days.

There followed seventy years of peace; the nomadic central Asian hordes appeared exhausted. The fourteenth century saw Europe in the turbulence of the Renaissance; in both China and Europe it was an era of sea voyages and exploration, for the Ming empire was far more sea-oriented than its predecessors. The Renaissance in Europe brought the liberation of scientific ideas, the end of feudalism; capitalism began its accumulation of wealth; the Spaniards erected an overseas empire on the slaughter and enslavement of the populations of Mexico. In China encyclopedic compilations were undertaken by the scholars, there was a great expansion of handicrafts and even of commerce and foreign trade, chiefly through Canton. Voyages were made to Indonesia, Malaya, India and Africa. The acreage under crops was increased and, thereby, agricultural output. But once again landlordism, ever rapacious, produced intense land concentration. Corvée increased to seventy-five and ninety days a year; landless tenants increased in number and peasant uprisings broke out, "unparalleled in magnitude in Chinese history".

The weakening of the power structure brought the inevitable invaders from outside, this time the Manchus, who crushed the peasant revolts and the battling cities with terrible slaughter. The struggle against the Manchus, continued for over forty years, led to wholesale depopulation in certain areas. Secret resistance movements, a peasant underground with strong Taoist overtones, were to promote more revolts; but the bureaucratic *élite* surrendered quickly and now served the Manchu emperor who had been satisfactorily civilized and wrote most elegant calligraphy.

The Manchus began with a policy of conciliation of the peasantry. Unpaid labour (corvée) for the State was reduced to twenty-five days (increased later), irregular taxes were abolished (reinstalled after 1800), and internal migration of peasants to sparsely populated areas was encouraged. But the landlords' exploitation of the peasant continued, keeping the latter's purchasing power at very low level. Usury became prevalent, interest being at sixty to one hundred per cent a year. Taxation fell heavily on industry and commerce, and restricted handicraft expansion. Trade was impeded. China remained cramped within the medieval framework, both mental and physical, its ruling bureaucratic-landlord-official class petrified, its examination system based on the "imperishable classics" of 500 B.C. more and more inadequate to promote independent original thinking. The sea-orientated dynasty of the Ming had given place to the sea-fearing Manchus. It became a capital offence for a Chinese to leave the country; exploration was ended, another avenue of experience closed. Meanwhile industrial Europe's capitalist enterprise roamed the world for markets. The peasant question ceased to dominate the European social context, as masses of them were forced into the new factories for wage labour. The manufactured goods from these factories needed export markets; military domination of areas with rich resources and cheap labour, colonial conquest, the partition of Africa and Asia, the slave trade, augmented the capital accumulation upon which Europe and the United States founded their modern imperialist affluence. It denuded and impoverished Asia and Africa, and slaughtered whole populations in America.

The economic, political, social and spiritual consequences of imperialist exploitation in China, from 1840 to 1949, form part of the accumulation of anguish which is ours today, as we reap the results of these historical actions and perceive their true implications. Present-day China is a product, not only of her own long feudalism, but also of the last one hundred and twenty-five years of bitter struggle against occidental exploitation. On the Chinese time scale, events from 1840 to 1965 are recent, history is measured by its distance from colonialism to national independence, rather than by the actual run of the years. In 1949 over a century of bitter servitude, misery and exploitation came to an end.

China today, therefore, is only seventeen years away from feudalism and from colonialism.

Again to get our time scale right, let us remember that until the first half of the nineteenth century came to an end land rent was the largest source of net income in many European states. In southern Italy and Sicily, as in Latin America, a feudal system of land tenure is still in operation today. In the United States, the abolition of slavery only dates back one century, and its residual problems, racial and economic discrimination, are not solved. Slavery persisted in the Western world, sanctioned as "normal and humane", into the nineteenth century. It is only two centuries ago that Europe made her great leap forward in scientific knowledge and achieved her industrial revolution, only one hundred years ago that industrialization on a mass scale began.

America exploded her first nuclear device in 1945, Russia in 1948 and China in 1964.

The Acceleration of History: 1840–1949

The period 1840–1949 is characterized by repetitive violence, practised either singly or collectively by the European nations, the USA, and an Asian capitalist power, Japan, upon China. To these one hundred and nine years belong the burden of unequal treaties, extra-territorial rights, war indemnities, the concessions, occupation by foreign troops, massacres, and the sacking of Chinese cities. All this would have truly become "the past", but that *the attitudes engendered then are perpetuated today*.

The "historic past" is still, therefore, very much persistent in present-day China. Only her own increasing power and strength can safeguard her.

The dual impact of Western aggression and internal disintegration due to the corruption and inefficiency of the Manchus wrecked the Chinese economy. The destruction of the economic basis of feudalism, the peasant economy, created both a commodity and a labour market, and opened the possibility for the development of capitalism in China. But this could not develop for in possession was another, far stronger capitalism. Mao Tse-tung writes: "The establishment in China of a capitalist society, under bourgeois dictatorship, will in the first place *not be permitted* by international capitalism, that is, imperialism. The whole history of modern China is indeed the history of imperialist aggression upon China, of imperialist *opposition* to China's independence and *to her development of capitalism*."

Precisely because Western monopoly capitalism was exporting capital to dominated areas in order to profit from their cheap labour and raw materials, and feared the rise of rival Asian industrial powers, and had overwhelming superiority in controlling outlets for export, all native Chinese attempts at capitalist development and industrialization met

with controlled obstruction. A rudimentary capitalist class
did emerge, an offshoot of the landlord bureaucrats and
the traders; the first industrialists of China were provincial
governors and imperial ministers. They were allowed to
form companies, which ostensibly promoted native industries,
but were dependent upon Western machinery, spare parts,
technical advice, and inevitably dependent upon large foreign
monopolies; they then performed the role of middlemen,
facilitating the further exploitation (by foreign monopolies[1])
of large areas which otherwise could not have been reached.
No massive industrialization with a powerful, independent
bourgeoisie was possible. No protection of native goods
within the internal market was allowed. Financial control
by Western capitalism of the customs, the tariffs upon
imports, the import-export trade, and communications, was
imposed; the revenue of customs and railways was earmarked
to pay for war indemnities and loans, payment which
obliged the Chinese government to resort to self-mutilating
taxation such as the *likin* (or internal transport tax) which
worked to the disadvantage of native goods, restricted commercial transport within the provinces, and drove provincial,
native capitalist enterprises to bankruptcy. Foreign industries
were installed in the seaboard and city concessions, in
Shanghai, Tientsin, Hankow, and whatever Chinese capital
was available gravitated there; thus a comprador-middleman
class was produced, adjunct to and dependent on Western
capitalist enterprise in China.

The Revolution of 1911, which overthrew the Manchu
régime, could have brought into power a national capitalist
class, however weak; for it was essentially a "bourgeois

[1] The same phenomenon occurs today in other areas of the world (*see*
Chase Manhattan Bank Report 4th November, 1966); national capitalist
industries are destroyed or absorbed by giant foreign monopolies, and end up
by serving as their subsidiaries.

democratic revolution", promoted by bourgeois elements who backed Dr. Sun Yat-sen. But it failed, because of their weakness, because the Western powers bolstered the feudal forces with arms and money; and went on backing them. The weak national capitalist class did not control armed power; it was, in the hands of military satraps, essentially feudal; it could not rally the peasantry or the very small proletariat—the workers in the foreign industrial concerns. The rise of a new kind of intellectual, influenced by Japan's nationalism, created intellectual discontent, which could not find an outlet. Sun Yat-sen, until 1919, seems to have believed in Western-type democracy; but the betrayal of the Versailles Conference convinced him, as it did tens of thousands of Chinese intellectuals, that talk of liberty, self-determination, and the rights of nations, was only a sinister farce. "No sun rises in the West for China."

The First World War of 1914–18 provided for China a temporary relaxation from the economic and political strangleholds she suffered. As the European powers, engaged in mutual massive slaughter, withdrew from China, national industrial enterprise increased; machinery was bought from the USA; China exported wheat, flour and cotton yarn and cloth; cessation of the export of commodities from the West to the Chinese market reflected itself in the rise of provincial industrial commodities and the balance of payments, permanently at a deficit, showed a decisive upturn. But this temporary retreat of Western capitalism provided Japan with an opportunity to increase her own economic invasion of China. In 1915 she presented the then Chinese government with a virtual ultimatum, known as the Twenty-one Demands, so as to secure China as her sole colony. Western Europe, suffering from a manpower shortage, asked for China's participation in the war and in 1917, 200,000 Chinese workers and students were recruited to man public utilities in France, the USA and other countries. China's entry into the war was due to persuasion from the United States, who had promised to use her good offices, at the Peace Conference, in order to revise the unequal treaties.

But in October 1917 the Communist Revolution in Russia took place; Russia withdrew from the war and in a moment the "balance of power" was upset. America now felt it imperative to utilize Japan against the newborn Soviet State, which threatened her interests in Asia. In November 1917, the USA made a secret agreement (Lansing-Ishii)[1] with Japan, under which Japan's special interests in Shantung province and special rights in Manchuria were recognized in exchange for Japan's participation in an invasion of Siberia.

At the Peace Conference of Versailles in 1919, the Japanese delegate could boast that no less than six such secret agreements, with six Western powers, had been concluded at China's expense.

The outcome of this betrayal, was the 4th May, 1919, demonstrations.[2] The May 4th Movement, as it is called, is a decisive date in China's history; from that date to 1949, history is in one piece; three decades form one single, solid whole; that of the rise of communism in China, the overthrow of the forces which, like "three large mountains", sat on the back of the Chinese people, feudalism, Western imperialism and the Kuomintang government. The three were linked and interrelated; they were overthrown together in 1949 by the triumph of the communist armies under Mao Tse-tung.

"The period [1912 to 1923]", says Fairbank, "has been difficult to study. Historians have sadly neglected it . . . it should appear in time to have been one of the great germinal

[1] A photograph of this document was taken by Eugène Chen and exhibited to several US Congressmen at the time as evidence of Woodrow Wilson's double-crossing.
[2] See Bibliography.

periods in the realms of Chinese thought. . . ." May 4th, 1919, is today regarded as the direct predecessor of the Great Cultural Socialist Revolution of 1966–7, in the same way as the Taiping peasant uprising is regarded as precursor of the communist agrarian revolutions of the 1920s to 1940s.

Beginning with a student demonstration of three thousand, the May 4th Movement unfolded across China; two hundred cities and towns demonstrated for the next eighteen months with marches, strikes and hartals, involving twenty million students, professors, workers, shopkeepers and merchants. Described as sporadic "rioting"[1] by Western newspapers, the movement was, as Mao Tse-tung was to analyse it, a leap in cognition, a *crise de conscience*, unprecedented in its fertilizing and sensitivizing effect. It sowed in the minds of millions of young Chinese the seeds of greatly heightened political consciousness—including in Mao himself. Mao Tse-tung was to notice as the special characteristics of this movement (*a*) that the strikes which it engendered were purely political: *no* demand for wages or benefits was made by the workers, which denoted a high level of political consciousness; (*b*) that shopkeepers, merchants, and small national capitalists contributed money, and also demonstrated together with workers, thus forming a *united front*, a multi-class movement; (*c*) that the closure of shops, public utilities, such as bus lines, telephone and telegraph companies, railroads, steam navigation; the strike in printing, paper milling and factories; the work stoppages of painters, carpenters, masons, drivers and scavengers, none of whom made any economic claims for their own betterment, were nation-wide and spontaneous, demonstrating a tremendous capacity for *mass action*.

It is from this manifestation, later reinforced by the mass action of the peasantry during the 1925–7 Agrarian Revolution, that Mao's understanding of the "mass line", his trust

[1] See PUTNAM WEALE, *Japan and China; Why China Sees Red.*

and confidence in the masses, basic to his thinking and actions, proceeds.

Not only Mao Tse-tung, a young student then, but many thousands of young intellectuals found in this first soul-shaking experience the catalyst which set them in the mould for national and later communist revolution. The May 4th Movement was both anti-imperialist and anti-feudalist, directed equally against foreign oppression and against the feudal militarists who had sold China's interests for personal lucre; it thus represented a total break with the past, the beginning of a new stage, which Mao Tse-tung was to name "the new democratic stage" in the national revolution of the Chinese people. This in time gave rise to another development in Mao's thought: that of the two-stage revolution, the first being a new democratic stage, the second a socialist stage. In the revolutions to come, this concept of stages—so runs the Chinese thesis—will apply; in each the elements of a united front, a multi-class struggle, will begin the process.

The new democratic stage in the Chinese revolution was to last from 1919 to 1956, for it was in that year that socialization of the economic base was completed, by agricultural collectivization, and the takeover of private enterprise (with compensation). The Great Proletarian Cultural Revolution of 1966 would complete the inception of a second stage, the socialist stage, in China's revolution.

Two years after the May 4th Movement, in July 1921, the Chinese Communist Party was officially organized; Mao Tse-tung was one of its twelve founders. From that date to the present, it was to be the spearhead of all progressive movement in China.

Each passage from one epoch to another in history has been heralded, accompanied and confirmed by its own cultural aspects. The feudal system of Europe with its ballads, its tales of knightly deeds and ideal love, its religious iconography and music, its scholars and their debates, was abolished by the Renaissance, which brought new writing, music, painting, ways of thought and behaviour, and vocabulary. In England the Puritans and in France the French Revolution were also to destroy and rebuild, to abolish the past and create their own artistic expression and values. Each new epoch is iconoclastic, denying or destroying its predecessor, in order to create its own values.

In China, too, a cultural movement, starting at the end of the nineteenth century, a reflection of the travails and throes of new ideas, sought the overthrow of the classical language; there was a renewal of art and music, painting and literature, manners and *mores*. Confucius is repudiated not only in today's China, but also from 1890 to 1919; it was from 1905 to 1919 that the demand for women's equality was made; a cultural renaissance began to make itself felt after 1911, and the May 4th Movement was as much a cultural as a political movement; it was anti-Confucianist, anti-feudal, anti-imperialist, it repudiated tradition, it demanded reform of the language and votes for women. The use of the vernacular in literature began then, a whole school of social novelists was ushered in, among them, most prominent of all, the great Lu Hsun. Newspapers could now rise to a considerable circulation, even if only five per cent of the nation was literate. Ideas could travel up and down, instead of horizontally among a precious *élite*. The petty bourgeoisie of the cities produced its own intellectuals: women entered universities, students formed political associations. An enormous number of pamphlets, magazines, articles was produced, all highly charged with political consciousness; Marxist study circles and debating societies were started almost everywhere. Peking University became the focus and centre of intellectual ferment, there Li Ta-chao taught, and Mao Tse-tung as assistant librarian read and thought and worked. In all this activity, Mao Tse-tung was one of many who took part, creating magazines, joining or forming debating circles; but Mao also ran evening schools for peasants, wrote articles supporting the emancipation of women, took part in strikes and demonstrations and carried on agitation among the Anyuen coal miners.

From the May 4th Movement began the tremendous *acceleration* of history in China which continues today. Professor Fairbank puts it clearly: "Since China is the largest unitary mass of humanity, with the oldest continuous history, its overrunning by the west in the past century was bound to create a *continuing and violent intellectual revolution, the end of which we have not yet seen.* For a full century after 1842, China was subject to a system of international relations characterized by the unequal treaties, not formally abolished till 1943[1] ... but within the space of three generations the old order was totally changed. Rapid change is nothing new to westerners, but the rate of social change in modern China has exceeded anything we can imagine ... *It is on a scale and a tempo unprecedented in history.*"[2]

The thirty years from 1919 to 1949 saw the birth and ascendancy of New China, through the most epic and prolonged, heroic and violent armed struggle of modern times, in which colossal numbers were involved.[3] And the outcome was bound to be a communist China, since no other kind of China was possible; Western "democracy" had made quite sure of that.

The thirty years between 1919 and 1949 were a prolonged

[1] Actually their practical abolition only occurred in 1949.

[2] SSU-YU TENG and J. K. FAIRBANK, *China's Response to the West. A Documentary Survey 1839–1923* (Athenaeum, New York, 1963).

[3] "In China the struggle ... is bound to assume a profoundly popular and distinctly national character and is bound to deepen step by step, developing into desperate clashes with imperialism and shaking its very foundation throughout the world". J. V. STALIN, 1927 *Works*, pp. 262–3 quoted by Chen Po-ta.

period of violent armed struggle, which forged the CCP[1] into the most widely experienced party, both in military and in political matters, that has existed. By the time it took power it had accumulated an enormous amount of experience. All through these thirty years, Mao Tse-tung was deep in the *mêlée*, never for a single day did he leave the work of the Revolution.

Whereas Russia fought its civil war after the October 1917 Revolution, the Chinese won their civil war, their mass bases among the peasantry, and their organizational experience *before* they came to power in 1949. Whereas in Russia the Revolution proceeded from the revolutionary proletariat of the cities to the countryside, in China it was from the countryside, from this enormous, staunch, heroic, many-millioned reservoir of humanity, tempered by centuries of privation and injustice, that the cities were surrounded and conquered. In this crucial difference lies the clue to other historical divergences. But it is because of this particular historical development, that China's revolutionary lessons are of such significance for "the world of the peasantry"; the rest of Asia, Africa and Latin America, the two-thirds of humanity deprived of wealth through the exercise of economic colonialism similar to that which prevented China's capitalist development, where agricultural feudalism still continues, and where the same kind of exploitation as in China is on the increase.

That the Revolution of 1949 should be communist and could not be otherwise was inevitable, and so it will be (says Mao) for other revolutions to come. And since 1949, all that is taking place only further confirms Chinese views that the present epoch is one of world revolution; following national-liberation movements socialist revolutions will continue the process. This is *because the capitalist road is made impossible*

[1] Chinese Communist Party.

for all underdeveloped countries seeking industrialization and economic independence: the chronic insolvency, the deficiency in the balance of payments, the widening gap between the affluent one-tenth of humanity who control and exploit eighty per cent of the world's wealth, and the forever more hungry and restless majority, the gloomy reports of the UN and FAO, rising expectations of famine and revolt everywhere, all seem a confirmation of the view of the present epoch as one of world revolt.

Meanwhile, the crisis of capitalism is becoming ever more clear. It began, actually, in the 1920s when a new pattern of indirect intervention, of financial manipulation, rather than obvious occupation, was adopted; this, in itself, confirmed the change in the balance of power, though Western military forces were to be found garrisoning Chinese cities till 1949.[1] The Washington conference of 1922[2] introduced new techniques of financial domination towards the "backward" nations. It is the continuation of these techniques we see today in action in the exploitable two-thirds of the world, often, as in China before 1949, with the active collaboration of the servile, Western-oriented ruling clique intent on personal profit. It is this layer of *élitist* exploiters which the revolutions to come must also overthrow, for they are the

---

[1] *See* G. BARRACLOUGH: "The Dwarfing of Europe". Barraclough attributes this to "differentials in population growth" but this is actually incorrect. The crisis of capitalism, as evidenced by the depression of 1929, the stock market slump, the disequilibrium in Europe after World War I, the Western powers' fear of communist infiltration from Russia all precluded further and more extended military adventures by European powers in Asia. From that time they played a mainly *holding* role, until America's return to the shores of Asia in recent years, in a new aggressive tide.

[2] "Rival aggression by the imperialist powers has now turned into concerted aggression . . . which is bound to deprive the Chinese people completely of their economic independence and reduce them to slaves of the international trusts, these masters of a new type. The time has come when we cannot but rise to give battle, for the Chinese people now face a life-and-death struggle." *Chinese Communist Party Manifesto: Second Congress*, 1922.

"new millstones" round the necks of their own people[1] and another factor of the resentment against Western stereotypes[2] in the rising tide of nationalism in Asia.

Viewed in the time scale of the Chinese Revolution, Chiang Kai-shek and his rule of twenty years (1928–48), were but an episode. Chiang did achieve personal power, but could not achieve the reconstruction of China, nor its freedom from financial enslavement; he could not solve the problems of the peasantry, nor organize a viable economic state.

From the inception of the two-stage revolution to its end, from the new democratic stage begun in 1919 to the Great Cultural Socialist Revolution of 1966, the whole Chinese revolutionary process bears the stamp and characteristic of Mao Tse-tung. Militarily, politically, economically, culturally, it is Mao Tse-tung who has saved, studied, debated, guided and created, to lead the Revolution through the protracted, devious and difficult struggles of these forty years;[3] for struggle there was, even after 1949. His have been the clearest vision and the most remarkable grasp of historical realities. There are no other examples in history of such a career, on such a vast scale, developing such a momentum, acting on so many millions, nor of transformation at such speed operated throughout the length and breadth of a country larger than all Europe.

The May 4th 1919 Movement, by Mao's own avowal, was the starting point of his illumination; July 1921, when he became one of the twelve founder members of the Communist

[1] See KEITH BUCHANAN, Pacific Viewpoint, September, 1964.
[2] The author Lu Hsun was always satirizing the "modernized" Western-oriented Chinese intellectual. See "The True Story of Ah Q".
[3] 1927–67.

Party of China, was its consecration; the period August to
October 1927, when he organized the Autumn Harvest
uprising and withdrew to the Chingkang mountain[1] with a
small band of followers after the almost total annihilation of
the Chinese Communists by Chiang Kai-shek, was the
beginning of his outstanding career.

It was at Chingkang mountain, the first Red base, that the
special genius which has made it possible for Mao to be what
he is today manifested itself. It was there that his ideas on
many issues, which finally led to victory, began, in those
hopeless hours when all seemed lost, to develop. Whereas
others failed either because they were intimidated into abdica-
tion or because they hypnotized themselves into copying
revolutionary programmes from other countries, Mao
Tse-tung's genius was that he could never be lured by
facile formulas, but always sought the concrete objective,
the reality of China, upon which to test Marxist-Leninist
theories. Possessing a meticulous, painstaking, scientific brain,
he grasped the essential importance of China's social system,
its differences from the West; by adapting communism to
Chinese conditions he was to evolve a new blue-print for
revolution, to aggrandize, create and develop the science of
revolution to a precision, exactness and flexible imaginative-
ness, which forty years after 1927, in 1966, would be proclaimed the guide to action for future world revolutions.
Today Mao is acclaimed as the Lenin of our epoch, his thought
the apex of Marxism-Leninism and the experience of Chingkang mountain "the road world-revolution must take",
that is, the road of armed struggle in a long, protracted
militancy lasting many decades.

In 1949, when the Communist Party came to power, the
condition of China, physically, was worse than it had
been even in 1919. The country was devastated by the

[1] Chingkang mountain is also known as Chingkanshan in this text.

war with Japan (1931-45) and the civil wars with Chiang Kai-shek. The five hundred million peasants laboured as they had done two thousand years ago; famine, disease, dilapidation, were everywhere. It was a ruined land of colossal needs which the Communist Party took over. But there was one asset which Mao had, and which he understood from the beginning, which he never underestimated. "What is the most precious thing on earth? It is Man ... our people are poor and blank but the most beautiful poem can be written on a blank sheet of paper ...". With this faith in Man and Idea, China's second Long March, to the next fifty years, began in 1949.

II

TRANSFORMATION AT THE BASE—
AGRICULTURE: RESHAPING THE
CHINESE EARTH

Demand grain from nature, and declare war against the great earth.

Peasant song

CHINA was, and still is, essentially an agricultural country. Before 1950 over eighty-five per cent of her population (today over seventy per cent) were engaged in the production of primary commodities which involve growing, planting and harvesting.

As Buchanan and Tregear[1] point out, the chief features of the Chinese earth are its diversity, its extent and its untapped resources. Appraisal of its natural resources has changed considerably since 1950, illustrating, as Buchanan puts it, "one of the most important concepts in geography, the concept that natural resources are cultural appraisals". As in history, so in agriculture and in other subjects, studies abound, based on presumptions: "China has no resources in oil"; "only thirteen per cent of China's area is arable land". China's poverty and scarcity of mineral resources were confidently held up for decades as "evidence" that she could never become industrialized. In the agricultural sector the methods of cultivation existent before 1949 and the density of certain lowland areas were held as proof of her having reached an agricultural maximum. Both these premises have now been proved wrong. The calculations of economists,

[1] *See* Bibliography.

34

based on Western standards of capital investment necessary for development, have consistently underestimated another, unsurveyed dimension and form of capital, which René Dumont calls "the most important and precious source of capital", human labour investment. The transformation of labour into capital, which has formed the basis of capitalist accumulation in the West (through slavery and cheap colonial labour) has been derided and denigrated for China itself, where the mobilization of labour resources under conditions entirely different from those which were practised in the factories of Europe in the nineteenth century has been consistently successful over the past seventeen years.

The Communist Party was already well experienced in most types of agricultural work when it came to power. Mao Tse-tung had called for such studies throughout the period of the Red bases (1928-48);[1] in Yenan, during the economic blockade by the Kuomintang, a large area at Nanniwan had been worked to grow crops under dry farming conditions, and handicrafts stimulated to supply much needed cloth and other articles. Collection of salt (still a government monopoly under Chiang, and forbidden for the communist enclaves) had led to the restoration of peasant devices to collect salt from ash and rock.[2]

Agriculture is still the broad base of the national economy in 1967, though industry, practically non-existent then, is now well-established, and industrial goods and products (including those processed from agricultural sources) now

[1] "Pay attention to economic work"—MAO TSE-TUNG, 20th August, 1935. In this essay the mobilization of the masses, rectification of the work style of some party members which "hinders economic reconstruction" are amply discussed; the same words would be applied again in present-day China's construction of an economic base.

[2] It is said that Mao deliberately chose Yenan as a base because it was near salt-producing areas; the Red armies had suffered greatly from salt deprivation in other bases.

comprise forty per cent of China's exports compared to five to
ten per cent pre-1949.[1] The Chinese leadership is convinced
that self-sufficiency in *food* is a major cornerstone of independence for a sovereign country; India's situation is an
example of a major country with immense potential crop
resources being held down and compelled to submit to foreign
dictates because of her lack of agricultural independence. It is
the countryside, not the city, which is the socialist base upon
which China's system is constructed; agriculture, therefore,
will retain its primacy. In this matter, the Chinese leadership
do not suffer from hyperfascination with "industrialization"
at the expense of agriculture.[2] "Man must eat before he can
do anything." Self-sufficiency in food is the first *sine qua non*
towards self-reliance.

The land reform movement of 1949–52 was a class struggle,
an educative process, an abolition of feudal landlordism, and
the beginning of collectivization in agriculture. From 1952
onwards, collectivization, through mutual-aid teams, lower
co-operatives, then higher co-operatives, proceeded step by
step, ending with the setting up of the communes in 1958.
These steps were achieved more quickly than the planners
themselves had expected, as all reports indicate. The surprise
factor of this transformation is its achievement in a non-
mechanized, labour-intensive agricultural country, reversing
the Russian model of "tractors first, then collectivization".
It was another indication of the Chinese preference for their
own independent development; a trait which was not acknowledged then by many experts. Only now, seventeen years
later, is the "Russian model" no longer invoked by Western

---

[1] Most of these "industrial goods" were from the light industries (chiefly
textiles) situated in the eastern seaboard cities; over half of these industries
were foreign-owned.

[2] It is claimed that the stabilization of crops has now been achieved in eighty
per cent of the areas under cultivation.

experts (and by non-Western ones) as *the* model of communist development; rather, it is the Chinese model which pre-occupies them.

Land reform began with the elimination of landlordism: but a redistribution of land, which results in a small-producer individual economy, among five hundred million peasants,[1] does not solve the agricultural problem, which is one of increased output. The average farm, on redistribution, would be less than two and a half acres for a family of five to six people. In the 1930s, already the average farm was estimated at 3·3 acres; it declined to under three acres in the 1940s. (Comparative figures are 77 acres per farm in England and 157 in the USA in 1939.) The output of food grain was reckoned at 140 million metric tons in 1936. It was 108 million metric tons in 1949. Tools were most primitive, as iron had almost disappeared; ploughs of wood, pulled by people, were the main instruments of production. Spades and hoes were hard to find. Only fifty million beasts of labour existed, their redistribution would not have brought any increase in efficiency. Of 245 million acres of cultivated land only forty million were irrigated; no chemical fertilizers were available at all. Dykes were in a ruinous condition. Disease, hunger and disorder ravaged the country.

True to the vision of interlocking, at all levels, theory and practice, land reform was not only a concrete abolition of

---

[1] See ALEC NOVE, *Collectivization of Agriculture in Russia and China*, Hong Kong University Press, 1961. PROFESSOR TREGEAR in *A Geography of China* gives an estimated six acres per farm for each peasant proprietor, but this appears too high; a three-acre farm in Hunan province already qualified for the status of middle peasant—but less than twenty per cent of the peasantry owned land up to three acres, eighty per cent farmed less than two acres, of which over seventy per cent was *rented land*. The income derived from the land, after payment of land rent (from fifty per cent up to seventy per cent of the crop) by the average tenant farmer was not enough to allow him to improve soil, or seed, or to accumulate savings. The slightest disaster precipitated him into irrevocable misery.

feudal landlordism, a preliminary step towards collectivization, but also an educational process laying the psychological
groundwork for a socialist education. The key words of land
reform were *class struggle* and *struggle for production*.

Vivid descriptions of land reform are penned by William
Hinton,[1] an American who was able to observe land reform
over several months, and by many Chinese writers. One
Chinese writer described his own experience to me. He was
the friend of a landlord, who not only kept six women, but
also bought or took away the male and female children of
his tenant farmers. His personal army of thirty armed body-
guards terrorized the district he ruled (for he was also a
magistrate). "How could I call such a monster my friend!"
exclaimed this writer, when at last he witnessed the execution
of this landlord in a peasants' court.

Land reform began the process of releasing *the productive force
of the rural regions*, first by abolishing the inhibitory factors,
excessive rents, usury, oppression, and landlord banditry.
By 1952 this has been done with some thoroughness. Secret
societies, private armies, Kuomintang organizations had been
put down; Taoist secret society emblems were taken away
or painted over (they represented associations which for the
last twenty years had been in league with the landlords and
Chiang Kai-shek). Few landlords, comparatively speaking,
were executed, only those who had committed crimes apart
from the usual exploitation; many were put on probation
"under the supervision of the masses". They received their
share of land to work;[2] they were deprived of legal rights but
their children were not deprived of the opportunity of labour
and education. Rich peasants were not thus deprived, and
remain to this day in many communes, often as a source of

[1] *Fanshen*, W. HINTON (Monthly Review Press, N.Y., 1966).
[2] Land Reform Charter and Constitution of the People's Republic of China,
1951.

trouble, for clan feudalism still subsists, disguised landlords' offspring and relatives reappear masquerading as poor peasants in certain areas, some had even, by 1961, become cadres, party members, bookkeepers and accountants in the production teams of the communes. In 1966, a girl peasant, aged twenty-five, in charge of a production team, said in an interview: "to have a rich peasant or ex-landlord about in a commune is like having a snake in one's pocket. The moment things go wrong, he takes advantage of the situation."

Physical elimination of *kulaks* had been on a much larger scale in Russia, probably because no meticulous distinction was made between the classes in the countryside, whereas in China this has been done.[1] In China physical liquidation did occur, but re-education and labour under supervision were primary instruments of change.[2]

By 1952, with mutual-aid teams functioning, the food grain harvest was 150 million tons. In 1953 the first Five-year Plan was launched and co-operatives proposed. At this juncture a division of opinion within the Communist Party arose over the question of agricultural collectivization.[3]

"It is an invariable law that, once the feudal land system is overthrown, a struggle begins in rural areas, in which the choice lies between the capitalist and the socialist roads. It is either the one or the other; there is no middle course. Some comrades take quite a radical stand in their attitude towards the bourgeois-democratic revolution, but they remain quite content with the peasants' having got back their

---

[1] MAO TSE-TUNG, *How to Differentiate Classes in Rural Areas*, followed by other works on the subject.

[2] Altogether including the clean-up in the cities of counter-revolutionaries, 500,000 people were reported physically eliminated by 1954. But these figures are only approximate.

[3] This division of opinion was not new; as we shall see later, the CCP has always at all times carried out an "intra-party struggle", "between two roads"; Mao Tse-tung considers this "a healthy sign of life . . . without contradiction there would be no progress in the Party".

land. . . . So they loiter at the cross-roads, between socialism and capitalism, and are actually more interested in preserving the small-peasant economy than in giving a lead in its transformation to a socialist agriculture. Such comrades fail to realize that small-peasant economy is not a paradise for the peasantry, but a garden in which capitalism grows. . . . Small production engenders capitalism and the bourgeoisie continuously, daily, hourly, spontaneously, and on a mass scale."[1] The general line of the Party, which means, among other things, speeding up the socialization of the countryside, won over the loiterers at the cross-roads. In 1952 there were already 50,000 families in collectivized farms; in 1955 17 million, in 1956 110 million, or over ninety-five per cent of the peasant population.

The "spontaneous return to capitalism" by the peasant in the countryside, already noted in 1953-4, was time and again to be one of the adverse factors which planners would have to take into account; until such time as a "new socialist man, whose ideas of self and property were thoroughly different", would come into being. It is agreed that these capitalist tendencies have not been eradicated yet,[2] for they are part of the peasant's traditional involvement with land as security. Hence the socialist education movements of large amplitude, and also the present Cultural Revolution. All these are designed to transform this attitude, otherwise the reshaping of the Chinese earth cannot be achieved. The rising standard of living, the increase in technical and scientific knowledge, and

[1] *Agricultural Collectivization in China*, 1955. Report.

[2] In 1953, in some areas, the mutual-aid teams fell into the hands of rich peasants, with the advantage of superior tools, the possession of beasts of labour, and better know-how. In 1961, again, agricultural difficulties led to a pull-back and relapse into spontaneous capitalism. Had these relapses been successful in halting collectivization, Chinese agriculture would remain a small-scale, small-producers economy, incapable of efficient capital accumulation, increased yield, mechanization, electrification and modernization.

the participation in collective work by the peasantry, also help to promote a new level of consciousness. And finally, political and social-economic studies, chiefly of the works of Mao Tse-tung, help to form in the (now literate) peasantry a unifying, scientific attitude, with a heightened awareness of the great goals and an abatement of private greed.

The establishment of a collectivized socialist agriculture, in the conditions prevailing in China, is essential to its future mechanization and electrification. Upon the steps to make the commune a success depends the whole architecture of the future of China as an "advanced, industrial, modern and comprehensive socialist state".[1]

Only collectivization would make possible the conditions under which the feudal peasant would become an educated, literate, scientifically minded man, the counterpart of an educated, literate, technical factory worker. From the vast man-ocean of hitherto degraded, downtrodden, peasantry, would come forth millions of innovators, inventors, experts, technicians, to create science, art, literature, a new world. *"To minimize or abolish the difference between town and city, between rural worker and factory worker, between manual and mental labour"* was the long-term aim of collectivization; in construction as in revolution the peasantry was the essential base, both material and social, of the whole structure.

The movement towards setting up communes began spontaneously in the merging of certain collectives in Honan province, eighteen months before the communes became an official programme in 1958. In six months 26,000 communes were established; by 1962 these 26,000 had proved too bulky, in the primitive state of communications which existed, and the relative inefficiency of lower-level cadre administration. They were divided into 74,000, an average of ten co-operatives per commune (760,000 co-operatives were in existence in 1956).

[1] CHOU EN-LAI, December, 1963. *Report.*

The communes were a direct personal creation of Mao Tse-tung, after months of personal tours of investigation. Derided as failures because of the initial mistakes and dislocations augmented by weather calamities, they have survived and flourished, and proved themselves the best type of organization yet devised for the attainment of China's goals, not only in the agricultural sector, but also in the speedy socialization of the entire population, and the thorough decentralization of industry begun in 1956. The communes are indispensable to the nation-wide strategy of self-defence by multiplying the centres of self-sufficiency in the event of bombing attacks (nuclear or conventional). They make China regionally self-supporting, decentralized,[1] a cellular living assemblage rather than a mechanical system; and, in the event of massive bombing, unconquerable.

In 1958, again, two tendencies were manifest within the Communist Party leadership. One was to press on, to "mobilize the masses" and "let the upsurge in revolutionary enthusiasm realize a material transformation"; concretely expressed, it meant that the communes could realize the pooling of labour power necessary in a labour-intensive production system to engage in basic capital construction such as massive water-conservancy works, terracing of hills, digging of canals and reservoirs, afforestation, soil improvement, utilization of waste land, etc. These all involved expenditure of labour on infrastructures whose benefits would not be immediately noticeable. The other trend was in favour of "going slow", a moderation which was actually the recurrent expression of the "pull-back" and which, in the long run, would have proved contrary to the long-term interests of the nation. The majority of the poor peasantry was reported to be in favour of the speed-up, certainly torrential enthusiasm was marked during the years 1958 and 1959, the first years of the

---

[1] "Several Special Characteristics of Peoples Communes", 1958. Draft.

communes and the First Great Leap Forward in industry. Obviously Mao Tse-tung had been in favour of going "all out" with the communes programme, to increase output so that a Great Leap Forward could be undertaken in industry. It is this strand of daring and boldness, often depreciated as "extreme" and "bound to fail", which, in the circumstances in which China is placed, has been repeatedly proved correct. For Mao Tse-tung's "war" on timorous feudalism, on servile imitation, on immobility, on what he called "the resolute shrinkers" in the Party, is of a piece with his entire conduct of the Long March and the Civil War with Chiang Kai-shek (1946-9). The cyclonic pace of change achieved would not have come to pass without him. For China, the attitude which was propounded by the experiment of the communes and the Leap in 1958 was an intellectual and psychological bounding into the twentieth century. Boldness and experimentation were to replace safe, traditional habits. "To dare" is the motto impressed upon youth, where once it was "to obey".

The communes had their share in the success and failure pattern of every new experiment, for they were a form as yet unknown anywhere else in the world.[1] High-level socialist collectivization, in the form of the commune system, *before* mechanization was accomplished, drew criticism from other socialist States; China's alleged claim that she would reach communism "within a few years" implied a parity, if not a superiority, in ideological excellence,[2] and this was irritating to Moscow.

The theoretical quarrel, whether a society can enter the

[1] Kropotkin's "agro-industrial complexes" presupposed an industrial base. The Russians criticized the communes: "It is not in Marx."

[2] TUNG TA-LIN, *Agricultural Co-operation in China* (1958-9): "We had to create favourable conditions primarily to develop agricultural production so that socialist industrialization would be assured of a reliable base, supplying it with enough grain and raw materials."

communist stage before abundance is created, depends, first of all, on a definition of "abundance" for the masses. Practically speaking, where Chinese conditions were concerned, Mao replied that "we cannot wait and hope that machines will drop from heaven", while the small-producers economy, the feudalism-riddled agricultural base remained stagnant, pulling China back into poverty. Only through the efficient pooling of labour-capital (China's main source of capital), only through the improvement of this capital (by education, both political and technical) would transformation occur.

The Twelve-year Plan for the development of agriculture from 1956 to 1967 provided the outline for the elimination of illiteracy, the establishment of schools, the elevation of socialist consciousness among the cadres as well as the peasants, the training of millions of lower echelon cadres in agricultural techniques.

The idea of the remaking of man as well as man's transformation, on the basis of the material gains achieved, of the earth he lives on, is the essential characteristic of Mao's approach to the whole problem of achieving socialism.

Literacy before 1949 in the countryside was (at its highest) five per cent. Today, no person *under forty* in the communes is illiterate.[1] This means that well over sixty per cent of the total population of rural China has now become literate. In 1949 *no* peasant knew anything about scientific experimentation; in 1966, a pool of six million peasant-scientists not only knew about soil and seed improvement but could carry out experiments, hold conferences, and pass on their knowledge at scientific meetings.

Differences from, rather than similarities to the Russian model strike one in Chinese agricultural development.

[1] Report at Ministry of State Planning Conference, November 1966.

Machine tractor stations were part of the Soviet collectives from their beginning; labour-intensive methods remain until today the main means of socialist construction in China's countryside, although mechanization and electrification are definitely increasing.

By 1966, 1,300 out of 2,613 rural counties had electricity, unknown in 1950; it is chiefly used for water pumps for the fields. Some communes are now mechanized, meaning that most of the work that used to be done by hand labour is now done by machinery of one kind or another; but for the bulk of the communes mechanization is only beginning—chiefly in the irrigation sector. Electric pumps release at least one-third of labour for other jobs. But seventy-five per cent of rural work is still labour-intensive; whether large-scale infrastructure building or routine production. It is hoped to complete mechanization and electrification in all communes *within* twenty years.

But the economic scope of the commune is to be more than an agricultural mechanized unit on the Russian model. The commune is to become the basic social, economic, cultural, educational, political and military (self-defence) unit of the socialist State. And this means industrializing the commune as well as establishing it as a farming collective, proof against drought and flood.

In 1958 Mao Tse-tung stated that the commune "includes industry, agriculture, culture, trade, military affairs ... includes the people of all professions and trades ... the people's commune is different in *nature* from the agricultural co-operative ... referring to the *urbanization* of the countryside, *the ruralization* of the cities, we imply that new changes have come to society *as a whole*."[1]

The commune will take over all local government organizations; it is the instrument for the elimination of the private

[1] *Several Special Characteristics of the Peoples Communes*, 1958. Draft.

ownership of means of production (the private plot, retained until today but now disappearing).[1] Each commune will become an agro-industrial complex, running its own affairs, a small state on its own, but connected with all other communes by the bonds of cultural, economic, political and military unification. The wage system, introduced to the peasantry through the workpoint, will gradually eliminate the difference between him and the industrial worker.

A decentralized, flexible and yet solidly interwoven social economic pattern comes into existence; a pattern capable of modification; it predicates the ruralization (even, perhaps one day, the abolition) of the cities as they were created, as strongholds of property and wealth, fortresses against a peasantry in revolt. Traditionally, the city has been a bulwark of exploiting systems against the assaults of the countryside; the development of cities in history is one of despotic power in the hands of the ruling class. In Europe the feudal city developed round the castle, where the landlord-baron held power; at its foot nestled the trade and marketing centres. The capitalist city is the seat of money, banks and other "fortresses of capitalism". In Asia the city has become in a sense the *étouffoir*, a senseless megalopolis drawing the hungry millions of the country into a horrifying belt of slums round its glittering, moneyed core. The giant megalopolises of the Third World have an economy which actively oppresses and exploits their own rural areas. The city is also the stronghold of essentially bureaucratic functions and departments; incitement to immobility, soft living, luxury and corruption. Mao Tse-tung knows what he is talking about; the rush of Party members to soft cushioned seats behind desks in the great cities is a tendency which has had to be actively combated time and

[1] The private plot and its retention till 1966 has been held up as evidence of the failure of socialized agriculture. The Chinese view is quite different; their gradual elimination is certainly the aim within the next twenty years.

time again. In 1958 no fewer than six million city cadres were "sent down" to the countryside to renew contact with reality!

The commune renders superfluous the *idea* of the city as a centre of culture, a repository of science and art, a stronghold of institutions, the seat of government. It is a feature of the massive decentralization, in process today, that the city as such *must not* draw brain, talent, and technique *away* from the countryside. Indeed, it is the *reverse process* which is being carried out, with millions of educated young students, and professionals being planted away from the cities into communes.

The social organization of the future communist society will be centred in the commune, which is at once city and countryside, trade market and production centre, with no distinction between peasant, worker, military, and white collar staff, no division between industrial, agricultural and intellectual labour. As modernization brings more abundance, the dream of a communist society in the commune will be realized, "though it may take a century", at the same time as the remaking of man, concomitant with the remaking of the earth, is achieved. With its own foci of culture, communication, defence, education, its own factories, its own food production, and its own exchange markets, the commune becomes a cell, a flexible miniature of the whole State. Again we find in this concept the non-mechanical, adaptive, "human body" touch which is peculiar to Mao Tse-tung. His vision of rational living is certainly essentially feasible, in a modern state endowed with television, telephone and jet transport (as China plans to be). The many problems of living which the out-of-date cities of the West create, with their slums, transport jams and overcrowding need not occur in China tomorrow. Supermarkets for consumer goods, parks, factories, schools, hospitals, recreational areas, totally non-existent in the Chinese countryside before 1949, are already *coming into being* in China's communes. "The whole of China will be one vast garden" may be an exaggerated lyrical description for the present; but to someone like myself who has paid repeated visits to the same spots and noted the rapidity of the improvements, it is not too far-fetched a dream. "We are not going to build any more cities", said a member of the Economic Planning Commission in Peking recently.[1]

There is not a building, road or factory, in China today, a canal, school or hospital which does not fulfil three "main" provisions—

(*a*) How best to serve the people's long-term interests, not only in the present, but within the next thirty years (this includes calculations for a fifty per cent increase in users).

(*b*) How best to achieve the maximum at minimum cost, the least amount of expenditure to the State, through volunteer, unpaid work by the community itself.

(*c*) How to fit these plans with overall considerations, both as regards development in peace, and as regards strategic defence in war.

Though reduplication of effort is unavoidable at the present stage as each commune tries to be self-reliant in as many ways as possible, regional planning, as transport improves, is already taking place.

The commune, therefore, is the plan upon which China in the year 2001 will be founded; the strong, stable food and industry unit of the country.

In the last four years, some one and a half million young intellectuals have become established in the communes for all their lives. In the next decade, twenty times as many, most of them under thirty, will be working in the countryside, to

[1] November, 1966—interview.

build up 74,000 techno-industrial pools. Workers, technicians, handicraftsmen have already moved into communes to start factories, electric pump stations, fertilizer plants and small steel furnaces. Siting larger plants (machine tools, trucks, petro-chemical and fertilizer, extractive industries, textile mills, cement works, and precision equipment units) in rural areas surrounded by communes which provide the food and also manpower reserves both for skilled and semi-skilled labour (such as building), has been the practice since 1958.[1] Commune organization is, say the Chinese, the major way in which a country deficient in capital but rich in manpower can organize production, and use manpower efficiently to produce capital construction and accumulation at top speed. As an educative mass base, too, the commune is proving its advantages. Universities, agricultural colleges, industrial and technical schools, will henceforth move away from the cities, into the countryside; within another twenty years there will be no illiteracy in China, and a vast reservoir of scientific-technical peasants will have been created. By that time, the mechanization of agriculture, it is hoped, will be completed, thus releasing half the population now in agricultural activities for industry. But this industry will be sited in the communes themselves, at all levels, and not in cities.

The first years of the communes were characterized by Utopian excesses, widely publicized in the Western Press—

(a) Manpower allocation was badly organized, the requirements made upon the labour power both in industrial projects (such as backyard steel furnaces) and in water-conservancy and afforestation projects were not correlated

[1] A rotation system of peasants on contract work in factories, and industrial workers working in agricultural pursuits for a certain number of months each year is being put into effect in certain areas as an experiment in widening experience and narrowing differences between peasant and worker.—Author.

to the demands of harvest and planting. As a result, the most enormous harvest that China ever had, writes A. L. Strong,[1] was, in 1958, left for the greater part lying in the fields, while the peasants went off to build large water-conservancy works. It is reported that seventy million peasants worked on water-conservancy projects, another eighteen million or so were drafted into technical institutes in the cities, the latter being "lavishly built" and at great cost; or in newly erected factories, where they waited for months for machinery and raw materials which never came, meantime being fed and paid wages by the State.

(b) The backyard steel furnace campaign took away another forty million from agricultural production. As a result large areas of cotton, wheat fields and other crops were left to wither on the stalk. The steel-making, the water-conservancy plans, the influx into the new factories and into the cities of peasant labour created a chaos of man-power. In one province alone, twelve million peasants were thus kept "in reserve" for large projects which did not materialize.

(c) Unscientific methods were employed by inexperienced cadres newly arrived in the countryside, who heedless of the experience of "conservative" peasants began to experiment with their own pet theories, for example cutting down banana trees in order to plant more rice, thus imperilling village economy which sold bananas as produce. The practice of the cadres in ordering unsuitable crops to be planted, and other manifestations of the bureaucratic desire to command was due to inexperience, haste, and the recurrent "feudal" petty tyranny which, as Mao Tse-tung wrote, "is so strongly entrenched . . . even among Party members".

[1] A. L. STRONG, The Peoples Communes and More on the Peoples Communes, Foreign Language Press, Peking.

(d) In 1960 the sudden withdrawal of Soviet technicians, the sabotage of machinery, and the stoppage of supplies of all spare parts and equipment brought industry almost to a standstill. It took nearly a year for reorganization in certain essential industries, more for others. The damage done reflected on agriculture also, as improved tools, pumps and steel for ploughs were not made for a while.

(e) Last, but not least, the ravages of nature.[1] That the years 1958 to 1961 were exceptionally bad years for floods and drought is fully documented. I personally visited areas in Szechuan where even bamboo dried on its stalk as a result of drought, a phenomenon which had not occurred for a century. In the north, areas on the Yellow River had continuous drought (three hundred days without rain) for two years in succession. Added to these calamities were insect pests, including locusts.

(f) In addition to this the sudden collectivization of vast numbers of pigs and other livestock, with inefficient and insufficient allocation of fodder and space, provoked the onset of certain diseases, which in the north-west for instance resulted in an epidemic of pig cholera which reduced the pig population.

(g) The inflated statistics of 1958–9, provided by over-enthusiastic peasants, were further inflated by hyper-fervent cadres. Utopian excesses occurred in some communes, whose members, persuaded that an era of plenty was forthcoming, killed and ate all their pigs; assets were squandered on such things as cinema houses and television in communes; two million men were engaged for the

[1] It is known that both in China and India an average, yearly, of ten per cent of cropland is affected by natural calamities. When this average increases to fifteen to twenty per cent (as in China during the three bad years, and in India in the last two), agriculture is seriously affected.

huge Sanmen dam project and the whole thing was left flat by the Soviet withdrawal (even the blueprints were taken away).

Yet prices remained stable, rationing ensured fair distribution of food, the system did not break, and there was no famine or mass starvation.[1] Within three years, the country had recovered, and in 1964 there was the beginning of a small surplus in meat, eggs and vegetables.

Strict rationing averted famine; the countryside ate, on the whole, better than the cities; many communes kept their grain for themselves; other communes sold too much to the State and were left short. No one died in the floods, for relief services were instituted, even by helicopter, with the army playing a great role in salvage operations. In the cities shortages were great and there was hardship, but distribution remained fair, and prices stable. There was no inflation. A system of free markets was instituted in rural areas, hailed by the Western Press as proving the "failure" of the communes and a return to free enterprise. Likewise the private plots, which sustained the peasant during the bad years, were announced as the doom of collectivization. Both these were temporary measures to offset the chaos resulting from the dislocation of manpower mobilization. Though palliative, the answer to China's agricultural problems does not lie in the private plot and the free market; modernization, and vastly increased yields, would be attained only through commune socialism.

In the upturn after 1962, the vast irrigation works and afforestation projects undertaken by the peasants in 1958-9 began to pay off.

---

[1] Though there was widespread malnutrition; the feat that the Chinese government performed in being able to maintain stable prices and fair rationing of over 600 million people has never been estimated at its proper significance. Yet it remains an incredible performance of organization.

Irrigation, in 1950 counted at 40–45 million acres, by 1957 covered 70 million acres. In 1958–9 another 58 million acres were irrigated, giving an area of 128 million acres out of the now cultivated 280 million acres.[1] If one discounts the irrigation works that were completed too hastily and led to soil alkalinity, one could estimate (and this is a low deflationary estimate) that possibly in the two years 1958 to 1960 over 100 million acres were brought under irrigation. In Kwangtung province alone over ninety per cent of the land is now irrigated in comparison with thirty per cent before 1949. In 1966, it was claimed that the total area of irrigated land was increased two and a half times, giving an area of 150 million acres irrigated, or half the cultivated land compared with one-sixth previously.

Before 1949 only five per cent of China was forested, during the first few years tree planting went on, but it took the installation of the communes to produce afforestation in a major way, with thirty billion[2] trees planted in the two years 1958–9. Tracts of desert land a thousand kilometres in length were reclaimed with criss-cross tree belts. Since then afforestation has continued and within another fifty years twenty per cent of China will be well-wooded land.

The years 1958–60, known as the years of the communes and the First Great Leap Forward in industry must be re-assessed for their overall achievements as well as their failures; gruelling lessons were learnt; experience was acquired; in-experience, as well as the weather, played havoc. But out of all this emerged the solidity, strength, resilience and enter-prise of the Chinese people and the usefulness and reliability of commune organization.

[1] The total cultivated area increased from 245 to 280 million acres between 1950 and 1960; it is nearly 300 million acres now, but no great increase in cropland area is contemplated; increased *yield* per acre is the target.

[2] One billion = one thousand million.

Readjustment was announced in January 1961. Errors and mistakes of judgement were freely aired. The subject the Chinese did not discuss was the withdrawal of the Soviet technicians, and the attempt to cripple Chinese industrial advance. It was not until eighteen months later that this was made public.[1]

Since 1964 the food grain harvest, which was below 200 million tons, has begun to increase; in 1966 it was 220 million tons (a ten per cent leeway for the harvest before storage is allowed; this ten per cent is probably used for commune reserves, and animal fodder). Decisions on production, administration and bookkeeping resulted in a streamlining of commune administration. "Under no circumstances may people other than those familiar with local conditions have the right to require production teams to plant crops that are not suited to concrete conditions." A most explicit directive.

Because the communes were responsible for the welfare of their members there had not been a major famine or breakdown, and hence the commune was now called The Iron Rice Bowl. The purchase of wheat in Canada to feed the coastal cities started in those years, and it has continued since. This is regarded as an avowal by China that she is not yet completely self-sufficient in wheat, and it is not denied.

However, there is a large increase in the rice-cropping area, extending even to Manchuria, rather than in wheat-growing areas, rice is being exported to the markets of South-East Asia, to Albania and Cuba and other regions. Ton for ton rice brings in more foreign exchange than wheat; but it is true that there is a gap, though small, which the Chinese will do their best to eliminate.

[1] The Nine Open Letters published between 1963 and 1964, addressed to the Communist Party of the USSR.

The further development of the agricultural sector rests on the reclamation of cultivable land, irrigation control, and the improvement of existing cultivated land. Reclaiming land is left chiefly to the State farms, of which there are about 3,000 manned by People's Liberation Army personnel; they produce about twelve per cent of China's food crops, and a few years ago a third of the tractor pool was at their disposal. At this moment the tractor pool has increased and the communes are being supplied with them, but tractorization is not a priority, for several reasons.

In Soviet Russia, where tractor stations were considered indispensable to collectivization, there was a shortage of manpower labour whereas in China the abundance of manpower labour is only too obvious. A stable and high yield, and *not*, primarily, saving in labour, is the requirement. Therefore the first priority of mechanization goes to mechanical drainage and irrigation (now the main target of mechanization) and not to tractors. Tractors were supplied to the State farms because these were manned by the veterans of the People's Liberation Army, many of whom had had some technical experience as drivers. Chinese tractors are being made, small and cheap, to suit the communes' requirements; they are not supplied free but are sold to the communes; tractor drivers are trained among the peasantry and they are paid, as other peasants, by workpoints. The Chinese aver that in Russia a "new class" of technicians, tractor drivers, was formed in the agricultural co-operatives.

Apart from reclaiming marginal land and improving yield on existing areas by building raised fields, filling gullies, and supplying irrigation and fertilizers, the communes will not, within the scope of the third Five-year Plan (1966–70) reclaim additional unused land. They will, however, concentrate on irrigation, and improving existing soil with fertilizers, on planting techniques and scientific rotation of crops.

High yields on the present cultivated land is the aim. Intensive farming, seed selection, insecticides and above all fertilizers, can treble the present yields.[1]

The labour put into water conservancy is impressive and can be divided into State projects for the control of great rivers, and commune regional projects. The latter are multiple-purpose affairs, aiming at flood control, generation of power, creating navigable waterways, multiplying irrigation canals. The regional projects depend almost entirely on manpower labour, and increasingly also on commune funds rather than on State funds, although the State does spend several billions a year on these infrastructure works. Multitudinous small-scale works, forming networks of canals, reservoirs, aqueducts and small hydroelectric plants over gradually extending rural regions, are undertaken by many communes grouping together; an average twenty per cent of the commune labour force may be engaged in such capital construction projects and these are carried out during winter and slack periods, whereas eighty per cent is engaged in production labour. Increasingly, as mechanization sets in to relieve a permanent labour force, a larger amount of manpower can be diverted from routine production to construction projects, to the industries which are becoming such a feature of the commune, and to State industries. The participation of city cadres, intellectuals and students in all these construction plans is helping to unify the country and to achieve the necessary levelling between intellectual and manual work, also part of the reshaping of China.

Only a few examples of the work thus achieved can be given: a giant irrigation system in Anhwei province, which

[1] This multiplication of output per acre is the chief preoccupation of the Chinese Press. Certain results are impressive: from 140 catties to 800 catties of grain per unit acre; from 30 catties to 150 catties of cotton. But "our national average is still low" and hence a massive drive for chemical fertilizers will occupy the next decade.

has been under construction for nine years, linking three rivers by numerous canals excavated among mountains and hills; it irrigates about 350,000 hectares, providing an inland navigation system, breeding grounds for fish, and power generation. The work was done by 400,000 builders from the communes. This year twelve canals and thirty related major installations (hydroelectric) will be added.

One winter 450,000 peasants dredged and drained a 164-kilometre river, and thus secured soil conservancy, water, and power for 1·3 million hectares of farmland. The same 450,000 are now digging a new outlet to the sea for a 140-kilometre river tributary; it will be completed within six months.

Higher yields depend on seed selection, adequate care and pest control, but the main problem is chemical fertilizers; China requires at least twenty-five million tons of chemical fertilizer; she provides herself with possibly fifteen million tons of non-chemical fertilizer (pig and human manure, and nitrogen-fixing (leguminous) plants now grown extensively as fertilizers. But these cannot replace chemical fertilizers. The fertilizer industry is a "leaping" industry. Today nine million tons of chemical fertilizer are produced in China; another three million are bought abroad; the building of another twenty large and small fertilizer plants to be completed within the next three years is in hand.

Until 1965 China had to pay her debts to Russia[1] chiefly in meat and oil; now that her debts are paid meat is not only abundant but in some areas there is a surplus. This is openly acknowledged by Australian meat exporters. The surplus, however, is not to be judged by Western standards of consumption; the average consumption of meat per year is still in the region of 12 lb per person (an average of 7 lb in the north per person per year in 1949) though Mao Tse-tung

[1] Debts: Korean War debts as well as industry capital equipment purchases.

in 1959 urged the peasants to consider 200 lb per year per person consumption of meat as the ideal to be reached. The large grain consumption of the average Chinese (55 lb per month for worker and peasant, down to 28 lb per month for a sedentary clerk) provides a high proportion of carbohydrates, which is necessary to offset the (until now) lack of protein food. In India six ounces *per day* of carbohydrate is the ration provided. It is said that the consumption of milk makes up for the diminution of carbohydrate consumption, but the average consumption of milk in India is probably even lower, as far as protein average is concerned, than the consumption of bean-curd in China. All that can be said is that the Chinese are today better fed than they have been in recent history; that rationing is not only adequate but plentiful by Chinese standards, that the consumption of protein foods is rising and will continue to rise, which is a desideratum and also a food policy of the State. The consumption of meat, fish, milk, and other protein products is being *urged* by the government upon a (sometimes) unwilling population. Food habits are the last to be given up. Thus in Canton in 1965 people were being urged to be "patriotic by eating meat!"

Canning factories, as well as refrigerating units, are urgently required for pork and mutton. Tibet's very first refrigerating unit has now been installed in Lhasa, because the Tibetans, unlike the Chinese, prefer meat and milk. The problem of the vast pasture lands in the western regions of China, Tibet and Sinkiang is lack of population, for some of the areas contain fewer than one person per square mile; efforts in investment and technical personnel must also be combined with the settlement of State farms manned by ex-soldier labour. A fourfold increase of livestock in the last seventeen years has been recorded. A road from Tibet to Nepal, to supply the latter with frozen meat, among other things, is one of the outlets created for supplying meat to Asian markets. The supply of vegetables, vegetable oils and beans, and fruit[1] exceeds consumption many times; processing industries for all these products are being developed in the communes themselves, and the by-products are to be utilized as fodder and fertilizer.

Although cotton production has recovered (it suffered grievously in 1960-1) the country's clothing problem is not and cannot be solved by cotton planting alone. Cotton is the favourite wear of most Chinese, who, even in winter, will wear cotton padded garments and not wool. The increasing use of synthetic fabrics will decrease the demand for cotton; but this too depends partly on re-education of habits.

In any large self-sufficient, modern economy, it is the internal market flow and exchange of goods which assure a safe, reliable base.

The problem of the monetarization of the peasant has been solved through payment of wages by the workpoint, which is equivalent to piece-work payment; a wage increase in the last eight years to the peasant was achieved by a fifty per cent rise in the prices of agricultural produce sold to the State.[2] However, there is still, on the average, a two-to-one difference in salary compared with that of the lowest paid worker, though this is said to be offset by the fact that many basics (housing, water, vegetables) are free.

Each commune runs its own budget, which is divided into accumulation and consumption funds; accumulation (capital investment) for construction is about five per cent of the total; sixty per cent of the commune budget must go into

[1] Millions of orchard trees were planted in the last decade; fruit is now a common item of consumption in the communes.

[2] According to Commission of Economic Planning, there has been an eighty per cent increase in average payment from the State to agricultural production in communes; however, this depends on whether the date 1952 or 1956-7 is used. A thirty per cent increase was registered in prices paid in 1956-7 over 1952 averages; another fifty per cent between 1957 and 1966.

payment of wages to commune members; thus any increase in payment by the State for crop quotas is passed on in increase to peasants. The agricultural tax, which used to be twelve per cent, is now seven per cent, and in communes with quick turnover and perishable goods, only four per cent. The total agricultural tax levied represents only eight per cent of the revenue in the yearly State budget.

Each commune has its own veterinary stations, agricultural research stations, cultural groups, libraries, and hospitals and clinics. All have primary schools, and many also middle-schools. Trucks, tractors, barges, boats, fishing equipment, small railways, repair shops, building and carpentry shops, flour mills, extra industrial or handicraft workshops are found in every commune. Factories, canning plants, cement works, brick kilns, small steel furnaces, fertilizer plants, insecticide stations are being developed in the decentralization and overall industrialization process.

Networks of hospitals and clinics, provided in each commune, are of tremendous importance, both for the achievement of nation-wide public health measures, for providing the peasantry with a comprehensive health scheme and also for an efficient and comprehensive drive in family planning. This could not have been successful unless tackled in the "mass line" way, which is now being done.[1]

The problems of commune organization are not all resolved; they stem from many causes. The recidivist return to petty capitalism has already been noted; old habits of selfishness and greed die hard; they found expression again after the three bad years, from 1961 to 1963; a large and arduous socialist education movement in the countryside to eradicate them is still going on. The difficulties of preventing commune leadership from being taken over by ex-landlords

[1] HAN SUYIN, *Report on Family Planning in China*, New York, October, 1966.

or rich peasants recur; the clan aspect of village feudalism remains in some areas a deeply rooted psychological problem. Whole villages have only one surname, the inhabitants being all related to each other, and also related to the ex-landlord. Family ties, fear of reprisal, clan loyalties, allow the more clever, better educated sons of landlords to acquire new power through entering the commune leadership, often as book-keepers. In one such village recently, the only scholarship was given to an ex-landlord's son; in another, it was found that among fourteen families, one was the landlord family, and it had "returned to power" by becoming the heads of the production team! The produce of this area was being sold on the free market by the landlord-cadre as his own property. Mao Tse-tung had already pointed out this difficulty in 1929: "the unit of social organization is the clan ... in the party organizations in the villages ... a Communist Party branch meeting virtually becomes a clan meeting." On top of that, there is what we have mentioned before, the habit of com-mandism in the bureaucratic cadres. Again Mao Tse-tung, who knows his people very well indeed, pointed out: "The evil feudal practice of *arbitrary dictation* is so deeply rooted in the minds of the people and even of the ordinary Party members ... when anything crops up they choose the easy way, and have no liking for the bothersome democratic system ... of meeting and debates and criticism." Constant rectification campaigns have only begun to eradicate this tendency; the present Cultural Revolution is the most profound and deep of these movements to change the attitudes and behaviour of the past, both among Party members and the general popula-tion.

Each commune also has its own corps of militiamen for self-defence, but this has not always been entirely satisfactory. In the process of cleaning up the communes (1962 to 1964) the discipline of the militia was tightened, and this job was tackled by the PLA.[1] Many militia units are drafted for major projects, such as water conservancy, building roads, railways, etc., in conjunction with the PLA.

The question of accountancy and bookkeeping is an important one in the communes; as Lenin pointed out, it is important in the whole process of socialization. Only with an efficient and honest computing staff can the labour-wages, based on workpoints, be calculated to the satisfaction of commune members. This problem, again, recurs; it has been mentioned among the complaints which the peasantry made against the cadres in the three years, 1962–5.

The argument that collectivization has not benefited the peasantry is untenable; that it has not benefited agriculture in China is also proved erroneous. Yields have increased; agricultural production as a whole has doubled in output over the past seventeen years. The rise in the standard of living is noticeable; the peasant of China is now a literate, informed, knowledgeable man, who understands what he is doing and why. Industrialization has come to the commune, mechanization and electrification of the rural areas will be accomplished within the next twenty years (some say less). Enthusiasm within the communes is real, for they are on the whole successful. But this enthusiasm must not be self-centred. Everywhere one goes, one is told: "But we work not only for ourselves, we also work for the other two-thirds of the world, who are still exploited."

This is the almost automatic response everywhere; this feeling that the work done is revolutionary, not only for personal comfort, but for the fruit of success to be shared with others, is an important aspect in the development of the socialist education of the peasant in China.

The incentives to work must be non-material; they must

[1] The People's Liberation Army, known as PLA for short.—Author. See Chapter VII for the clean-up in the communes and the role of the PLA.

be revolutionary. Though in the case of the peasant socialization has been accompanied by a raised standard of living, money in the bank, security, schooling for the children, the continuing socialist education drives must teach the peasant that this material betterment is not the main goal of communism, but will also be acquired and ever more swiftly as he learns to be unselfish, dedicated, doing his best for the collective. It is this change of motivation, which is really the power which can move mountains, change heaven and earth; and though it still needs millions of hands, millions of baskets, already the earth is changing and the peasants can see the changes happen in their own lifetime.

Not for material rewards, but for the good of the community, not for self, but for others; the inspiration which will provide this change of the content of motivation and heighten collective awareness is acquired step by step, and the first step and springboard is the study of the thought of Mao Tse-tung, because the kind of thinking, the world view, and the revolutionary aims embodied in this work are "the best and most effective guide". Mao's writing is comprehensible to the peasant, who can apply it immediately. "Why cannot the 600 million peasants, poor and blank, build a socialist China, rich and strong?" Mao Tse-tung, too, is a peasant, and it was from the peasantry that the forces of the Chinese Revolution drew their strength. For them to read Mao is to read about themselves and their power to master their own destiny. Today, each commune is exhorted to become a "small Red base of the thought of Mao Tse-tung".

For a long time yet, the communes will use the "walking on two legs" methods, part mechanized, part labour-intensive, using all the ingenuity and short cuts that man invented empirically before science was understood. The replacement of costly and rare materials by local ones and the "thinking out ways and means", where there is a task ahead which looks difficult, involve a thorough reappraisal of attitude. It is this new confidence and pride in achievement so different from the old miasma of despair and resignation which are striking. Every commune member takes pride in subscribing to the Three Don'ts—

Don't ask money from the State (in loan for projects; try to do it yourself).

Don't ask help from other communes (in labour hands; try to cope with your own needs).

Don't be put off by any difficulties (we can order sun and moon to change places—we can change the earth).

And indeed, when 100,000 orchard trees are planted by 480 members of a production team in their spare time, to bring in extra income of 30,000 yuans; when a canal 340 kilometres long, is *dug in nine months* by voluntary labour without costing the State a cent . . . the distinction between "labour" and "capital" becomes invidious. It is not possible to calculate, by capitalist standards, the cost of reshaping the Chinese earth so that it shall produce, in abundance, for those who work it.

III

INDUSTRY—DESIGNING A NEW
HEAVEN AND EARTH

Do not say the strong pass is girded with iron. This very day we shall take
the first step, to scale the summit.   MAO TSE-TUNG, *Poems*

ALEXANDER ECKSTEIN[1] points out that fifteen years of
communist rule have produced a "united totalitarian State . . .
with a *compelling urge* to develop China into a major industrial
and military power in the shortest possible time". Most Asian
countries have the same "compelling urge" as China to
become industrialized independent states. The speed of China's
progress in industrialization, starting from a lower level than
Russia did in 1917, is impressive enough; what is more
impressive is that she has in certain sectors, already reached
advanced international levels.

Both from her geographical extent, material resources and
population, China can become, "one of the three major
modern powers in the world in the near future".[2] This
requires industrialization, intensive, swift, and of the highest
technological standards.

China's natural resources are far larger and more diversified,
than previous geological surveys estimated; in 1949 she was
still geologically an unexplored country. Surveys have since
been made by the Chinese themselves, resulting in the discovery of more underground wealth than had been reported;
this includes oil, gold, platinum, uranium, thorium, and work-
able quantities of minerals previously believed absent.

[1] ALEXANDER ECKSTEIN, *Communist China's Economic Growth and Foreign
Trade*, 1964. *See* Bibliography.
[2] FRITZ BAADE, *The Race to the Year 2000. See* Bibliography.

65

China's coal reserves are enough to meet the needs of any amount of industrialization. Her iron deposits are more widely scattered and richer than previously estimated. Tungsten, antimony, lead, nickel, vanadium, molybdenum, zinc, mercury, magnesite, manganese, aluminium, tin, asbestos, etc., are all found. Copper may be the only mineral that is not too plentiful, at least in Manchuria, but the proved reserves of oil in Sinkiang alone are more than sixteen times those of Iran.

"Natural resources are cultural appraisals." The geological finds continue; only recently another coalfield, oil deposits, as well as natural gas in large quantities, have been found in Szechuan province.

But before discussing China's industrialization we must know: "what *kind* of an industrial power does China want to set up?" China wants to establish a major *socialist* industrial power, with emphasis on the word *socialist*; at one time this meant following a Russian pattern, but it no longer does so; China is building her own pattern and has been more clearly building it in her own way since 1956. This pattern depends in a great measure on ideological considerations or, as the Chinese call it, the socialist world-view; but it also depends on strategic evaluations, and on the principle of developing to the maximum the inventiveness, and capacities for intelligent labour of the Chinese people within the context of the Chinese resources.[1] Why is it that China's industries have *not* followed the Russian pattern? Because in industry as in agriculture, the Chinese maintain that the general line of development must be unswervingly socialist, unswervingly independent, and adapted to the realities of China.

It has been argued that heavy politicalization would be

[1] This point is important; for Western capitalist industrialization was accomplished at the cost of exploitation of *other* lands and resources and labour power.

"disastrous" and lead to failure in China's efforts to indus-
trialize. And yet it is *because* of its socialist pattern in industry
that Soviet Russia achieved tremendous industrial growth in
such a short time during the 1930s, at a pace unknown in
Europe till then. And it is also because of the conviction that
"politics is the lifeline of economic work", that today China
can boast a sizeable industrial achievement.

The example of Japan, always held up as the pattern of
an Asian "major industrial power" can surely not be seriously
entertained; her first capital expansion was financed by war
in China in 1894–5; the invasion of Manchuria in 1931 was
precisely the same type of colonialism as that practised by the
West in order to reap further capital accumulation through the
exploitation of colonial raw materials. And her role in the
Second World War led to Pearl Harbor in 1941. Her present
prosperity is due to the injection of USA capital; it is as a USA
satellite, against China's growing power, that Japan survives
at the cost of great exertion. Can anyone rationally wish that
China should have done the same?

At the present moment, measured by the USA's or
Russia's standards, China's industrial base is still small; but
her capacity for speed of development and growth is quite
another matter; a growth of nine to fourteen per cent[1]
has been the average in industry for the past seventeen years;
Soviet Russia in the first fifteen years of its existence, also
grew at a rate unprecedented in Europe. It is an open secret
that within the next decades the economic breakthrough and
emergence of China as a comprehensive, totally self-reliant
industrial power will be recognized, for already she is on the
verge of breakthrough. A war, if war comes, in which the

[1] Figures of rate of industrial growth vary wildly; twelve per cent average
for the first Five-year Plan was recorded; it then leapt in 1958–9, then receded.
No statistics have been published since 1961 but in 1965–6 well-informed
French sources suggest a growth-rate of fifteen per cent.

bombing of industrial sites to cripple China is openly discussed in the Western Press, will not prevent this outcome; the grand design to "bomb China back to the Stone Age" will not be easy to achieve; since 1956, certain that she will not be allowed to progress, nor be left in peace, she has adopted measures for self-protection which comprise the planning of industrial sites in a way designed to mitigate the bombing that is to come.[1] "The enemy dares to cheat us, because we are still poor and blank—but wait eight or ten years, then they will see what China is. . . ."[2]

In 1949 China's heavy industry was almost non-existent and all comparisons with Russia only point out this extreme lack. The USSR in 1917 produced 4·1 million tons of steel and 4 million tons of petroleum, had a fairly large technical and managerial personnel, 5 million *skilled* industrial workers in all types of industries for a population of 130 million. In 1948, China's production of steel was 40,000 tons. Though the Japanese had managed to produce 1·34 million tons of steel out of Manchuria, at peak, these steel plants had been stripped in 1945 (by the Soviet Union). China herself never produced more than 50,000 tons "not enough for nails or needles."[3] In 1952, Russia produced 60 million metric tons of steel, and in 1965, 91 million metric tons. China's steel production in 1952 was an optimistic 1·1 million tons[4] from rehabilitated plants; and in 1960 (according to Chou En-lai) 12 million tons (of which 4 million had been produced in the backyard furnaces and was not industrially useful). For 1965 figures are "inspired guesses", since no statistics or figures are

[1] "A rain of nuclear bombs, the dirtiest we can get . . . that is the only way we can deal with the Chinese people." Dr. Ralph Lapp, 14th February, 1966.

[2] Quoted from *Jen Min Jih Pao*, 13th August, 1960 (a few weeks after the withdrawal of the Soviet technicians).

[3] Quoted from Yung Lung-kwei. Author's private interview, July 1962.

[4] But the actual production was under half a million, the rest being purchased from the USSR and not really produced by China. Author's note.

issued. Some scholars put it at between 10 and 15 million tons, but others think that it is much nearer 18 million tons, taking into account not only the large, medium and small steel plants, but the three thousand five hundred odd converter and blast furnaces of modern type now scattered about the land. The Chinese estimate that their industrial growth aiming at ten per cent in a year, but which seems to have reached fifteen per cent in the last two years,[1] will permit them to achieve their goal, proclaimed in 1958, of catching up with England in steel production by 1972 (26 million tons).

The years 1949 to 1952, as in agriculture, were years of rehabilitation for whatever industry there was. Engineers and other personnel rallied to get the mines, railways, etc., working again, for neglect, disrepair and war had disrupted almost every one of these.

Light industry in the form of textile mills, flour mills, paper mills, bean cake factories, situated in Shanghai, Tientsin, Hankow, a large proportion foreign-controlled, was put back in working order. There were no machine plants of any kind, only machine repair or assembly shops; no building industry, no rubber industry, motors of 20–30 kW could be assembled but all parts were imported. In Hankow there were the Japanese-controlled Han Yeh Ping steel plants, the only heavy industry present in China proper; they produced the famous 40,000 tons of steel. In Manchuria there was the Anshan Japanese-built steel plant. It was to be completely rebuilt, on the Russian model.

Half of the railway system, four-fifths of the coal production, fifty-seven per cent of electricity, gas and water supplies were still under foreign control in 1949, the takeover and control of these assets was part of the "industrialization" process in

---

[1] *Far Eastern Economic Review*, 29th September, 1966, p. 621. Hsinhua News Agency estimated industrial growth in 1966 at over twenty per cent.

its initial stages. The return of the concessions with their fixed assets and public utilities, the barracks of foreign garrisons, the banks, gold, and properties of the Japanese and the Kuomintang, the customs (foreign-controlled till 1949) provided an initial source of capital equipment and funds. Dockyards, telegraph and telephone services, undersea cables, weaving mills were requisitioned; compensation was to be given (these were foreign-owned). Small individual, national capitalist enterprises continued on a private basis till 1956.[1]

A licensing system of import-export for foreign traders was instituted in 1949, and the Bank of China was appointed for foreign exchange transactions; the ruinous inflation of the Chiang régime was checked.

Though the State devoted over forty per cent of the national State budget to national defence during the two years 1950 and 1951,[2] by 1952 the economy was in a far healthier state than it had been all through the decade since 1939. Industrialization then began in earnest, with the first Five-year Plan (1953–7). It was preceded (and this was to become almost a feature of each industrial plan) by an ideological, political movement or campaign.

The Three and the Five ante-campaigns[3] took place in 1952–3. The small sector of light industry which had remained in private hands was reduced. Revision, in 1962, of the rates of interest paid to capitalists on their investment in such enterprises[4] was due; but an extension till 1966 was granted.

[1] 1956 is regarded as the year in which socialist transformation at the base (agriculture, capitalist concerns, industrial and business concerns) was completed, or almost. A number of small shopkeeping and retail stores remained on a part State part individual footing till 1966 (curio dealers, antiques, restaurants).

[2] Korean War expenditures.

[3] *See* Chapter V.

[4] Originally the payment of interest at five per cent (up to eight to nine per cent) was due to expire in 1962, it was then renewed for three years, 1962–5 and was due for reappraisal in 1966 (interview with Yung Lung-kwei, 1962).

The first Five-year Plan (industrial sector) thus began with the propitious psychological groundwork of the anti-corruption drives, the Korean War of national self-defence in which patriotic fervour gave an impetus to the initial process of industrial construction, and a stable countryside. It also began with China having to "lean one side", upon her (then) only friend, Soviet Russia, because of the embargo, United States hostility, and USA support during the civil war to Chiang Kai-shek. Today, reappraising the first Five-year Plan, it is conceded that many mistakes were made in planning large heavy-industry complexes on the Russian model, for these were not adapted to China's needs.[1]

The emphasis of the first Plan was on heavy industry and particularly on the production of industries manufacturing means of production, seventy per cent of the investment of the first Plan being in steel and machine-building plants (producer goods industries) and thirteen per cent in consumer goods industries (textile, shoes, etc.). It was estimated that half the capital goods and machine equipment needed for industrialization would be manufactured in China within the first Five-year Plan. All the heavy industries other than steel, that is to say alloys, nonferrous metal, machine construction, chemicals, petrol, precision instruments, transport, refineries, fertilizers, would have to start from nothing. A phased staging of industrial development, with priorities, was therefore essential.

Steel came first, with new steel complexes in three regions; followed by the Sanmen hydroelectric project, and over one hundred and fifty key industrial projects, all on "normal" commercial terms, to be paid for (with interest in some cases).

[1] This question was already raised in 1956. *See Eight Party Congress Documents: Reports* by CHOU EN-LAI; also *Jen Min Jih Pao*, 11th April, 1957. "There is ... too much emphasis on large, modern, mechanized, high standard construction with no regard to conditions in China . . ."

By 1956 the Chinese had realized that the Soviet model was not ideal for conditions in China, primarily because in the planning of heavy industry in China, outside planners forgot the primary economic base, the agricultural sector; and even heavy industry had to be geared to this base. Secondly, these enormous plants with their many labour-saving devices did not have a secondary line of industries to utilize their products; thirdly, spare parts were frequently in demand and extremely expensive (they became more so in time). Fourthly, the concentration of these heavy industrial plants, and the cost of building, was extremely high and the return slow.

Nevertheless the growth rate in industry was around twelve per cent a year for the years 1954–7. China's intention to catch up industrially with the West was to be done in "leaps"; the theory of "leaps" is a Leninist and dialectical materialist principle, applied to knowledge, as well as to material and historical advances. Mao Tse-tung basing himself on the long experience of the Red bases, their survival and triumph, made it clear that the principles of socialist construction must not be given up for the sake of industrialization; and the emphasis on heavy industry was producing a disequilibrium in the national economy.[1]

Neglect of the peasant agricultural base was not Mao's idea of socialism. Two problems thus confronted the government, the problem of psychological transformation of incentives which in Mao's view was essential to increased socialization, both in agriculture and industry, and the problem of overall equilibrium between heavy and light industry and agriculture. Needless to add that the "Right wing deviation" which was already mentioned in official reports, and the growth of bureaucracy and armchair

[1] See MAO TSE-TUNG, "China's Path to Industrialization", in On the Correct Handling of Contradictions among the People, 27th February, 1957.

leadership, already manifest, added to these problems. In 1956 also came the first signs of revisionism in the Russian Communist Party superstructure.[1]

That Russian aid, both technical (machinery and men) and financial (loans) was essential to China's industrial beginning cannot be denied. Whatever the present relations, the setting-up of a heavy industry base in Manchuria and other areas and the 156 main projects between the years 1951 and 1955 (of which 145 were in hand or accomplished by 1958) still form an important part of China's industrial base. When I visited Manchuria in the summer of 1966, most of the heavy industry plants working were on the Soviet pattern, although other machine plants existed. Technical innovations by Chinese personnel were pointed out in almost every branch, and in the Anshan and Wuhan steel complexes these innovations are shown to visitors, with references to the "sabotage" by "revisionists" and the abrupt withdrawal of all engineers and technicians in 1960; but the help and hard work put in by Soviet personnel and engineers (some of whom wept when recalled) is also remembered.

That the Chinese benefited from the inevitable short cuts, due to the more advanced stage of Soviet industrialization in 1950 than in 1930, has also been pointed out. The subsequent inventions and improvements however, made by the Chinese themselves, are becoming a significant factor in progress since 1960, pointing to a rapidly sophisticated technical personnel. This personnel is derived from among the workers themselves, many being "inventors", and this significant and rapid "technicalization" among the worker masses is a

[1] The Marxist classics define the base as the means of production and relations of production, and the superstructure as the administrative, cultural, political and leadership complex which guides and directs the transformation operated upon the base. Interreaction between base and superstructure is constant, therefore, and hence revisionism in the superstructure (or nerve centre) affects the whole State.

factor of great importance, which answers the often repeated question about China's "lack of trained personnel".

A French economist, touring factories and plants in China in 1956 and again in 1964, complained to me of the "low" level at which "decision making" and plans for the working of the factory, the equipment and machine buying, were inaugurated. By this he meant that it was the workers themselves, in meetings with the administrators and engineers, who participated in what is considered top-level decision making. I tried to explain the policy of the socialist government, that action must follow the "mass line", and that mass democracy was the goal, not bureaucratic tyranny, nor technical dictatorship.[1] This implied that in every such decision making, whether in factory, mine or commune, the total participation of the workers, or peasants, was sought by meetings and discussion, often lengthy and tedious, and that this was the essentially broad democratic way of doing things; that this was what Mao Tse-tung sought to implant in the minds of the people, the masses, what he had described as the touchstone of success, back in 1928.[2] Any factory, steel complex, industrial plant has "three-corner consultations", meaning the party leadership or administrative staff, the experts or high-level technical engineers, and the workers themselves. This produced the best results in the long run. "But how tedious", was the reply of this French engineer. Tedious or not this policy is not only democratic but educative, it is the best way of galvanizing and mobilizing resourcefulness and inventive power; workers are not machines, they are the men who work the machines, and they must be made to feel that they control the machines, and not the other way round.

[1] "The people need democracy. . . . The Army needs it." MAO TSE-TUNG, 25th November, 1928.

[2] "We have always maintained, that the revolution must rely on the masses of the people, on everybody taking a hand, and have opposed relying merely on a few persons issuing orders." MAO TSE-TUNG, 2nd April, 1948.

The rapidity with which technological personnel has been created is due precisely to this practice of democracy in its application to all workers in industry.

In 1950 technological personnel was very insufficient; their training was undertaken together with the setting-up of industrial plants. Fifteen thousand students were sent to the USSR and other socialist countries. Today over 250,000 engineers (fully trained) exist in China, the majority (eighty per cent) are under thirty-five years old.

The First Great Leap Forward in industry, 1958, was coupled with the creation of the communes, in an all-out drive for a crash industrialization programme. The thinking behind the First Leap Forward was already evident in 1954, when references to "leaps" were made.[1] But there was more than Marxist economic theory behind the decision taken at that time. In socialist China, the bulk of funds for capital construction could only be derived from such sources as profits of State industrial enterprises (more than eighty per cent), agricultural taxes and customs (around twenty per cent) and the native capitalist sector (very little, practically none after 1956). By 1956 the accumulation fund (proportion of national income saved for development) was roughly twenty per cent per year of the revenue, and it has remained so on average till 1966. This high rate of saving coming entirely from domestic sources is directly related to the continuous and even increasing emphasis on thrift and frugality, cutting down of waste and extravagance, to finding time-, fund- and material-saving innovations and to "turning labour into capital" policies, an investment contribution made by all citizens in working overtime without wages in industry (or in the communes).[2] The slogan of the Leap was "doing more,

[1] The theory of leaps in development is a basic one to the theory of knowledge in dialectical materialism.
[2] "Building our Country through Thrift and Frugality" occupies a whole

quicker, better, and with more economy", and this has remained
the basic definition of all the strenuous efforts for an industrial
breakthrough. By 1957 the gross output value of industry
had increased two and a half times since 1952; the decision to
leap, based on the increased agrarian output, then obtained
was bold, but not unreasonable. But its success was contin-
gent upon two things. One was continued good harvests.
The smooth passage to collectivization induced hopes that
the communes, pooling labour-intensive methods, would
provide, without much surplus investment, a stable and
increasingly productive base to subserve the industrial leap.
This calculation did not materialize immediately, as described
in the previous chapter. The second was the continued supply
of capital equipment and spare parts for the machine tools
from Russia (there was no other source) and the implementation of accords signed in autumn 1957, promising further
and expanded technical aid. The accords also promised military
help in the form of nuclear knowledge.

The second Five-year Plan, 1958–62, envisaged expansion
of heavy industry, especially in hydroelectric power and
chemical fertilizer plants; already the need to streamline
industry in some respects to harmonize with agriculture had
been pointed out; and a warning not to follow "foreign
stereotypes" had been issued.[1] The Yellow River, Liuchua and
Sanmen dams (two million kilowatts) projects were to be
continued, and would have furnished power for the electrification of a large region and also dealt with the irrigation
of at least twenty million acres of notoriously arid land; this
scheme, as well as a similar but even larger one for the

---

[1] Proposals for Second Five-year Plan, 27th September, 1956. CHOU EN-LAI,
Report on Proposals for Second Five-year Plan, 16th September, 1956.

---

chapter in the booklet: *Quotations from Chairman Mao Tse-tung.* "This principle
(of thrift, economy) is one of the basic principles of socialist economics", 1955,
Socialist Upsurge in China's Countryside.

Yangtze River, and many other projects, was arrested in 1960 by "the sudden complete withdrawal of 1,390 Soviet experts, tearing up of 343 contracts for experts and the supplements to these contracts, abolition of 257 items for scientific and technical co-operation, and since then reduction in large numbers of the supplies of complete equipment which caused huge losses, upsetting our original plan for development of our national economy, and greatly aggravating our difficulties."[1]

The story of the First Leap Forward in industry has been told many times: the first ecstatic frenzy, the extremes of enthusiasm, the thousands of small backyard furnaces to make steel. Though the whole story, if one only concentrates on the errors, sounds lunatic, yet a more dispassionate appraisal will show us that it was necessary to pass through such revolutionary enthusiasm in order to operate a net qualitative change, and that under the circumstances, the Chinese did not lose their heads completely, and recovered very swiftly.

Thus the backyard steel furnace episode was really an exaggerated instance of the new stress that was going to be laid on Chinese self-reliance, on going her own way without imitating Russia any longer. In China these directives have a way, at first, of provoking an over-reaction, sometimes rather terrifying in its literal-mindedness. I have noticed this quite often, and it was again apparent in 1966 (though mitigated by the fact that limits had been placed to mass hysteria by preliminary recommendations to prudence). But in the first decade no such safeguards were at first thought of; and so it was sufficient for someone to launch the slogan: "We shall do it all our own way" for a campaign of massive proportions to start in which machinery was badly over-used; the warning not to "imitate slavishly foreign stereotypes" led

[1] CHOU EN-LAI, 4th December, 1963, quotation from *Report*.

to a movement in which it was, for some weeks, very fashionable to look down upon anything foreign. The early excesses of the young Red Guards in cutting some girls' hair (in the first two days of their activities) was prompted, no doubt, by the fact that "long hair" was associated with "romance" and therefore with revisionist selfishness. And so it goes on. A people, in the process of learning how to think and to act in an entirely new way, succumbs perhaps more easily to these massive and enthusiastic hyper-obediences; the process of teaching the masses to think for themselves, to debate and to reason, is one of the aims of the Cultural Revolution but the mental leap from feudal obedience to scientific socialist rationale is gigantic.

In such an atmosphere (and I have now twice had the experience) bureaucratic pettiness and tyranny make the situation even worse. A certain regard for rationality and a little less literal-mindedness are very much needed by Party members; and these needs were evident in certain aspects of the First Leap Forward. Many factories were built, which would never be utilized because no machinery came for them; steel was made, or rather a crude kind of steel, which was never carted away for there was no transport. Roads were built by labourers recruited from the villages, while the harvest went rotting on the ground. "Even without natural calamities, some readjustment was due", writes Anna Louise Strong.

Readjustment was made; it began in late 1961, and went on through 1962. The orientation of industry was totally redesigned. The motto: "Agriculture as the base of the national economy with industry as the leading factor" established an equilibrium. Industry began to be geared to the production of agricultural tools and machinery, and irrigation pumps especially, were made in vast quantities. A better distribution of investment to light and heavy industry followed. The drive to build more fertilizer plants was increased. Already three had been built during the first Plan; from 1959 onwards five more large and several small ones were to be built. Decentralization of heavy industry also proceeded swiftly. The shaping of industry on the Chinese model, and away from the Russian model, had started in earnest.

The allocation of investment in transport was also increased greatly from 1958 to 1961. Transport bottlenecks had led to much difficulty during the first Five-year Plan in getting raw materials to the factories. An extensive network of commune-built roads now trebled the kilometre length (46,000 km in 1949 to 93,000 km in 1958 to 150,000 km in 1964). The distribution of Chinese railways, until 1949, had reflected the priority of the colonized seaboard and external commerce over the provincial and "backward" inland—a corollary to the fact that China did not have a real national economy, nor a unified internal market. This changed. Railways increased from 13,000 km to 48,000 km between 1958 and 1963; the linkage of five rivers by canals to form an integrated water-transport system covering almost half of China was achieved, and aviation routes were developed. Telephone linkages (so that, for instance, Peking–Lhasa conferences and meetings are held by telephone) have strengthened the cohesion. Industrial production leapt in 1958 to a twenty per cent growth rate,[1] but then decreased to nothing in the years 1960–1; in 1962 and 1963 it grew at a rate of about five to seven per cent (allowing for readjustment). The rate of growth was ten per cent in 1964, fifteen per cent in 1965 and is expected to remain between twelve to fifteen per cent in the third Five-year Plan which began in 1966.

[1] Some observers report that this increased production also broke many machines. While it is probably true that there were excesses, there was also a good deal of work done in industry as in agriculture, whose after-effects would be beneficial.

The geographical distribution of industry was changing, as the Second Plan outlined, moving inland. At present some of the most sophisticated types of machine tool seen at an exhibition of industrial equipment in 1966 came from Chinghai province in the west. Very large and important industrial projects exist in the autonomous areas of the national minorities, in Sinkiang and Tibet.

A new regional equilibrium has now come into being centring round industrial locations near new and extensive sources of mineral wealth. The discovery of oil wells in Manchuria and in several regions of Sinkiang, opened up in record time by combined teams of technicians and army men, has made China self-sufficient in oil requirements for her present development; Chinese refineries now turn out a whole range of petroleum products; 10 million tons of crude oil a year (375 million in USA) a figure that will probably be doubled by 1970.

The siting of industries in sparsely populated areas depends not only on communication but also on developing a food base nearby in order to spare transport. In the ever-present drive for economy and to cut down transport wastage each "economic region" must become as self-sufficient as possible. During the "three bad years" 1959–61, each organization, each unit, including banks, stores, schools and ministry departments, grew its own food (sometimes in flower-pots on window sills) and sent its staff to the countryside, in rotation, to work lots, raise pigs, etc. This experience has been profitable.

Today each industrial plant grows, or provides by contracts with surrounding communes, its own food. Taching oil wells complex for instance has its own communes, to supply it with grain, meat and oil; the same is true of many other new industries, such as the Sian precision instrument complex, located in the countryside, which has its own vegetable farms and contracts with neighbouring communes for oil, meat and eggs.

The policy of "walking on two legs", applied to agriculture, also applies to industry. Thus a great variety of stages of development exists at the same time. Highly sophisticated, automated plants are neighbour to small, old-type ones; in certain industries some of the processes outdate others by twenty years; in a canning factory the meat will be processed most efficiently, and the end product conveyed in wheel-barrows to the depots.

Large comprehensive industrial complexes, such as the Russians built in Manchuria in the early fifties, are costly, vulnerable to air attack, and in a labour-intensive country do not fulfil the educative functions required. Thousands of small steel plants scattered over the whole country whose output serves local industry by the manufacture of agricultural tools and water turbines, cutting blades and presses are far more useful. This is the pattern of the steel industry today; several large complexes built before 1960 and over 5,000 smaller ones, using the latest techniques, but scattered in every region.

The replanning of industry, and transport, involved the wholesale moving of personnel and labour. The call to youth, made in 1958, to participate in socialist construction resulted in a large movement of young people from the more sophisticated centres to the Western hinterland, such as Sinkiang. Young students, from the cities, PLA men, and young militia from the communes form the bulk of these pioneer settlements.

The new orientation has produced new centres of communi-cation: Szechuan, now an important industrial and agricul-tural economic centre serving also the vast Tibetan region; Sian and Lanchow, foci where rail, road and air routes that serve the Inner Mongolian and Sinkiang regions meet.

Kansu, whose underground mineral wealth is vast, is an industrial, mining and agricultural base, now that tree belts and irrigation are taming its deserts. China's newest and most up-to-date factories are found in such once remote wildernesses. A million students have been settled in Kansu alone. The Shanghai dialect is heard from Harbin to Urumchi. Yunnan is also a developing economic base linked with the Burmese–Indochinese frontier areas. Most transport developments are carried out by PLA army units (as was the road to Tibet) aided by local labour and commune militia. Many of the new factories built since 1961, mines, and heavy industry sites also have PLA staff or are under the supervision of PLA cadres, who work together with technical personnel and workers from all over China.

Medical and technical colleges and institutes are transferred from Shanghai, Peking or other cities to serve the demands of these new industrial locations. Schools follow.

There are, to summarize, two "sets" of industrial development in China today: the State-financed, large-scale, heavy industries and light industries (large and medium size) and the smaller factories, workshops, etc., growing in number in the communes, chiefly processing agricultural goods. The policy of "walking on two legs" to "achieve more with less, faster, more economically, more efficiently" also is part of China's strategic outlook. A widely scattered multiple industrial base,[1] by which each region becomes industrially as well as agriculturally self-reliant, makes China unconquerable by bombing.

By utilizing the *ad hoc* with the planned, by combining

---

[1] During the steel campaign, a number of roads and even wooden railways were constructed by commune labour, to and from the communes to the centres of coal, iron deposits and lime quarries. Today, these are in use for the new factories, which are developing within the communes and which form the commune industries.

archaic types of small semi-mechanized factory with modern factories with a high degree of automation only a few kilometres away the whole industrial field has, since 1965, been girding itself for an enormous forward movement, a Second Great Leap Forward.

The "redundancy" of personnel which some visitors notice in Chinese factories and plants is due to apprenticeship, for the need for skilled workers is increasing very fast. Each worker usually has two "apprentices" with him who are actually students, being put to "university" at the work-bench. Today, each factory, each commune, each plant is also a school, not only technical but also ideological, since politics must be in command. Education thus conceived cuts cost to a minimum; supplemented by lectures, television courses, and short-term courses at technical institutes, it is satisfactory and practical and integrates the young workers into the social context of their work immediately. The rapid expansion of industry envisaged from 1966 onwards will not lack skilled young workers. Today they number around forty million and in State enterprises the intake is one million a year. These forty million also comprise workers in commune factories, who are only semi-trained, artisans and craftsmen rather than workers. The raising of "scientific experimentation" to a revolutionary mass movement with its emphasis on audacity and innovation has continued ever since 1958, and it is openly avowed that the disastrous Russian behaviour acted as a spur to self-reliance and to ingenuity.

A large degree of independence is given to factories and industrial units in the provinces; they are under local or provincial authorities and this, while releasing spontaneity, may have certain drawbacks in asserting overall economic planning. In certain regions capital construction accumulation is faster than in others for there are still difficulties of supply due to unequal distribution, allocation, priorities and use of funds. Kwangtung province, for instance, ninety-five per cent electrified, is probably the most efficient both industrially and agriculturally. The largest number of export market industries are still in and around Shanghai, which had the biggest light industry base in the past (now multiplied thirtyfold and with heavy industry and machine tools added), Manchuria is still an advanced heavy industrial base, skilled model workers from there being found all over China. The steel works at Anshan have now expanded to four times their size in 1953. Szechuan is becoming a very large industrial base, as are Kansu, Sinkiang. Even Yunnan and Tibet are being transformed. This speed creates bottlenecks in raw material allocation and supply, as competition for machinery between the several regions develops, the demand being always greater than the supply in personnel, in funds, in transport, in equipment. These teething troubles are not yet ended. However, in the perspective of China, in the vastness of her problems, and the vastness of her solutions, such things as temporary reverses, bottlenecks, stoppages, are considered from a different viewpoint. Indeed, with the whole picture, both in agriculture and industry, in mind, it is the successes, the achievements in a short seventeen years, which count and not the failures. When all these difficulties, the inexperience and errors, the embargo, the Korean War, the transformation of the social system, *and* the Russian let-down in 1960 are taken into account, as well as the tumult and chaos of the First Leap Forward, one can only agree that China has done well, and those who belittle her endeavour and her courage are neither objective, nor able to view her achievements impartially.

Today, China can build machinery for industry, agriculture, defence, transport and scientific research. She can produce all kinds of motor vehicles, ships, aircraft, high-precision machine tools, instruments and meters, locomotive engines, and whole textile plants. She produces synthetic materials, plastics, computers, hydraulic presses, she can set up fertilizer plants, steel plants, and refineries, all on her own. Whole plants are being sold abroad, and she is also buying whole plants. She is able to design independently and to build modern coal pits each with annual output of one million tons, integrated iron and steel works each with an annual productive capacity of 1·5 million tons of steel; chemical fertilizer plants, each with an annual productive capacity of 25,000 tons of synthetic ammonia, various heavy machine-building plants, power stations each with a 650,000-kilowatt capacity.

China can now make ninety per cent of the machinery she needs. Sufficiency in steel products climbed from seventy-five to ninety per cent during 1958–65. Changes in distribution in industry allow every province and autonomous region in the country to establish modern industry to some extent. In the space of only a dozen years, the foundation of socialist industrialization has been laid. It could be surmised that China might be able to maintain the same leap-forward speed in order to carry through the socialist industrialization of the country within a reasonable period of time.[1]

The third Five-year Plan, 1966–70,[2] which lays continued stress upon agriculture as the base of the national economy with industry as the leading factor, increases investment in heavy industry, fertilizer plants, petroleum, petro-chemicals and steel, these being the "leaping industries".

In 1949, 27,000 tons of chemical fertilizers were produced. In 1966 fertilizer production had reached nine million tons.

Emphasis on developing industry according to the policy of taking agriculture as the foundation of the national economy

[1] Chou En-lai, *Report*, 1964.
[2] *See* interview with Han Suyin, "China's Third Five Year Plan", *Far Eastern Economic Review*, 24th November, 1966.

and the carrying out of socialist economic construction centring on heavy industry are not contradictory; the two are a unity. The Third Plan gave, therefore, emphasis to the growth of the means of production so that social expanded production might be realized, and advanced technical equipment, provided for the technical transformation of the entire national economy including agriculture. But the over-emphasis on heavy industry, pleading that this was the only way to strengthen all sectors, including national defence, was to be guarded against; the results indicate that so far the warnings from the right-wingers, that the national economy would remain backward if priority to heavy industry was not given were baseless, and that these pleas covered political motivations such as "economism" which are being denounced as revisionist today.

Today industry, science and technology have reached a stage where China can go forward industrially even if completely blockaded. Every plan for industrial expansion takes the coming attack by the USA into account. The "second front" in industry, that is the small industrial sites in communes, is also directed towards the strategy of a long protracted war. The emphasis on defence and on combat readiness is evidenced by the military training in which, regularly, all workers and administrative personnel in every industrial concern take part. The demand for increased accumulation of savings inevitably points the way to another large "thrift and frugality" movement combined with the Second Leap. The thrift, frugality, the cutting down waste and saving campaigns go on all the time and receive a fresh stimulus every two or three years.

Consumption is antithetical to net investment. A rate higher than the twenty per cent savings so far effected must be realized by a self-imposed control of consumption; and an extra sustained amount of "invisible" investment in the form of voluntary unpaid labour of all kinds. The satisfaction humans derive from self-denial and sacrifice has proved, historically, more meaningful and creative than selfish greed; and here the building and transformation of a quarter of humanity is a colossal undertaking.

Availability of export markets, and the rate of population growth are other factors affecting industrial expansion; a movement for planned families, already begun in 1962, will continue; here youth is the target, the emphasis is on late marriage, dedication to high revolutionary ideals, voluntary self-control; this forgoing of individual satisfaction is repaid in group approval and the meaningfulness of its value for the community.[1]

Industrial products[2] now form more than sixty per cent of export goods (including processed and semi-processed) in value; though agricultural produce still remains the largest single item to subserve these processed goods, this will decrease gradually in the decade to come, remaining at about thirty per cent for a good while.[3]

In conclusion, it cannot be denied (says *Far East Trade and Development*, October, 1966) "that the general line for socialist construction contributed very much to increasing social consciousness and determination to overcome difficulties". The 1966 proletarian Cultural Revolution is now persevering in this line, and making this leap method the *standard* to be followed; opening up new vistas in speed, technical education, and public consciousness and creative enthusiasm, those

---

[1] HAN SUYIN, *Report on Family Planning in China*, New York, October, 1966.

[2] Forty per cent of raw materials used in industry come from the agricultural sector.

[3] It is computed that a diminution to thirty per cent is possible, but will then level off and stabilize around that level in the next decade, though semi-processed goods will yield to finished goods (canning of meat, fruit and vegetables will expand considerably).

incalculable sources of energy whose effectiveness in transforming our earth is only beginning to be realized. The momentum towards self-reliance has increased; the capital for socialist construction has been obtained within China's own economy. By 1966 China did not have any debts anywhere. Even the National bonds (internal) of 1951, 1957 and 1958 were to be repaid in full, with interest before the end of 1968.

The appearance of revisionism in Soviet Russia, and the experience China had of its effects, led to very thorough investigations and assessments about the possibility of revisionism in the Chinese Communist Party and also in every sector of the economy including industry. Revisionism in China, with its material implications of profit and material incentives, would not lead to independent industrialization, but would be a disaster, starting a spiral of craving for luxury items which no poor country in the world today can afford without verging on bankruptcy. Industry would be hobbled by private selfishness; its growth directed towards making profits for *external* monopolies would be abetted by a comprador class; the Chinese peasant would not become a technical, intelligent, modern man but would fall back into a private small-producer economy. Within ten years the hardwon gains, the independent economy, the self-reliant industrialization, would be corroded into the type of economy it was before 1949. China, weak and rotten, would once more become everyone's prey.

The battle against "revisionism" in industry is part of the building of an independent national economy. Along with this goes a problem of overriding importance for the future; the problem of incentives. Will China's national economy and its growth resort to capitalist material incentives or will it maintain the correct Marxist line of revolutionary incentives?

The economic changes in the Soviet Union and in East European countries, which imply the return of material and personal profit in the shape of a salary hierarchy, bonuses and other material incentives, as well as profit-sharing in industries, have been watched carefully by the Chinese Communist leadership. Economic "decentralization",[1] regard for market demand, accounting in terms of profitability, and additional norms of material incentives now practised along the lines proposed by Liberman in the USSR or Ota Sik in Czechoslovakia, are thoroughly repudiated by China.

The move towards this return to a non-socialist type of economy was initiated by Yugoslavia in 1951. After Chou En-lai's speech of 1956 at the National Peoples' Congress[2] certain Western observers thought that China might also follow this liberalization, especially as "decentralization" was featured in Chou En-lai's speech. This view was disproved; for actually Chou En-lai did not speak of *material* incentives, but only of giving more authority to local and regional organizations over industrial projects. China today is further away than she was in 1956 from a return to capitalism; the present Cultural Revolution is moving her along the road to constructing a socialist economy on incentives very different from the ones prevailing in Russia today.

A Chinese economist pointed out to me that Yugoslavia's present precarious economic position, with devaluation of the dinar and soaring prices, was an example to all those nations who trust to aid (in this case USA aid) rather than to self-reliance and hard work, as China does. Even if one feels that this explanation is naïve the fact remains that only an

---

[1] "This 'decentralization' is quite different from that begun in China, which is strategic and geographic." CHARLES BETTELHEIM, *La Construction du Socialisme en Chine* (Ed. MASPERO).

[2] Speech by Chou En-lai in June, 1956, at NPC.

inflexible stand on socialist principles in the socialist construction of the economy can bring success, and that means the *abandonment of material incentives*. The thorough socialist education and re-education of peasants and workers, to change their thinking and attitudes, would be instituted instead. Hence the intensive campaigns to study the thought of Mao Tse-tung, the "Great Socialist Cultural Revolution" being carried out at the moment, which is the culmination of several years of "socialist education" movements in the communes and factories, now extended to the entire nation.[1]

Not only will the present Cultural Revolution consolidate and expand gains achieved in the material base but it will also prevent the re-emergence of selfish motivations, of a high salaried new class in the superstructure: administrators, intellectuals and technocrats in industry.

Marx states: "The labour of the individual under communism is taken from the start as social labour. Therefore, whatever the specific *material* form of the produce which he creates or helps to create . . . that which he has bought with his labour power is not a specific product, but a specific *share* of the communal production. . . ." This principle is to be carried out to the letter in China, with the abolition of a hierarchy among various forms of labour. The appearance of a high-salaried class among workers and foremen is also thoroughly repudiated; this phenomenon corrupts the working class and is most apparent in the revisionist parties of Europe.

The abolition of bonuses in China's factories is now being achieved by the voluntary, mass line consent, of the workers themselves. The criterion of profitability is never to be used; "the introduction into a socialist economy of *motivations* which are foreign to it, will prevent the very progress of

[1] A. L. STRONG, *The Remaking of Man*; letter, September 1966.

socialism" says Bettelheim.[1] Socialism does not consist of clever economic bribery to induce people to behave like "socialist man". The incitement to increased production by the stimulus of personal gain only defeats the purpose, which is to create a socialist society of socialist-minded beings. This can only be done by inculcating *unselfishness*, a whole-hearted dedication to the community and to the aims of the revolution, a brotherhood of feeling, international solidarity, the knowledge that whatever work one does, however menial, has a *universal* purpose and usefulness in propelling the advance of humanity towards happiness and abundance. The continuation of class struggle, *against* the return of "bourgeois dictatorship" in any form, becomes therefore a state of conscience. The struggle in the mind itself between unselfishness and greed, between "the others first" and "me first", must become the worker's creed.

Appendix

In 1919 an analysis of the classes in Chinese society would have revealed the development of two classes since the 1880s, heralding the change from feudalism—

1. A small national capitalist class, whose development had been most prominent during the years 1914–19, but whose growth was constantly checked by foreign monopoly capitalism in China.

2. A proletariat of workers, the "antithetical twin" of the first class. These, by 1920, were reputed to number "about two to three million". Seventy per cent were employed in foreign enterprises, in the seaboard cities of China; they were therefore subject to direct exploitation by foreign concerns. They were also extremely concentrated. By 1949 their numbers were still "under five million".

[1] CHARLES BETTELHEIM, *La Construction du Socialisme en Chine.*

This concentration of the proletariat was to make it both easy to reach them with propaganda but also easy to deal with them by foreign troops—as proved by the 1927 massacre of workers in Shanghai by Chiang Kai-shek. Twenty-five million workers were reported in 1960; with the extension of mechanization in the communes, semi-skilled workers probably totalled ten million or so, but most of them were really "craftsmen", smiths, etc., as well as builders, bricklayers, and carpenters. There are, today, over forty million workers of skilled, semi-skilled and craftsman grade in China.

IV

TRADE, POPULATION, RESEARCH, NATIONAL ECONOMY, FACTORS OF INHIBITION

It took us thirty years to learn how to make a revolution. Let us hope it won't take that long to learn how to build a national economy.

CHOU EN-LAI

HISTORIANS still castigate China's reluctance to trade with the West as a reprehensible peculiarity. This reluctance was not peculiar to China. England did not admit crews from foreign ships to her shores in the eighteenth century; Japan and India, for a long time, imposed restrictions on intercourse with foreigners. The resistance to invasion of the Chinese market (in goods and principally in opium) is well documented, as are the unequal treaties, starting in 1842 and lasting till 1943. From 1842 to 1949, Chinese tariff rates were fixed by the unequal treaties to about five per cent *ad valorem* on many goods.[1] This limited the revenue of the Chinese government to a nominal sum, the greater part of which went into repayment of interest on loans previously contracted.

[1] After 1932 tariff rates varied from seven and a half to twelve per cent on certain imports but this list of "surtax" imports was limited; extensive smuggling, especially by the Japanese, negated this increase, which was actually earmarked for the servicing of foreign loans.

The Chinese Customs Office was under an Englishman from the 1880s to 1939, and an American from 1946 to 1949, with a small interim during the Sino-Japanese war when customs and revenue fell into Japanese hands. The Chinese government did not assume *de facto* control of its own maritime customs and their revenue until after the Communist Revolution of 1949.

93

Indebtedness in the period 1895 to 1910 amounted to 270 million US dollars, from 1911 to 1922, 520 million US dollars and between 1927 and 1937, 1,680 million US dollars. There were 8,000 non-Chinese enterprises (import-export, insurance, banking, mines, docks, etc.). The profits derived from these and sent back to the West have never been reckoned.

Eighty per cent of China's imports were controlled by foreign firms and so were sixty-six per cent of the exports. Imports were: foodstuffs twenty per cent; consumer goods and luxury items seventy per cent; capital goods, machinery ten per cent. Harbour administration, pilotage and foreign exchange control were under foreign supervision as were customs, salt gabelle and railroads.

Extra-territoriality allowed the export of Western capital to erect factories and industries in enclaves in China without any possible control over these, and profits were remitted back entirely to Europe or the USA; besides preventing the growth of local manufactures, this system also permitted flagrant economic pillage, distorted China's economy and trade into an adjunct of Western capitalism.

Silk, the chief export of China from 1914 to 1922, declined to a fraction of the Japanese silk trade after 1922. The tariff imposed by England on Chinese tea broke her tea trade. Fifty per cent of Chinese exports was tea in 1883, only two per cent in 1921. Cotton manufactured articles were imported from England, the United States and Japan until 1949.

"China finds a place at the bottom of every list showing the *per capita* trade of the countries of the world" said Remer. It was about 1·5 per cent of the world trade in 1900, 2·2 per cent around 1930 and less than 2 per cent in 1949.

China's trade relied almost wholly on the export of agricultural produce (ninety per cent) and this sector was also largely in the hands of foreign import-export companies;

comprador middlemen bought the produce, and prices were controlled by foreign monopoly. She imported almost every item of manufacture required, from batteries and bicycles, to sewing machines.

After 1915 Japan implanted her own textile industry in China, thus restraining the growth of the Chinese textile industry. Sixty per cent of the textile mills in Shanghai were foreign- or part-foreign-owned. Forty per cent of the coal production in China came from mines under foreign control till 1938, when eighty per cent passed under Japanese control. The iron industry was also in the hands of foreign companies; even with Chinese partnership the commanding sectors were non-Chinese. The same picture of insolvency, deficiency in balance of trade, and financial control by foreign powers, as is reproduced today by almost every "underdeveloped" nation, such as India, or in Africa, Latin America, was the picture of China's "national economy".

The annual unfavourable balance of trade in China was 200 million Haikuan taels of silver from 1899 to 1913; it dropped to 48·4 million Haikuan taels from 1915 to 1919 (the First World War), but after 1919 again climbed and China ran a deficit (largely unpublished) which was offset by large amounts of "aid" in the form of foreign loans after 1935.[1]

Between 1942 and 1949 inflation occurred. Partly owing to manipulations by Kuomintang officials, this became catastrophic by 1949. China had a large reserve of foreign exchange in 1945,[2] since disbursement abroad had been small and receipts substantial owing to a USA loan of 500 million dollars and USA military expenditure in China.

Between 1946 and 1948 most of this was squandered on a large import surplus (luxury goods, and military equipment for

[1] S. ADLER, *The Chinese Economy* (Routledge and Kegan Paul, London, 1957).
[2] ibid.

the New Army of Chiang Kai-shek). By 1948 foreign trade had fallen, hyper-inflation set in; corruption, smuggling, and a large flight of gold bullion (to Formosa in 1948) disrupted the economy further.

In 1950, as a result of the Korean War, a total embargo and blockade were proclaimed against China. Because of this embargo most foreign firms (granted licences by the new communist government to continue trading) had to stop. "This was not China's fault" a Chinese economist told me. "The door of trade was closed by the USA not China."

Foreign Trade

In any country foreign trade is the single most important source (apart from tourism and "aid") of foreign exchange. However, it must be pointed out again that no real national economy has sprung from anything but the intensification of internal trade, sheltered by protective barriers in adequate proportion. Within this framework, foreign trade plays a useful and often extremely important role but *only if* the State is in complete control of it and can *plan* it for its best interests.

As early as 1948, the Chinese communists expressed their desire to trade with foreign countries on the basis of mutuality, reciprocity and equality.

Trade returns are estimated today at over US $5 billion in total volume (US $1·5 billion in 1952). That foreign trade is small when compared with internal exchanges is a characteristic of all very large, continental countries (such as the USA with a very large internal market and almost total self-sufficiency). The character, direction and growth of trade, the balance of payments resulting from it and how trade affects relations with other countries are relevant to an understanding of Chinese construction plans. The planning and protection of the internal Chinese market is now total, since the State controls all import and export outlets.

Before 1949 Chinese trade with Russia was insignificant, and with other Eastern *bloc* countries non-existent. Between 1945 and 1949, the USA dominated the Chinese trade market; between 1949 and 1951 owing to the Korean hostilities, the UN embargo, and the freezing of Chinese funds in American banks by the US government, political interest coincided with economic interests to shift the almost total volume and direction of Chinese trade towards the Soviet *bloc*; the subsequent needs of Chinese industrialization confirmed this process. The proportion of Chinese trade then conducted with Russia and the Eastern *bloc* rose from twenty-seven per cent in 1950 to over eighty per cent in 1954.

In 1956, with the opening of the Canton trade fairs, a shift in emphasis occurred, a reflection of the Chinese desire to widen foreign trade. The period 1956 to 1962 will be considered as the period in which China's increasing emphasis on self-reliance, her increasing refusal to become a satellite appendage of Russia (militarily, economically, politically) and an increasing insistence on establishing an independent comprehensive national economy in her own way, led to gestures towards another equilibrium in all sectors of relations with the rest of the world. In 1956-7 the UN embargo on China began to be eroded, many European nations making it clear that they could not continue to adhere to its terms; today no nation refuses to trade with China except the USA.

In 1966, the percentage of trade with the USSR and the East-European *bloc* stabilized at round about twenty-five to thirty per cent of the total; seventy to seventy-five per cent of trade is conducted with the rest of the world. The gainers so far have been Japan, Great Britain, France and West Germany. But there is also a very significant increase in trade with the countries of the "Third World", Latin America, Africa and South-East Asia, with which the total volume of trade has trebled in the last few years.

The "crucial and strategic importance of Hong Kong" for China's economy has been emphasized as the most important and secure source of foreign exchange earnings. But trade figures with Hong Kong are deceptive since many of these purchases are for re-export to other countries; and now it appears that Hong Kong's importance in the future will decrease as direct trading at Shanghai and Canton and other ports takes over.

The years 1950 to 1954 were characterized by a preponderance of imports over exports to the USSR, due to the needs for capital industrial construction; these were partly financed by the sale of meat, oil, grain, partly by Russian credits. After 1954, however, the situation was reversed, with China exporting to the USSR more than she bought, but with respect to East-European countries this only occurred after 1959.[1] This was chiefly due to the repayment of the loans to the Soviet Union. By 1966, all loans and bills had been repaid, including the Korean War debts, which were wholly paid by China. China owed not a penny to anyone, and was very proud of this state of affairs, perhaps an old-fashioned feeling in these days of aid and loans.

An export surplus has been the significant and gratifying feature of China's trade since 1956; even during the agricultural crises of 1960–1 China continued to export more than she imported; this is due to the strict control of the overall balance, maintained between export and import. This persistent surplus from foreign trade is the main source of foreign exchange.

There are no other sources of aid, grants, loans, or long-term credits. "Hard currency" payments are made promptly

[1] A. ECKSTEIN, *The National Economy of China*.

and scrupulously; the credit payments accorded to China are nearly all short-term.[1]

As China becomes more industrialized, trade patterns with Western nations will become more markedly selective. To some areas of the Third World she will become a supplier of machinery, whole plants and producer goods as well as textiles and other consumer goods, thus challenging both Japan and the West.

The participation of China in economic exhibitions and international fairs in over forty countries to date, the solo exhibitions of industrial goods and machine tools, and the reciprocal exhibitions held in China all mark her entry into the internal arena of industry.

The export of technical services of many kinds to certain countries in Africa and Asia is a form of aid which China began some years ago; the technicians she sends live on the same scale as the workers in the country they visit, and leave as soon as they have finished their work. All aid is granted free of interest, and there are no stipulations of any kind. This is in accordance with the Eight Principles of Aid enunciated by Chou En-lai in 1963.

The large-scale purchases of wheat every year represent about three per cent of China's consumption of food grains; and they are the single main item of expenditure in her foreign exchange surplus; thirty per cent of her foreign exchange goes into paying for this wheat. The drive for higher yields will continue until there is total self-sufficiency in food. "Our yields, though rising are still low in comparison with certain countries, but we can certainly double or treble them."[2] The latest indications are that it is hoped to achieve this by 1975.

[1] The single exception so far is a recent 1966 accord for the purchase of nickel, 9,300 tons, the first long-term (four years) credit agreement signed with France.
[2] Commission of Economic Planning, November 1966.

The foreign exchange surplus is, to date, US $ 1·5 billion per year and increasing.[1]

China's capacity to buy industrial equipment and heavy machinery is limited by the necessity of immediate repayment, it is also limited by scrupulous control against any tendency to a deficit, but it is increased by swift improvement in her own industrial production, and thus her earning capacity. This is already making her an exporter of machinery. The Canton twice-yearly trade fairs show these industrial advances. Ten years ago there were only four types of machine for export; in 1956, at the first commodities fair, the only instruments offered were drawing compasses, set-squares and other teaching instruments.

Today more than eighty types of machine, exported to more than forty countries and regions, are available. Also more than three hundred instruments were on the export list, including metal and non-metal testing machines, fault detectors, electronic instruments, electrical and heat engineering instruments, microscopes and micro-balances. High tension insulators are now made in China (up to 330,000 volts) and exported as well as whole telephone switchboards, high pressure reactors, TV and transistor sets, etc.

Since the agricultural sector still provides the bulk of export goods (whether raw, semi-processed or processed) the capacity to buy is also limited by the success of the agricultural sector. The increase and stabilization of yields, whatever the weather, is the aim in agriculture for both self-sufficiency in food and industrial raw material demand; so is the expansion in the field of processed agricultural goods. The wide range of foodstuffs available, canned, refrigerated,

[1] Overseas Chinese remittances have always been held up as China's way of getting "invisible" foreign exchange; these remittances are becoming less and less important; not more than five to ten per cent of the foreign exchange *surplus* balance is represented by them, and this amount will dwindle further in the years to come.

processed (around 2,500 varieties) is also an imposing measure of the advance.

The French reports, based on data collected from various French experts working in China, is that the harvests have never been better, in spite of severe drought in some areas, because the irrigation and water-conservancy projects are paying off. Increase in vast numbers of electric pumps and simple improved tools (two-shear ploughs, rice planters and harvesters) is also reported. But the drive for fertilizers and insecticides to double and treble yields will continue and China will still be a purchaser of fertilizer for some years.

"We are against no one, except the domestic and foreign reactionaries who hinder us from doing business...." "When we have beaten the internal and external reactionaries by uniting all domestic and international forces, we shall be able to do business, and establish diplomatic relations with all foreign countries on the basis of equality, mutual benefit, and mutual respect for territorial integrity and sovereignty."[1] These words of Mao Tse-tung, quoted at the Canton Trade Fair, underline the fact that the Chinese do not regard trade relations as coming under ideological restrictions, but under the simple, pragmatic rules of equality and coexistence. However, it is certain that political hostility will not reinforce trade, but decrease it. And the declining trade with Soviet Russia is not likely to show a sudden increase for a very long time.

Population—a National Resource

Is a large population a boon or a curse? The idea is persistently put forward that an increase in population growth by itself negates economic growth, and the extra expenditure

[1] Peking, Hsinhua, 16th November, 1966.

involved in feeding and educating so many diminishes the national income of developing countries. Medical progress in not yet industrialized countries consists mainly in a decline in infant mortality. This immediately increases the number of consumers more than it increases the number of producers. Serious debate over these questions in China led to some fluctuations in the policy towards family planning until 1962, when family planning became a firm plank in the national framework of advance.

For a country with labour-intensive methods and semi-mechanization just beginning, a large population is also a blessing, though it imposes strains upon short-term agricultural prospects and also and perhaps chiefly on education and economic growth. True to dialectics, this dual aspect of demography can be utilized. China's large population is also one of its most outstanding national resources; like all resources, it has to be organized, put to work, and invested in, but also disciplined.

The dramatic increase[1] in population in Asia after 1900, indicating a major shift, with the demographic balance turning against Europe and America, has been commented on. In the nineteenth century the population of Europe had doubled, which enabled the export of forty million emigrants to Australia, America and Canada. But by the beginning of the twentieth century this demographic expansion slackened; it has now stopped.[2] In Russia after 1917 there was a decline in population, made good during the 1930s and again followed by a decline after the Second World War.

In Japan the population doubled between 1872 and 1930,

[1] *See also* BARRACLOUGH, *An Introduction to Contemporary History*, Chapter III.
[2] Except for the export of the poor peasantry of Southern Europe to Australia, Canada, etc., and the "brain drain" to the USA from Great Britain.

but at the moment the net rate of increase is 0·8 per cent and growth is almost at a standstill.

The population of India increased by over eighty million from 1920 to 1947; in China, the greatest increase has come about after 1949. In 1953 the first communist census of population in China gave over 583 million; until then figures had hovered between 450 and 500 million. Infants up to four years old constituted 15·6 per cent of the 583 million; which gives a round figure of ninety million infants under four years old in 1953. This astronomic increase in four years was due to the nation-wide and compulsory public health measures taken immediately when the communist government came to power, the immediate uplift in conditions in the countryside.

In the census of 1953, the total juvenile population up to age seventeen was 41·1 per cent of the total population. This gives us a figure of near 240 million juveniles in 1953.

No census of population figures have been published since; but the trend has continued towards a net increase as in India; the rate quoted by Chou En-lai being 2–2·2 per cent a year.[1] An inspired guess that forty-five per cent of the population is under eighteen years old and fifty per cent under twenty-one does not appear extreme. In 1966, the population was quoted as "700 million" by leaders of the government. If we take this figure of 700 million, we have a possible 315 million juveniles under eighteen in China, or 350 million under twenty-one years old.

The implications of these figures, by themselves, are sobering. A large young population, whose reproductive rate in the next decade will be very high, represents "consumption" rather than "production". This is adding to the already weighty problems of China. How are these 300 odd million young to be fed, clothed, educated and given a better life

[1] Interview with author, September, 1965; also with Edgar Snow, March, 1965.

than their parents? If "normal" Western standards are used, the task is obviously impossible.

Is this enormous young population a relative or an absolute factor in retarding China's progress? Can it be handled, as Mao Tse-tung says: "so that a bad thing becomes a good thing"?

The first notion we must clarify is that of over-population. There is no "over-population" in China.[1] A population of 700 million in China gives us a proportion of around 190 people per square mile, the average of Europe today. In India, one-third the size of China, the population of 520 million today gives us an average of 350 per square mile, less than half the number of inhabitants per square mile in Belgium, Holland and Japan. We must, I think, agree that population is also a cultural appraisal, and its evaluation depends on the development of resources, and their distribution and working. It is, in fact, a function of the economic system and of industrial development.

The *distribution* of population in China is uneven, the eastern seaboard, the deltas, the more fertile agricultural areas, low-lying rice-producing basins with double or treble cropping have a crowded countryside with 1,000 people per square mile; two-thirds of the Chinese population live on one-sixth of the area of China. The rest is sparsely populated; some areas have fewer than one person per square mile.

This uneven distribution corresponds to the Key Economic Areas of feudal China,[2] labour-intensive fields with almost certain harvests and established systems of irrigation. Historical attitudes, as well as the low level of tools, and the feudal system itself, prevented the clearing and pioneering of new

[1] As BAADE points out in his book, *The Race to the Year 2000*, the world could support ten times its present population, if all its resources were well used.

[2] CHI CHAO-TING, *Key Economic Areas in Chinese History*.

settlements. Superimposed upon the primitive means of production was a superstructure of inhibiting social habits and traditions such as filial duty, clan relations and superstitions.

The non-monetarized rural economy, laws restricting travel and commerce, inland transport taxes, landlordism and debt contributed to stagnation and lack of incentive to pioneer.

The tradition of the clan tended to keep all its members together, so as to have enough labour hands for the harvests. Tools and means of production were owned by the clan and could not be removed.

Today, the picture is different. Decentralized industrialization moves the young from the cities to new areas; wholesale commune-centred family planning, new methods of part-work part-study education are spreading out the population, limiting births, and cutting down the cost of education and consumption.[1]

Education is an investment in human capital, enhancing and multiplying its effectiveness. The scientific peasant, the worker-inventor, creates wealth. The forms, modalities, directions, emphases of education are therefore of particular importance. Making the whole system of education in China a part-work part-study system is restoring the juvenile half of the population in varying degrees to the production sector. On this all-important subject of turning consumers into producers, and turning education into a self-reliant, self-sufficient, self-feeding, self-paying sector of the economy, a new policy is being worked out; it is only possible to be sure of one thing, that all schools will be part-work part-study schools, and the same for colleges and universities.

At the same time birth control at commune level throughout the land, is also intelligently directed towards the most reproductive group, the under thirties.

[1] *See* "Education" in Chapter VII.

Late marriage and contraceptive techniques are being advocated with the same methods of appeal to revolutionary priority, this priority being not the self, but "production for the revolution". If within the next decade the population control techniques succeed, a stabilization of the population growth at around 1·5 per cent increase per year is possible. The emphasis on the absence of fear, and on the voluntary co-operation of married couples in wise family planning is, psychologically, the best approach and the most relevant to human worth and dignity.

If this succeeds, then by the year 2001 it can be safe to assume that the population could be stable round about 1·2 thousand million people or less, assuming that at the moment, with half the population under twenty-one and the family planning drive in the communes only beginning it takes another decade before reaching the desired rate. If the yield per acre has doubled and in some areas trebled, the food production will be sufficient. But it is a race, at the moment, between increased yield and increasing numbers of healthy babies.

Science—Development and Research

This subject, like so many facets of the Chinese policies of development, tends to be confused by contradictory reports. Studied emphasis is placed, as Dr. Ping Chia-kuo[1] pointed out, on "certain aspects . . . which are important only as symptoms, while deeper, historical trends often forgotten amidst the crises and passions of the day, and yet of lasting significance" are either omitted or ignored. *The interpretation of what happens in China is a function of the attitudes towards China,* and what happens in China cannot be

[1] PING CHIA-KUO, *New Age and New Outlook*, Penguin, 1960.

studied apart from what the Chinese themselves take as guide to their actions, namely, the ideological factors (known as the Thought of Mao Tse-tung); these, so far, have not received in the West the attention that is due to them.

Scientific research in China has received close attention since 1956. All of it has been overshadowed by the constant threat of encirclement, containment, and since 1962, of almost certain attack, within the foreseeable future, by the USA.

Geological surveys were hampered at first by lack of personnel, but this is no longer the case. Well over 10,000 qualified geologists today, instead of the 1,200 of 1950, have discovered in China, among other things, deposits of thorium and uranium, at present used in the nuclear research programme.

Speaking of the "new revolution in science, technique and industry produced by automation," Chou En-lai said[1] that this was a "revolution far exceeding in its significance the industrial revolution associated with steam and electricity". China would have to "leap" into the highest international standards within twelve years (1956–67). A Twelve-year Plan for long-term research projects was drawn up that year and is now coming to a close; an evaluation can therefore be made while the next long-term scientific research plan is being prepared.

In the decade since 1956, China has not only conducted the steps necessary for the first industrial revolution, but has also undertaken the second revolution necessary because of advances in automation and in the use of atomic energy; this overlapping has meant that the funds necessary for research and experimentation have been more than generous; that the creation of technological personnel has been a priority at all

[1] CHOU EN-LAI, *On the Question of Intellectuals*, Report, January 1956.

times, despite the political and ideological emphases on political purity which, however much it is always deprecated in the West as "stifling initiative" does not seem to have that effect.

Scientific know-how and achievement, in my opinion, coincide with the requirements of Marxism-Leninism; scientists are *also*, sometimes unconsciously, imbued with ideals of the Good Society. In the present Cultural Revolution, the movement includes *scientific experiment*, which is the spirit of innovation and research. This is significant, as is the extolling of scientific heroes and heroines and other worker-inventors.

Chou En-lai's emphasis on "bringing our country's most vital scientific departments near to the most advanced world levels by the end of the Third Five-year Plan" (1966–70) can also no longer be looked upon as a vain boast.

It was in this speech, notably, that Chou En-lai emphasized self-reliance and independence of the USSR. "To fulfil this task, we must discard all *servile thinking*, which is lack of national self-confidence. . . ." Although Soviet assistance was needed to do away with backwardness, one should "distinguish between what is essential and not essential . . . to seek a solution from the Soviet Union to every question, great and small" was "incorrect" and to "send mostly middle school graduates rather than scientists" to the Soviet Union was wrong. "The result would be *forever a state of dependence and imitation, impeding the systematic rapid development of our science. . . .*"

The best scientific forces and the best university graduates must be concentrated "for the earnest, and not merely nominal launching, of the march of science . . . *we must grasp the time element.*" All the necessary material such as books, publications, archives, technical data, and other facilities including translation of foreign works etc., are and have been available at all times, contrary to reports in the Western Press.[1]

There are two aspects to this research programme; one, the high level concentration of the best brains and talent on certain projects, the second, the most widespread diffusion, communication and facilities for creating a pool of technological personnel *of all types* at worker-peasant level. And though this seemed "impossible", it has been done, surprisingly well.

In agriculture the most important emphasis has been on the wide spread of scientific knowledge to the peasants themselves, and co-operation and co-ordination between scientist and peasant. Today the idea of research and the words "study and experiment" have become part of peasant vocabulary. "Co-operation, now a routine functional factor in China, has been a major element in the scientific and industrial success stories. . . ." [2]

In industry each factory has its one or more lines of research, all technical problems and improvements are discussed by co-operation between scientists, workers and lower technical staff, and the administrative cadres; the practice of sending students from technical colleges to the factories also results in their discovering problems in design and manufacture, and these become their chosen subjects of work; they get full co-operation in solving these research problems from workers and scientists as well as the approval of party cadres.

News such as, for example, that Anshan steel works has turned out one new product every day for the last two years, that technical innovations in this period are developed at an average of fifteen a day, that the steel complex has caught

[1] C. H. G. OLDHAM, "Science and Education in China", *Contemporary China*, USA, Pantheon Books, 1966.
[2] *Far East Trade and Development*, October 1966.

up or surpassed current world standards in twenty technical economic norms is a tribute to the technical innovation movement. Twenty-two special technical teams, including engineers, research workers, experienced workers and cadres, were employed on these technical questions; in the process, several young inventors (post-1962) made innovations; 40,000 technicians are employed in this one complex alone; they have produced alloy steel in open-hearth furnaces, a kind which could only be made previously in electrical furnaces; these technicians are now organizing conferences and demonstrations and sharing their experiences with other steel complexes, big and small, all over China; and the number of technicians capable of making these alloy and special steels has doubled in two years.

The pure oxygen top blown converter process introduced recently in China will not only make steel at far greater speed and lower capital investment, but also allow the recovery of waste materials (gas and soot) for the production of fertilizers and other chemicals. It takes less than one year to design and build such a converter in China.

Scientific breakthrough has occurred in all sectors, and not only in nuclear development; synthetic insulin has been produced and also synthetic benzene, a basic raw material for the manufacture of plastics and other synthetics. Fermentation dewaxing is another recent breakthrough made by young Shanghai workers and scientists. (This process removes paraffin from crude oil by bacteriological action.) A fireproof chemical which resists 1,000 °C is produced by a small chemical workshop in Manchuria. In medicine, a recent[1] delegation of seventeen Belgian doctors reports impressive surgery techniques, even in country hospitals; research in medical and surgical fields continues; all medical instruments, of the most complex type, are produced and

[1] 1966.

made in China; heart, lung, and liver surgical techniques are of international standard.

The Institute of Automation of the Chinese Academy of Sciences is producing automatic control motors; already several factories, entirely automated, are functioning (as models for the future). The expansion of technological personnel is no longer a function of academic diplomas; it is at the very base, among the ordinary workers, that science begins; there must be no hierarchy among scientists confined to "top level" men or experts or technocrats; the present Cultural Revolution reaffirms this principle and will strengthen this policy.

Like all aspects of the Chinese Revolution, the theme of research and development is accompanied by a "two lines" contradiction; there is the contradiction between the technical and scientific personnel, who at least until 1960 were mostly of bourgeois origin, and the demands for political meetings and discussions; during the First Leap Forward there was widespread grumbling over the interruption at research level; in today's Leap Forward, however, special care has been taken to reiterate that scientific personnel must be protected, just as special care has been taken that all must proceed "by reason and not force", and also that "the minority is not always wrong, truth is sometimes with the minority". Local party interference and high-handedness with intellectual personnel still occurs, and it has been more obvious in the realm of pure research than in that of practical application. However at the 1966 Physicists Congress in Peking a galaxy of young investigators read papers on original research of international calibre. Special consideration to the scientific branches is increasing, as after 1962 more and more scientific personnel was of worker and peasant origin; the acceptance of "intellectuals" as part of the proletarian society and their fitting into the social system is becoming easier.

The nuclear programme development has also been swift; as far as is known, this is the one programme where from the start China has had to go it alone, since the Russians refused to share their knowledge of nuclear weapons with China (as revealed in 1963).[1]

Until 1956 the attitude of the Chinese towards nuclear weapons was disparagement of their power (as implied by the Rand Corporation expert, Alice Langley Hsieh in her book, *Communist China's Strategy in the Nuclear Era*, the Rand Corporation, 1962). This attitude was embodied in Mao Tse-tung's statement on 13th August, 1945, that atom bombs could not decide wars; "some of our comrades, too, believe that the atom bomb is all-powerful; that is a big mistake . . . the theory that weapons decide everything, the purely military viewpoint, a bureaucratic style of work divorced from the masses . . . all these are bourgeois influences in our ranks".

The equating of fear of the atom bomb and the conviction that primacy of weapons decided everything was classified by Mao, as on a par with bourgeois thinking.[2] This was in 1946; in 1965, with the issue of Lin Piao's *Long Live the Victory of the People's Wars*, this thesis was reasserted.

The unwavering principle that "people, not weapons" are the factor that makes for victory, therefore, has not changed in two decades. China would not give in to nuclear blackmail.

The charge that China has "changed her mind" about atomic weapons, because she has now had to develop her own nuclear armoury for self-defence is specious;[3] it is still

[1] The unilateral abrogation of the accord reached in autumn of 1957, a few days before meeting Eisenhower, at "Camp David", is fully documented: GUILLAIN, *Dans Trente Ans la Chine*; p. 187; KLAUS MEHNERT, *Peking and Moscow*; HARRY SCHWARTZ, *Tsars, Mandarins and Commissars*; JEAN BABY et al.

[2] Interview with Anna Louise Strong, 1946.

[3] The solemn and repeated reiteration that "China will never use nuclear weapons first", and the call for complete, total nuclear disarmament and

people, not weapons, that decide the outcome of historical development.

In 1958-9, and again in 1962-6, there was active and tenacious intra-Party struggle, and struggle in the Army, between those who held the purely military point of view, and those who held to Mao's theory of people not weapons being the deciding factor. This "two roads struggle" is continuing on a world scale.

In spite of the accomplishment of a nuclear programme, the exploding of atom bombs and now the successful launching of a guided missile, and the declaration that China will persist in her nuclear development programme (which means that within three years we shall see a far wider range of missile development in China than has been guessed at by Western experts, and also probably the development of new and hitherto unsuspected weapons), adherence to the theory of people's war is maintained.

Where then does the nuclear development programme fit into China's conception of people's war? As a purely defensive tactic, and above all to break the nuclear blackmail of others.

China regards the "non-proliferation" treaty which is being discussed by the USA and USSR as yet another attempt at domination, since this treaty applies to every other nation, but not to the Big Two. The test-ban treaty of 1963 was similarly an attention-making stunt; by that year both the USA and USSR were relying entirely on underground tests, which have continued.

In nuclear knowledge, as in medicine, physics and industrial research, the Chinese are showing a capacity, second to none, for reaching the highest possible levels. It is certain that the

---

destruction of all nuclear weapons and stockpiling has been reiterated five times in the last three years.

next decades will see China taking her place in the exploration of space, and capable of developing new devices for this venture.

Round-up of the National Economy

In December 1963, after the readjustment of the First Leap was made, Chou En-lai gave a summary of the economic situation. The aims of the Chinese Communist Party in "building an independent, comprehensive, modern national economic system based on socialism" were reiterated. By that time the breakaway in economic, military and political sectors from Moscow was obvious; the factor of self-reliance which would guide the national economy in its further development, was therefore emphasized.

By 1966, it could not be denied even by the most prejudiced observer that China had achieved a national economy of her own; that it had made impressively good progress in seventeen years despite the setbacks of 1960–1, and that China was on the verge of an economic breakthrough. Although reports, arguing that the "growth rate" was "only" three per cent, or that there was now "stagnation", continued to be put out by the publications devoted to denigrating Chinese effort, it was the consensus among business circles in close touch with Chinese economic affairs that in almost every respect Chinese achievements had been long underestimated. This applied not only to the nuclear programme, but to all sectors of development in China.

Perhaps the most consistent denigration has been of the ideological programme because it is the one most repugnant to Western inbuilt ideas of "free enterprise". The scope, necessity, and particular aspects of the "politics in command" factor have not been studied adequately; they have been left mostly to propagandists in the British and American sectors;

the material transformation which a change of attitude can promote has therefore not been properly assessed. It has been dubbed "brainwashing" and "thought control", and attention has been centred on writers and artists of pre-1949 vintage, and their vicissitudes;[1] but the entire aspect of the ideological transformation necessary to build socialism, was not studied in its context. Again, the fixation on "the Russian model" and on the subsequent "Sino-Soviet split" has tended to obscure these developments, both in their interpretation abroad, and even in their internal application, in China itself. The "Chinese model" of development may not, in the end, prove applicable everywhere, but it certainly has been successful in operating change, at a quick pace, in a backward agricultural country with an economy warped by colonial exploitation; a situation which was not present in Russia at the time of the 1917 Revolution.

The transformation of the base, that is the agricultural and industrial sectors, into a socialist guided economy pattern was terminated by 1956. In that year the small capitalist light industry base till then co-existing with nascent State heavy industry was collectivized, with compensation and interest paid on invested capital, a step which, with ideological preparation beforehand, was responsible for the smoothness of the performance. A directing role by the State in trade and commerce, finance and banks, was also achieved. The breaking up of the old power structure and the substitution of a new were already achieved through the *military victory* of the Red Army and the *débâcle* of the Kuomintang. Land reform broke the landlord-based power in rural areas. Because of the large preponderance of peasants it was the alliance between worker-peasant (the peasant being defined by Mao as the semi-proletariat) which was to be the basis of

[1] But even in this respect, the fact that a good many of them, like Pa Ching and Tsao Yu, became well adapted, was not brought out.

the political power; the number of workers was small, and they were still close to the peasantry (many of them were only one generation away from rural areas, since industry was so young in China). The abolition of all foreign interests within the country, the takeover of foreign dominated enterprises, and Kuomintang-controlled businesses were achieved before 1956. Socialist transformation therefore can only be counted as a decade old, 1956 to 1966.

The building of this national economy was carried out under unified State plans, and their characteristic was duality, each one having both short- and long-term components. The short-term, Five-year Plans were geared to fit into long-term objectives and as such, were flexible, though no compromises or deviations away from the guiding principles of the general line of building socialism were possible. Short-term adaptations and temporary fall-backs were admitted and operated, such as private plot retention and free markets. But the temptation to fall back from socialistic principles was resisted and apparently attractive short cuts, expediencies, profit motivations were repudiated. Because of the ability to control prices, markets and wages, to plan ahead, and to stabilize livelihood, temporary setbacks did not shake the grip of the State on the economy, so that even in the three bad years (1959 to 1961) there was no inflation, little speculation or black market operations.

The freedom from any debt, mortgages, loans, both external and internal, means that all surplus balances from trade (and China has had a foreign exchange surplus balance since 1956) can be utilized for planned purchases for economic growth. Full protection of the internal market by total control makes manipulations and smuggling operations, such as occur in other countries, risky and difficult.[1] Likewise there

[1] Though limited smuggling by some Overseas Chinese does happen and continued till the Cultural Revolution of 1966.

is no earmarking of any internal revenue of any kind for repayment of loans. There is no problem of balance of payments; neither can foreign manipulation (as in India where two-thirds of the currency is today in USA hands) occur. Inflation is rigorously decried as it is not a principle of socialist economy. A relative deflation, due to increased production, in retail prices of certain consumer goods (such as vegetables, eggs and meat) and in services (bus and train fares) augments the real income of the workers though wages remain low; the price-fixing (of rents at four per cent, water and electricity five per cent of a worker's wages) of services to consumers, the augmenting of benefits and amenities at little or no cost (medical care, maternity full-pay leave of fifty-six days, pensions, canteens, free cinemas, transport, television, nurseries, etc.) augment the standard of living without being reflected in an inflationary tendency. On the domestic market, commodities have increased in volume by ten per cent a year since 1962, and articles of common use have decreased in price by one to three per cent a year. Improvement of livelihood is expressed in the fact that there is no unemployment, and that there is social security for all, old or young. Full employment has not been easy to attain. It is reckoned that on an average two out of every family of 5·7 persons *is* in employment; and this average of employment augments the family income (which is still pooled in families).[1] There is no income tax so that wages are not eroded. The average worker's wage today is 180 per cent compared with the average worker's wage in 1952, but marginal benefits and amenities make the increase larger. Meantime saving, on the thrift and frugality principle which is the basis of the economy, is encouraged and shows steady increase.

The scissors policy, by which industrial workers are favoured at the expense of agriculture and the peasants,

[1] Interview, November 1966, State Planning Commission.

in other "undeveloped countries" is not practised in China. On the contrary, the whole aim of socialist construction is *equality* between worker, peasant and professional. Therefore the peasant's income *must rise*, for his is still the lowest of all.

This is in process in various ways—

1. The agricultural tax, which was twelve per cent in the early 1950s, has been lowered to seven per cent and in some cases to four per cent (for communes producing perishable goods such as fruit and vegetables with quick turnovers). This gives direct help both to the commune accumulation funds and to the wages paid to the peasant.

2. The procurement prices for agricultural commodities have increased twice: once in 1956, by thirty per cent—at the same time as workers' wages were raised—and once in 1962, by fifty per cent; it is now eighty per cent higher than it was in 1952, just as workers' salaries were raised to become 180 per cent of what they were. This increase *must* be passed directly to the commune members. Commune members *must* receive *sixty per cent* of the revenue of the commune in *wages*, and therefore an increase in the procurement prices is passed on directly to them. However, this increase in the price of agricultural produce has not been passed on to the worker in the cities in increased costs, since prices are stable.

3. Where the peasantry is concerned, payment by workpoints[1] earned ensures that the income of the peasant family in money is assured. Payment in kind of basics (food grains,

[1] The workpoint is the unit of accounting in the communes; it is the allocation of work done, and makes it easier to share revenue between commune members on basis of work performance. Each commune decides the value of a workpoint by meetings and assent of all the commune members, men and women. The workpoint has been discussed in various articles and studies, but its effect on the attitude of the peasant in making him wage-conscious, and in monetarizing the rural economy, has not yet been assessed in full.

cotton cloth, oil) also occurs, thus obviating price manipulation at grass roots level. Increases, therefore, are immediately reflected in the cash income of the peasant.

4. The cost of the machinery used in factories is still high, but farm machinery and machines for irrigation are sold to peasants at cut prices. Farm machinery is one of the leaping industries, as are chemical fertilizers (an increase of forty per cent per year since 1962 in fertilizers is reckoned, and this will continue in the present Third Five-year Plan).

5. Electricity is supplied to the farms at forty per cent below city prices. The higher cost of delivery of electricity to rural areas is not taken into account, since "profit" is not the motivation; the State absorbs the loss. Petroleum products are also sold to the communes at thirty per cent discount; all these discounts add up to make a difference in living costs which tends to equalize the real income of worker and peasant.

The essential importance, in this type of economy, of revolutionary, non-material incentives, is obvious and has been amply discussed. Ideological education, making all workers and peasants politically conscious, is necessary in order to *change motivation and attitudes*, to generate the responsibility, consciousness and awareness of long-term benefits, rather than short-term immediate gratifications, which are essential in order to make the socialist system work with efficiency and grow with speed.

The soundness of this type of economy, therefore, depends on the socialist quality of the worker, and of the system in its entirety. It is, more than any other, a system where compulsion of any kind defeats its purpose and must be replaced by *conviction*.

We have already referred to the source of capital construction apart from the usual connotation of funds, and that is the investment of human labour whose "accumulation" produces and creates capital. The labour, overtime, voluntary, honest, efficient, of hundreds of millions of people animated by the will to do their best and *not* by material gain, represents billions of extra labour hours and is capable of creating capital wealth in the form of capital construction. How do we compute this form of capital increase? In the absence of colonial territories to exploit, cheap colonial labour (or child or woman labour), or slavery, which formed the basis of Western capital wealth, there is no other source but that of a large population imbued with zeal, enthusiasm and fervour for the tasks to be done. This is a source of accumulation which, in the next few years, will increase rather than decrease, by the mobilization and return to production, through the part-work party-study school system, of an enormous population reservoir of teenagers.

This labour-into-accumulation (capital wealth) is the most important source of capital acquisition for *all* "underdeveloped countries" which have inadequate financial resources; it represents the uncomputed and is, as René Dumont has written, "the most precious of all the categories of capital . . . human labour". But it means *hard work*, determination, thrift, unswerving far-sighted planning.

Consumption is antithetical to net investment, and hence the attitude of thrift and frugality, of cutting down waste and eliminating luxuries, as well as increased use of underemployed seasons (such as occur in agricultural countries, which all suffer from disguised unemployment) calls for inventiveness and innovation in making do (walking on two legs) in order to "produce more, better, faster and more economically, while maintaining quality and increasing quantity". It means that the *revolution in attitudes* must be thorough, must require the minimum of compulsion (for compulsion is after all very costly, requiring surveillance and

defeating its purpose) the maximum of voluntary and enthusiastic co-operation, initiative and inventiveness. This
Spartan programme may sound unattractive to affluent
societies accustomed to luxury; but it is not certain that the
Spartan and frugal teenagers of China are more unhappy than
the teenagers of affluent societies.

The Factors of Inhibition

There must be a thorough conversion from past values
for the carry-overs of traditional attitudes are inhibitory. Of
such are the contempt for manual labour and the exaggerated dignity attached to being literate, which immediately made an intellectual an over-prized being, and the
literate minority a class in itself. These attitudes still
remain. Peasants, for instance, when their children become
literate, immediately want them to become "officials".
What is the point of being educated, they argue, if their sons
and daughters must remain peasants? And instances where
boys are sent to school and girls kept at home abound.

Without this revolution in attitude, the resurgence of a
new class, equivalent to the mandarinate class and the swift
deterioration of cadres at grass roots level were certain. Deep,
long and long-enduring the feudal roots of bureaucracy are
entrenched in 2,500 years of the past. It would be impossible
unless this reorientation occurred, to make the commune
work as it is intended to.

The workers' mentality also had to be changed in order to
get away from the "engineer-foreman" complex. Workers
in highly sophisticated complexes tend to have amenities
denied to the decentralized but numerous, small-scale, not
so sophisticated commune factories. The dispersal of seedling
industrial potential over as wide an area as possible in case of
nuclear devastation, the necessity for a highly developed

consciousness, "high socialist morality" and preparedness become more significant among the workers in industries.

Far from being detrimental, superfluous, or holding back technical development and China's economic growth, therefore, the reinforcement of ideological education is essential, for advance and success.[1] Not only peasants and workers, but Communist Party members are prone to petty bureaucracy, ordering people about and opposed to democracy and to expressions of criticism. This bureaucracy is perhaps the chief and foremost plague of the Chinese system, its roots are in the literocracy of the past. How, and in what ways, the ideological problems sketched here are being solved, and with what result, we shall now describe.

[1] And also for the strategic conditions of military preparedness which the threat of nuclear annihilation and persistent destruction in other ways compels China's government and people to adopt.

V

IDEOLOGY IN COMMAND—THE
THOUGHT OF MAO TSE-TUNG
THE CULTURAL REVOLUTION

So many deeds cry out to be done,
And always urgently.
The world rolls on,
Time hurried.
Ten thousand years are too long;
Seize the day,
The hour!

MAO TSE-TUNG, Poems

THE relationship between the material achievements and the political or ideological goals of China today has been noted. The importance the Chinese leadership gives to the spiritual component is something which constantly surprises other communists. For the Chinese, dialectical materialism means that spirit and matter are both manifestations of matter itself, indissoluble. As a man thinks, so he acts, and the process of thought and its conditioning, have been the subject of intensive study and much debate. The remaking of man, the transformation of motivation, of the spirit's contents, are as essential as the remaking of the Chinese earth; in fact they must be done together. It is in the transformed spirit of the collective that the material strength needed to create a new society finds birth; without total understanding there is no total effort, and it cannot be done by individuals, but by the awareness of the working masses. This spiritual and social transformation is to be achieved, therefore, by *education* in socialist morality, heightening political consciousness,

123

accompanied by putting into practice the theories learnt, so that they do not remain mere verbiage. Studying, understanding and especially applying (with an emphasis on this idea-to-action causality) the sum of revolutionary theory and practice now known as the Thought of Mao Tse-tung, is averred the way to change, to learn how to think correctly, dialectically, scientifically, as a Marxist-Leninist should. Today seven hundred million people are learning to think and to act, using Mao's way as their guide.

The first time that the term "the Thought of Mao Tse-tung" was used was in 1945, at the seventh Plenary Session of the Chinese Communist Party Congress.[1] Again it was used in 1952, after Liberation, when the intellectuals of China pledged themselves to study, "Marxism-Leninism and the thought of Chairman Mao". In recent years, the emphasis on Mao Tse-tung's thought has increased, gradually replacing the former exhortations to read Marx, Engels, Lenin and Stalin, and Mao, although it is always made clear that "the thought of Mao Tse-tung is the summit of Marxism-Leninism in our time", not something new or different from Marxism-Leninism, but its completion. Communist Party members certainly are enjoined to read Mao's predecessors but the masses are not required to do this. For revolutionary understanding and especially practical application to living conditions they need only to study, and especially apply, the dialectical scientific guide-lines inherent in Mao Tse-tung's works.

That correct thinking is the essential requisite for effective practical work is a truism; but the people of a State which, for the first time, is bringing scientific (and Marxist) thinking to millions still so near to feudalism, require a programme of mental training to grasp objectives and scientific facts; and

[1] Report on the Seventh Plenary Session of the Central Committee of the Chinese Communist Party (Chinese version).

this is provided by the kind of thought processes (analysis—grasping the main problem, synthesis—solving it) which Mao Tse-tung exhibits clearly in his writings, and also the practice, or action that follows.[1] For thought can only be tested against deed.

The immense transformation required of a whole people to pass from a world of feudal superstition to a world of science is here doubled by the transformation of emotion, attitude and behaviour needed to pass from an exploiting to a non-exploiting society. This process is called ideological remoulding. Accomplished by the slow method of natural evolution in the past, it now has to be accomplished by a voluntary, consciously directed effort in study and awareness. For time is of the essence; and there are many centuries to shake off in a day.

In Mao, the two factors (Marxism-Leninism as a political philosophy, and science as knowledge of the laws of the universe) are completely fused; correct political thought and practice must lead, inevitably, to success in scientific achievement and other concrete objectives. Hence the call to the young to be "Red and expert". For if the motivation is correct, then the eagerness to learn and to do, the enhancement of zest in learning and achieving, will release creative capabilities and do away with lethargy, timorousness, and the acceptance of inadequacy—traits so common in the past of colonized peoples.

But this is not all; at all times an ideological struggle goes on, at all levels within society. It occurs between the classes, between individuals, and within each individual himself. In each the past conditioning of exploitation and class outlook

---

[1] The emphasis on practice as the test of correctness in thinking is reiterated; this is to get away from the typical (and endless) discussions and "philosophizings" which would otherwise result; "armchair Marxism" is much frowned upon in China today.

battle against the new demands: selfishness against the demand for unselfishness, the desire for personal gain, against the need for collective advance. It is a battle forever present within the Communist Party. Right and wrong, the past and the future, correct and incorrect thought and analysis ... this struggle spares no one, either high or low; at all times this angel–demon tussle between bourgeois or capitalist retardation and socialist advance, between enemy and friend, between "the forces of darkness" and the shining tomorrow continues. In a nation-wide aspect, this struggle takes various forms and shapes; it can be very complex, for in the transformation of China, ideological reshaping deals, in a period of transition, with fantastically diverse problems of class, personal ego-centrisms, exploiting tendencies and patterns. Remoulding can only proceed step by step; each of these steps, like the planned moves in the physical refashioning of the land, is linked to and dependent upon the current situation (both psychological and physical), the success of the last step, the intention of the next move, and in the context of the un-deviating aim—the creation of socialism on the way to a communist society.

Within this process we can place the various campaigns, or movements, which like tidal waves roll to envelop the whole population, with an amplitude and massiveness for which no other metaphor is possible. Untiringly thudding upon the shores of consciousness, such ideological movements begin sometimes inconspicuously, signalled by a speech, or even, as in the present Cultural Revolution, by one poster put up in an institution. This is "the single spark" which then sets light to mass participation, which expands until every person is involved in the process.

In the study of the transformation of the economic base, one must not be tempted by what appears as a reversion, or a failure, to believe that the aims will change. "Two steps forward, one step back" is still a movement forward into socialism; the same applies to ideological movements.

Since, as Marx points out, the economic transformation which is the first stage—conversion of private to common property—does not abolish the injustice which consists in the distribution of articles of consumption "according to the amount of labour performed" and not according to the need; it follows that at first, a revolutionary party cannot transform society ideologically except by stages; at each stage, according to the law of contradiction, the forward movement towards socialism will inevitably also give rise to its opposite, a conservative reactionary fall-back, which must be not only resisted, but also studied, and *urged to expose itself*. Mindless suppression will only cause it to "go underground" to hide in "positions of influence", so that, at a later date, a reversal can take place.

The struggle for economic transformation, from planning to performance, can never be divested of its ideological content and therefore political consciousness must always be put in the forefront, sacrificing even temporary material advantage for the ultimate goal. This dedication was never lost sight of during the seventeen years from 1949 to 1966.

"Between capitalist and communist society lies the period of the revolutionary transformation of the one into the other. There corresponds to this also a political transition period, in which the state can be nothing but the revolutionary dictatorship of the proletariat." (Marx.)

In Lenin's *The State and Revolution*, the transition period is defined as that in which there is dictatorship of the proletariat, but with an enormous expansion of what is called genuine democracy, "democracy of the poor, democracy *for* the people, *not* democracy for the rich".

In China, Mao Tse-tung worked out the theme of the New-Democratic Revolution—or the two-stage revolution—

on the way to a socialist revolution. The application of this step-by-step process to the complex and chaotic state of China occupied the period 1919 to 1966. The first thirty years, 1919–49, were occupied by armed struggle for the conquest of power, and the second, 1949–66, by the transition period of transformation. By 1956, the transformation at the base had been achieved; and this completed the first stage of the New-Democratic process, hailed, hastily and erroneously, as the triumph of Marxism-Leninism in China by the right wing. This was corrected in 1966 when the Cultural Revolution exposed the revisionist wing in the Party, and proclaimed the Thought of Mao Tse-tung the summit of Marxism-Leninism in the present era. Hence the necessity of thorough understanding of the class struggle, on all fronts, study, and application of Mao Tse-tung's thought in all domains, so that revisionism – bourgeois capitalism – should not occur in China.

The various movements from 1949 to 1966 will be briefly described; each was dual—ideological and practical; each had a definite purpose; in each total involvement of as many people as possible was assured. At the end of each movement assessment, summarizing of experience, and a period of watchfulness or consolidation set in, to see how well it had taken, to shape the next tidal campaign.

There is always this duality in all that China does or says, an ideological as well as practical component to any achievement or policy. Building a bridge is not merely building a bridge, but is charged with a significance beyond the mere concept of bridge building. Each economic plan has been preceded by an ideological mobilization, not only in order to have its aspects fully grasped and supported by all the people, but in order to "mobilize" all physical resources as well. Political enthusiasm combines with planned construction in an efficiency otherwise impossible to achieve; ideological incentives replace material incentives but generate material results.

In all these movements, certain features recur. One is the technique of the mass line. "From the masses, and back to the masses." Mao Tse-tung thus defined it: "Comrades should be good ... at going among the masses, and gathering their ideas ... these are then refined and discussed; the masses' spontaneous creativity is thus aroused and they will then move on their own." The mass line technique is the most effective way of achieving active involvement by millions of people, voluntarily and swiftly. It turns the masses themselves not only into performers of an action, but into their own source of enthusiasm in the performance, and their own innovators of techniques for its achievements. There is no need of coercion; *the masses exert their own pressure upon themselves.*

"Once the masses understand the objectives and aims, they support us with tremendous revolutionary enthusiasm." The development of the mass line from the first enthusiasm, through meetings, discussions, debates, into participation "strengthens the practice of democratic centralism"; the sense of involvement through discussion is enhanced; each movement is thus assisted by the maximum possible dissemination by all means available, processions with drums and flags, and on all media, radio, television, loudspeakers, and newspapers. Each movement generates its own collective heroes, has its own easily memorized slogans. Slogans do not translate well, though stimulating and often poetic in the original; they are repeatable, clear and practical directives with a positive content. One such ran: "strongly aspire to the best, with steady, forceful, hard work and true, create more, swifter, better and without waste, in spirit dare to be strong." Slogans can be chanted; like marching songs they recharge the individual with energy and trust in the meaning of his performance. The masses create their own slogans; each commune has its own in addition to the general slogans, as it creates its own songs and poems which often incorporate the slogans. To a visitor all this (and on the loudspeaker) may seem overstated and overstrenuous until one remembers that 700 million people have to be moved out of the rut of 2,000 years, educated out of superstition, fears and taboos, into new thinking and new doing. Physical coercion can never compel peasants to study, to keep accounts correctly, to respect trees, to dig canals in the slack season; only a tremendous psychological motivation, more compelling than any selfish interest, can generate such effort. High enthusiasm like ozone multiplies energy, "like an avalanche, like a roaring stream". Not to participate, to remain isolated from this activity arouses psychological distress, a sense of isolation almost unbearable. The reorientation of values, the transformation of motivation, the reshaping of cultural content and significance as well as relations between man and man, and man and his actions thus come to pass.

These movements do not spare Communist Party members. Many have been directed towards a "rectification" of faults in the Party. A responsible Communist Party reflects the "contradictions" within society, lives "in the masses" and not above them. Therefore what is found outside the Party is also to be found within the Party. Mao Tse-tung has been the first communist leader not to make the "baptism" of being a communist a factor of invulnerability, to be aware, as early as 1928, of the tendencies to bureaucratic abuses and feudal tyranny to which Party members become prone; and to institute constant shake-ups of the Party, the greatest of all, prototype of the present Cultural Revolution, being the Great Rectification of 1942–4.

The uninterrupted process of these movements starts from the beginning of Mao's career, with the first Red base at Chingkangshan, founded by Mao Tse-tung, in October of 1927. Later historians, studying the development of

Mao Tse-tung's thought will find this his germinal period. Today, forty years later, "the thought of Chingkang mountain" and "the road of Chingkang mountain", are held up as the correct revolutionary thought and road for all the peoples of the world. It was there that the concept of "the countryside surrounding the cities" was first conceived by Mao Tse-tung,[1] against the "city stronghold" theories of other communist leaders. The Red Guards, now back in prominence, also date from that time.[2] So does the insistence upon ideological work, the emphasis on correct thought, on education, on remoulding and not physical punishment, at that time applied to the Army, as was the creative concept of the democratic relationship between the Army and the people, fundamental to the success of the revolution. The emphasis on the Army as an intelligent vehicle of *ideas*, carrying out intelligently political tasks, including military action, rather than a brute, mindless, physical weapon of destruction alone, is again prominent today.

The belief of Mao that *unity*, rallying the people by force of ideas rather than physical force, rests on a process of debate and criticism which is a constant component of the political struggle, and must be carried out at all times, was also a fruit of revolutionary practice during the period of the Red bases, 1927–49. It is due to this constant process of debate that, so far, the Chinese Communist Party has not suffered the kind of physical liquidations and purges which occurred in Russia. The method of criticism is much more effective.[3]

Throughout the period of the Red bases, 1927–49, and even throughout the Long March, 1934–6, the internal Party

[1] *See*, in *Mortal Flower* by HAN SUYIN, an account of the "readjustment at Sanwan" Mao is supposed to have created the concept here in October–November 1927. [2] Mentioned by Mao in his writings of that period.

[3] Though in the first decade of its existence Russian methods were followed and there were physical liquidations in the Great Rectification movements, 1942-4.

struggle, between two policies, two lines of conduct, "correct" and "deviationist" (either Right or Left) went on. It also went on at Yenan, when the most important and significant rectification movement mentioned above, from 1942 to 1944 occurred. Its significance lies in the fact that many of the issues and problems and even personages, of that time reappeared in the Cultural Revolution taking place in 1966; and that Mao Tse-tung's writings and speeches during that 1942 Rectification Movement have become the standard of correct thought and action now, in 1967.

Throughout the years, vigorous "thought struggle", with continual debate, study and practice, was the chief method practised by Mao of forging unity and maintaining discipline in the Chinese Communist Party. Unity—debate—criticism—more unity (an unending duologue) presupposes a necessary dialogue and endless dualism, and Mao himself says that this dualism will continue for a very long time, *perhaps* even in communist society under other forms.

It was after 1949, when the Communist Party came to power, that the need to extend ideological movements to the whole population began. Military victory alone cannot consolidate a socialist State; it is in the hearts and minds that the battle is won or lost.

The first movement, inaugurated in 1949, was a nation-wide "study movement", to promote self-education in Marxism among all those who could be reached, and chiefly the civil service, many of them being ex-Kuomintang officials. A total drive to wipe out illiteracy began at the same time. Literacy in China before 1949 was accounted an average ten per cent; the Marxist study movement affected chiefly intellectuals, the civil service and a small segment of the urban population.

Intellectuals, or the professional non-manual class, were essential for the rebuilding process, and already in 1948 special directives to win over the intelligentsia had been issued to Party members. The reopening of schools and universities provided platforms for group study and discussion of Marxism.

The Land Reform movement, 1949–52, was also the largest, most important re-education campaign in the socialization of the countryside. It involved 500 million peasants, over two million cadres and about 100,000 intellectuals, teachers, students, artists and writers who participated, as onlookers, as helpers in this earthquake upheaval of a 2,500-year-old medievalism. They saw landlords being accused, their crimes exposed in people's tribunals manned by peasants. They also took part, interviewing peasants, reading land tenure records, writing down accounts of extortions by landlords. It was hoped that by their horrified discovery of what their own peasants had suffered, the intellectuals would understand the hard process of revolution and participate wholeheartedly in efforts for reconstruction. What effect this participation had upon them has not been adequately studied, except that in 1956 Mao Tse-tung wrote: "It cannot be said that all our intellectuals have as yet achieved remoulding."

Some, moved by the discovery of what they had ignored, did become "changed", but, as was later revealed, many did not, because their own personal grievances, diminished estate (they were often hurt by the roughness, suspicion and sometimes arrogance of Communist Party cadres, almost naturally hostile to "white-handed gentlemen" of the literocracy) personal affronts which took away their face outweighed their discovery of what the peasants had endured. The cadres, who had fought their way through guerrilla decades, had no consideration for the "fine feelings" or "subtleties of mind" of the intelligentsia. The Communist Party members who took charge of universities, schools, etc., occasionally rode roughshod over the professors and other luminaries. Until a new generation of intellectuals, bred from workers and peasant families, would come of age and replace the older type, trouble would brew among the intelligentsia.

In 1951, another campaign for study and thought reform among teachers in middle and elementary schools was undertaken, also a campaign for writers and artists, in the wake of the Korean War. Mao's "Yenan talks on art and literature" of 1942 were given wide circulation. It was emphasized that literature and art should "serve the masses, the peasants, workers and soldiers". Intellectuals and writers were urged to go to the countryside or to factories, to "learn from the masses" and write about their epic sufferings. This line has continued with more or less emphasis, until the present day, but in 1966 there were still to be found recalcitrants who had not taken the trouble to visit even a commune!

The San Fan, or Three anti-campaign, started in 1951 was of a scope as vast as the Land Reform; it soon merged with Wu Fan or Five anti-campaign started in 1952. These were actual, real physical purges. By that time the communist hold over the cities (once the bastions of Chiang Kai-shek's power) was firm. The countryside was being cleaned up, the full force of purification concentrated on corruption, prostitution, sabotage, profiteering, gangsterdom and other evils. Many Kuomintang spies and counter-revolutionaries had been arrested; but there was still an enormous substratum of corruption, pimping, black marketing, secret society gangs, spies and agents of all kinds. It is estimated that in these two movements about 500,000 (official figures) were "purged".[1] These were two-pronged campaigns. One was directed against the members of the Communist Party becoming corrupted in the cities; the other was against swindlers, black marketeers, gangsters and pimps. Both were harsh. Party members who had indulged in bribery, misuse of public funds, and even

[1] Some say 800,000. Other estimates put it at one million.

gone into co-operation with State capitalists for smuggling
activities were purged, as well as the Kuomintang spies
planted among them. It was then that the mass line was first
put into effect in the cities; each street, each person, participated
in mass investigation campaigns; holding meetings, denoun-
cing and exposing suspects. The organization of street committees, so that today the policing of each street is done by
the people themselves, laid the foundation for the dictatorship of the proletariat.

Waste, corruption, bureaucratism, both in and out of the
party were thus erased, though they were to recur. The San
Fan and Wu Fan movements were not only purificatory
but also laid the ideological groundwork for the First Five-
year Plan (1953-7). The takeover or conversion of private
enterprises into State enterprises was thus remarkably smooth.
The guarantees issued to the capitalists, interest payments,
and the fact that their children were admitted to education,
eased the change.[1]

In 1954 the Korean War came to a stalemate; at the same
time occurred the first visible sign of the permanent intra-
Party struggle *after* the communist triumph of 1949. It
was terminated by the suicide of Kao Kang, a top-ranking
Communist Party member who had been in charge in Manchuria. The full story of Kao Kang, with his reported attempt
to set up an autonomous state in the north-east, as well as
"restoring capitalism", is held up today as an example of
"the struggle between two lines" in the CCP, mentioned
repeatedly. Whether Kao Kang was in collusion with certain
forces abroad is unclear. In 1955, a campaign against an intellectual named Hu Feng[2] who had switched several times

[1] *The Socialist Transformation of Capitalist Industry and Commerce* in China,
KUAN TA-TUNG, Foreign Language Press, Peking, 1960.
[2] A study of the biographies of many intellectuals who have run foul of the
Party is edifying. Many of them switched back and forth several times between
Communist and Kuomintang parties.

between Kuomintang and Communist parties in the last two decades, was the culmination of a large counter-revolutionary campaign which had begun in 1952. The campaign can be divided into two parts; one against open counter-revolutionaries, 1952–4; one against hidden counter-revolutionaries, 1955–6, that is those who masqueraded as communists. These two movements, even if useful in ferreting out spies (which they did) increased the pressures on intellectuals, and hostility against them among the cadres of the Communist Party. In January 1956, a special session to discuss the question of intellectuals was called by Chou En-lai.[1]

By that date the collectivization of agriculture had resulted in the co-operatives, and a movement for socialist education in the countryside and in factories was being elaborated, but it was piecemeal. The year 1956 remains known, in the West, as the Year of the Hundred Flowers, when the intellectuals were invited to criticize freely. Actually the policy of the Hundred Flowers, was not to let the intellectuals "go back to bourgeois capitalism" but to allow them to expand "towards socialism" by the method of debate and criticism which Mao had instituted. It was also to enable a survey and assessment of tendencies among intellectuals, and the exposure of legitimate grievances.

Socialist construction could not move ahead without the intellectuals, and mistakes in handling them had been made; the drawing-up of the Twelve-year Plan for scientific advance required a rallying of all those capable of being rallied to the policies of the government; 1956 is therefore usually thought of abroad as a year of relaxation in the sense of liberalization; but this is a semantic error; never did Mao Tse-tung[2] think of it as a step towards "bourgeois

[1] CHOU EN-LAI, On the Question of Intellectuals, 14th January, 1956.
[2] Here we must say Mao, because it is obvious that, within the CP leadership itself, there have always been two minds, two roads, a "class struggle".

liberalism", but instead as a step towards socialism. Events outside China, however, were soon to influence the course of internal movements, such as the Hundred Flowers; for the year 1956 was a year of tension, the year of Suez, the Polish and Hungarian revolts, and Khruschev's condemnation of Stalin (February 1956) at the Twentieth Congress of the Communist Party of the USSR.

1956 was also the year in which warnings of bureaucracy in the Party, and right-wing deviation in plans for industry and agriculture were made and these warnings were continued into the 1957 rectification movements of vast scale.

It was acknowledged that only forty per cent of the intellectuals "could be called progressive" in 1956. The rest were still either hesitant, or full of "incorrect thoughts".

The Hundred Flowers movement among intellectuals gained momentum in 1957; in the last two months of the movement an opposition, including certain Communist Party members, came out against the guiding policies and leadership of the Communist Party; thus turning what was supposed to be a debate to *help* the Party to rule, into what was considered a *challenge* to Party leadership, and to the policies identified with Mao Tse-tung. The first had received attention, the second was to be crushed; however, there was no "purge", though many intellectuals were criticized, few suffered more than heavy newspaper criticism and a term of manual labour.

By the end of 1956, the Chinese Party was well aware of the phenomenon called "revisionism" (a similar term would be *embourgeoisement*) at work in Yugoslavia, Hungary and in Russia itself.[1] The Hundred Flowers movement conceived as an increased attempt at unity with the intellectuals, wobbled inconclusively. The appearance of the booklet *On the*

[1] MILOVAN DJILAS *The New Class.* Also *see: On the Historical Experience of the Dictatorship of the Proletariat*, 1956.

Historical Experience of the Dictatorship of the Proletariat at that time indicates the beginning of Mao Tse-tung's concern with revisionism. In the summer of 1957 direct disagreement with the Soviets occurred, later to be patched up at Bucharest.[1] The rash of strikes among students in universities (in 1956, seventy per cent of university students were of bourgeois origin, in 1966, forty-five per cent were still of bourgeois origin) was scrutinized. An anti-Rightist shake-up within the Party itself began, and was extended to intellectuals outside the Party; there was also a rectification of the dogmatism and tyrannical behaviour among the cadres; again a two-sided campaign. Two years later many "rightists" were rehabilitated and reinstated, among them some who in 1966 were again thrown out of office.

The growing doubts about relations with the Soviet Union continued to give a bivalent impulse to events in China. It was in February (1957) that Mao made his famous speech on the correct handling of contradictions among the people.[2] This most important document which for the first time clarified issues concerning the basic principle of contradiction was neither understood nor valued at its true worth at the time, not even in China; certainly not in Russia.

Mao himself went to Moscow in autumn 1957 to celebrate the fortieth anniversary of the 17th October Revolution. With its out and out condemnation of Yugoslav revisionism and the Declaration of 1957, harmony seemed restored.[3] It

[1] It is not possible in this book to give details of the Grand Controversy. THEJA GUNAWARDHANA's *Khruschevism* and JEAN BABY's *La Grande Controverse Sino-Soviétique* as well as KLAUS MEHNERT, *Peking and Moscow* are to be consulted. (*See* bibliography.)

[2] MAO TSE-TUNG, *On the Correct Handling of Contradictions Among the People.* Where the author is concerned, this is one of the most important and fundamental documents illuminating the thought of Mao; it was rejected, however, by the Russian leadership.

[3] A new accord, on technical, industrial, and nuclear knowledge sharing, was signed then.

is said that some Chinese officials recommended to the Russians the study of Mao's *On the Correct Handling of Contradictions Among the People*. If this be true, it may have grated upon the Russians' sense of being "leader of the socialist camp" to find the Chinese (whom they obviously did not regard as their equals) proffering ideological advice, and daring to develop Marxist-Leninist theory on their own; and Mao's recommendation that they should "study ceaselessly" and "remould their thinking" cannot have been welcomed at all by the unstudious Khruschev.

For in this essay, as in *On the Historical Experience of Dictatorship of the Proletariat*, Mao was actually pointing out where Stalin had erred, where Khruschev was erring; urging upon the Soviet leadership the educational corrective, "gentle and clear as a spring breeze", rectification within the Party by study, and not by physical liquidation. Already, in 1957, corruption was fairly in evidence among communist members in Russia, as also among society in general. The appearance of the first prostitute on the streets of Moscow in 1953 had formed the subject of a special report in the Western embassies. "At last, corruption has set in", jubilantly exclaimed one diplomat in private conversation with me in 1957. He added that he was watching "for the same thing in China".

The Chinese take their Marxism seriously, that their "fraternal advice" might irritate the Russian leadership did not occur to them.

By early 1958, as well as the anti-rightist movement, and a rectification campaign in the Communist Party, the course was set for the First Great Leap Forward and the communes. In 1959, to celebrate the ten year anniversary (1949–59) many pardons were issued. It was pointed out to the author in an interview with Kuo Mo-juo, the writer, in 1956 that the suppression of counter-revolutionaries meant their uncovering, but not necessarily the death penalty in each case. It was through the directives of Chairman Mao, I was told, that the death penalty was actually meted out only to a small percentage; many of them received a death sentence but with reprieve for two years and reform through labour to give the criminals a chance to reform and become "new men". Thus a number of ex-Kuomintang officers were interviewed by some foreign writers in Shanghai in 1966.[1]

The decision for going all out in agricultural socialization was taken by Mao himself, and the Great Leap Forward was the outcome of Mao's decision to accelerate the industrialization process. Already the call for a "cultural revolution", doing away with bourgeois authorities and foreign stereotypes, was issued then, to be repeated in 1966. Bold independent thinking, and the participation of youth in productive labour, was called for at the same time. It was also pointed out that more youth of peasant and worker origin must enter higher institutions of learning. The entrance into a communist society was foreseen "in a certain number of years". This urgency was the response to an assessment of Russian revisionism and its betrayal of the revolutionary cause; an assertion of China's determination not to become an agricultural appendage of Russia. The streak of independence, asserted in speeches in 1956, confirmed by Mao's theoretical creativeness in 1957, followed by this concrete example of Chinese desire to become economically a power on their own, was not lost upon the Russian hierarchy. It represented a Marxist-Leninist challenge to the policies of "collusion with US imperialism".

The Great Leap Forward was a movement of tremendous scope, involving an exuberant utilization and mobilization of human resources and energy. That there were "some

---

[1] Altogether about 400,000 counter-revolutionaries were unearthed in the ten years, of whom 81,000 were found guilty, 190,000 were sent to labour, 100,000 were put under surveillance, the rest were pardoned.

people" against this speeding up, is quite clear from the statements made. The struggle between two lines in the Party was "very intense", according to newspaper editorials and reports. This very intense dispute was also present in the Army; it is known that in 1958 Khruschev made demands which were equivalent to a military occupation by Soviet troops of military installations in China. This the Chinese leadership refused. However, the demand of certain generals for an *armée de métier* rather than an ideological army reflected the influence of Soviet instructors. It led to the dismissal of several generals[1] and the return of Lin Piao, already famous during the Yenan period, in order to re-educate the Army, and clean out "bourgeois and right-wing elements".

In June 1959, Khruschev suddenly went back on the accord for nuclear weapons and other technical aid made in autumn 1957. He had decided to "drop" China and co-operate with the United States. His subsequent visit to Eisenhower and the Soviet attitude during the Sino-Indian border dispute in 1959, confirmed that he had decided to seek an alliance with the "foremost imperialist power", the United States.

The year 1960 was to see the sudden and abrupt cancellation of Soviet projects and the withdrawal of Russian technicians, which brought industrial projects to a standstill and almost wrecked China's economy.

During the years 1960-1, ideological movements did not take place on a large scale, meetings were cut down, the city communes were abandoned as were many of the more idealistic projects in the communes themselves. Economic "readjustment" was announced by Chou En-lai in a major speech in April 1962, but "readjustment" was already

---

[1] Including Peng Teh-huai, who had met Khruschev in 1958 and seemed influenced by Soviet thinking. This struggle was also characterized as "a very acute one".

mentioned in a communiqué of the Central Committee of the CCP in January 1961.

These years, 1960–3, viewed in the time scale of the next half century, may have slowed down China's economic growth and industrial advance for a short while, but in the end they had an enormous effect in deciding her future, her continued and accelerated development in self-reliance, the total break from the Soviet road, both politically and economically. But more than that was the ideological spur and development which it led to, and which it is not yet possible to encompass totally. All we can say is that Mao's decision to "take up the heaviest burden", the burden of revolution, and to become the leader of the world revolt in the place of the renegade Russian leadership was made then; that the subsequent course of events and China's emergence as a world power and the direction of that power will influence the course of history in the world for centuries to come. The spur towards this larger destiny was Soviet Russia's behaviour, the arrogant chauvinism and selfishness it denoted[1] which the Chinese took as a salutary lesson to themselves. It is also quite certain that the USA decision to shift back to Asia, and to re-establish domination there, dates from those years and the knowledge of the abandonment, by Russia, of the revolutionary cause.

In 1959, in view of the clear manifestation of revisionism in the USSR, and its potential threat in China itself, Mao Tse-tung consecrated himself to a thorough study of all the implications of this change in Soviet leadership, and also to the growing trend of collusion between the Soviet leadership and Washington.

The division of opinion within the Party and the Army concerning the role of the latter again occurred in 1961;

[1] It is said that in 1962 Khruschev offered to return technicians and specialists, and to reopen negotiations for industrial supplies, but this was rejected by the Central Executive of the CCP.

once again it was along two main lines: those urging caution, withdrawal from "hard positions", continued reliance on the Soviet Union (they were later to be accused of being dazzled by Soviet achievements and frightened by the nuclear blackmail) who wanted an *armée de métier*, with less political and more technical work and know-how, and those who insisted that "politics to the forefront, or ideology in command", should remain the slogan of the Army and that the Army should remain an ideological weapon of the Party. It was a continuation of the 1959 "struggle". Meanwhile, the conference over Laos took place at Geneva; it showed the Chinese plainly that the USA were preparing to re-enter into South-East Asia as a military power.[1]

By 1962 China was recovering from her setbacks. In September 1962 Mao then sounded the warning: "Never forget the class struggle." For in the period 1960–1, the retrograde forces had gained influence and begun to occupy positions of power within the Party. Ideological campaigns, held in abeyance during the worst period (1960–1 and early 1962) were to start again; readjustment was not only physical, but also ideological.

The years 1962–6 are extremely important, in respect of both material advance and ideological determination. The obvious evidence of an extremely swift recovery, increasing self-reliance, the general well-being, abundance of food, stable low prices, increased consumer goods, rapid advances in industry and technology were evidence of success; increasing confidence, an expanding economic base predicated a new leap. At the same time, it was clear that the "struggle between two roads" was by no means over. The rapid decline of socialism in the USSR and other socialist countries, the inroads of revisionism in every Communist Party in the

[1] The author was present at the Laos conference in Geneva as an independent observer.

world, had a great effect in China too. It can be surmised that it was then that a definite clique emerged, strongly revisionist-orientated, and working against Mao Tse-tung. Whether this clique actually had any contacts or collusion with revisionist agents is not known; though the departure of certain old-time right-wing or left-wing opportunists, such as Wang Ming, to Soviet Russia occurred.

Open polemics with the USSR began.[1] A series of statements giving a complete outline of the Chinese "world view" culminated in September 1965 in Lin Piao's pamphlet *Long Live the Victory of the People's War*, and indicated clearly that China elected to take up world revolutionary leadership, abandoned by the USSR. This shift to leadership in ideas coming on top of demographic power, and the evidence rapidly accumulating of growing industrial potential, culminated in the revelation of China's own development of thermonuclear weapons and, in October 1966, of guided missile weapons with atomic warheads. Immediately the whole "balance of power" was changed.[2]

In 1962–3 Lin Piao's clean-up of the Army, begun in 1959, was completed; the movement for "socialist education" in the countryside began. Parallel with it began, from 1963 onwards, a call to "emulate the PLA".[3] This could not have happened unless step one (Lin Piao's clean-up of the PLA) had been successful. The process was also hastened by the realization that China would be attacked by the USA and have to "go it alone", the attack would probably be by bombing to destroy or retard the industrial potential of China, and nuclear and bacteriological attacks to put down the population.

---

[1] *See* the "Nine Open Letters" to the CPSU beginning 6th September, 1963.

[2] *I. F. Stone's Weekly*, Vol. XIV, No. 35.

[3] PLA, People's Liberation Army.

As the war in Vietnam escalated and the threat to China increased, demonstrations for support of Vietnam, against America, blended with the call to learn from the PLA. The people's militia, reinstated in 1958, took on new importance in their supporting role to the PLA; in 1966 the Red Guards would become a mass reserve of thirty million recruits for the PLA.

In the Army itself the return of ideological study and firmness under Lin Piao was given a new dimension in 1963 by promoting Army cadres to participate in ideological movements among the people, thus reverting to their role in the Chingkang mountains. "Since the Army was never separated from the people the 'struggle between two lines' on the literary and art front in the society is bound to be reflected in the armed forces."[1]

The links between worker, peasant and soldier were to become closer; in a recall to the days of 1927–49, when the distinction between civil and military did not exist, soldiers not only manned the State farms but now also opened up and developed factories and plants such as the great oil wells of Taching, in fact, the control of *all* oil and petroleum resources came into Army hands; PLA soldiers helped in harvesting and planting, building roads and bridges; they took a lead in the Four clean-ups which went on with the "socialist education movement" among the communes; bookkeeping and accounting units of the Army especially rendered services then. All distinctions and badges of rank had been abolished as the Army was exhorted to return to the Yenan spirit and the spirit of the Chingkang mountain base.

The socialist education movement in the countryside began to get under way by 1963. During the hard years, the Party organizations had winked at many a deviation from

[1] *Peking Review*, No. 18, 1966.

the correct path, both in conduct and in ideology, among the peasantry and the lower cadres. Corruption, defalcations among the administration of the communes, the "return of spontaneous capitalism" in certain areas of the countryside, filching from the State, private enterprise among the peasants were noted.[1]

In 1964 exhibitions showing cases of injustice, corruption, nepotism, the return of "secret clubs" (possibly secret societies) in the communes were opened to the public, school-children were taken to see them and also to see exhibits of the "bad old days". Plays, dramas, stories, enjoining the young never to forget the past, all pointed to a development aimed at a massive re-education of the population. I have visited such exhibitions; 174 cases of murder, arson, violence, black marketeering, profiteering were shown to me in vivid posters pinned on walls, with drawings; thousands of school-children were being taken to see these demonstrations of "return of landlords and feudalism in the countryside". This was the beginning of a new thoroughness (derived partly from the lessons learnt in the preceding movements, in part from the knowledge and experience accumulated in the communes), the registration of every individual (now achieved through the workpoint registration and rationing) and extensive surveys by special study teams in 1961, 62, 63 and 64. The *hsia-fang* or sending of cadres and intellectuals to the countryside from the cities, which had started in 1958, and had continued all through the years, had greatly cut down the "ensconced bureaucracy" in the cities (in one case reported no less than nineteen "cadres" were found whose sole work seemed to be making tea for a total of four hundred employees!). Sending city people and students to the countryside achieved a dual result; they were to investigate conditions and make reports as well as help the peasantry, and remould

[1] Reports in *Far Eastern Economic Review*, 1966.

themselves by manual labour (which is today a normal feature of education, and not a punishment). This made inquiry into agricultural conditions, as well as the propagation of socialist education in the countryside and rectification of all errors, a movement of substantial value continuing until 1966. By diverting many of the younger age groups to the countryside, with the setting up of agricultural schools, and part-work part-study schools, the construction of the technical, scientific and ideological framework without which the communes would not have advanced at the necessary speed was hastened; socialist education of the peasantry was also promoted; millions of peasants began to read Mao Tse-tung.

From 1962 onwards, owing to the readjustment in planning, from priority in heavy industry to priority in agriculture "with industry as the leading factor", light industry boomed; consumer goods in increasing quantities came upon the market. The communes also got into their stride; planning and control of stocks and marketing were greatly improved, and rationing except in grain, cotton and cooking oils disappeared. Self-reliance now added stimulus, as also did patriotic emulation devices. It was with gratification that Mao Tse-tung could claim success in overcoming the arduous times, sabotage by the USSR leadership, and in the correction of weaknesses and deficiencies within the organization. But the "struggle between two lines" was continuing and the new modest "affluence" and security promoted a false sense of peace. In fact, the most noticeable thing, when one went to China, was the almost soporific sensation of relaxation, which did not tally with the tension and fear manufactured abroad, especially in the USA; I was continually travelling back and forth then, and found China most restful and serene, as did many Westerners. But this very ease lulled. The revisionist influence spread, particularly in cultural and art circles (cinemas, plays, etc.) and the improvement in living standards actually reinforced the false sense of security. For all that time, the Vietnam War was escalating. And it was necessary to prepare the masses for the coming onslaught, or else to surrender.

In the period 1958 to 1965, the following political attitudes, essential for the future, had been promoted and consolidated among the masses—

1. Manual labour was accepted as a normal part of education and of life. The contempt for manual labour has been definitely abolished. The drive to get intellectuals to go down to the countryside to live and work with the peasants was a revolution in itself and a successful one. The resistance to such a movement, the evasions, the "make-believes", the cadres and bureaucrats who ostensibly "went down to the countryside" only to give orders were also, however, still very much about. Though behaviour, attitude and deeds, rather than shouting slogans, became the test of trustworthiness in a Party member, and one criterion was participation in production, that is manual labour, there were still a good many who got away with it by "inspection tours".

2. Rectification movements to improve the quality of cadres in the countryside were vigorously pursued and led to the reactivation of mass organizations, such as the poor and middle peasants' associations, in 1964. These were a return to the Chingkangshan and the Yenan spirit, where peasants' associations played a great part in an extension of democratic procedures to curb the tyranny and arbitrariness of petty bourgeois cadres. This single event, little documented, actually was the presage of the present "mass democratization process" in the Cultural Revolution.

3. Besides rectification among the communist cadres, remoulding the ideas of intellectuals about the value and dignity of physical labour, the third achievement of these years has been to bring education to the countryside in the broadest possible way—education meaning not literacy alone but scientific reasoning and socialist consciousness. A completely different "mass base" for the next step had thus come into being, and chiefly among the under thirties now the majority of population, the young.

Superstitions, disgust for manual labour, refusal to volunteer for the Army ("good sons do not make soldiers, just as good iron is not made into nails," was a proverb twenty centuries old)[1] these anchored attitudes were now to be eradicated. Socialist education was coupled with emancipation from tradition with special emphasis towards the breakout of youth from the framework of "virtue". The Women's Federation co-operated everywhere by promoting the political consciousness of women in the countryside. The complete equality of women, the great number of women in leadership positions in the countryside, the marriage reform laws all became part of the social pattern of living, completely accepted by the under thirties.

Because of the difficulties in 1961-2, hopes were raised in the West of the "failures of the communes" and of "change" in China; China's "utter dependence" on Soviet Russia for her nuclear shield was the subject of Rand Corporation studies. The hopes of corruption extended to China's second generation; perhaps the required softening and disintegrating process would happen to them? A student of China whom I met in 1965 looked forward to the development of homosexuality in China, which, he averred, would be a "logical

[1] It was filial duty to look after one's parents and breed sons; it was unfilial to submit, for instance, to surgery for this was "spoiling the body given by one's parents".

outcome" of the abstemious sexual morals and the eradication of prostitution! And yet a little deeper study of Mao Tse-tung's works, and his performance, might have led him to a different conclusion.

The four clean-ups and socialist education in the country-side of 1963–6, restoration of "politics in command" in the PLA, "restoration of links between Army and people", return of the poor and middle peasants' associations and of mass democratic movements *outside* the Party hierarchical organizations, and a mass socialist education in 1964–5 in the cities, were all to culminate in the Cultural Revolution and the massive all-encompassing educational process known as studying the Thought of Mao Tse-tung, all over China. "Each factory, each commune, each institution, a school of Mao Tse-tung's thought, the whole country one great school of Mao's thought."

Mao Tse-tung's call "never to forget the class struggle" was the warning of the greatest ideological shake-up ever undertaken in history, the proletarian Cultural Revolution; its inevitable material concomitant is the Second Great Leap Forward which signals China's breakthrough into a complete, comprehensive, modern industrial and socialist State. In the short space of four years (1962–6) China demonstrated her enormous capacity for economic recovery and in the most prodigious industrial acceleration the world has ever seen made good the previous losses as well as asserting Great Power status by developing thermonuclear weapons and their delivery by guided missile (27th October, 1966) all on her own.

But, and there is a but, all of this was done in the ever-deepening shadow of a large-scale attack on China. The USA and USSR, the two greatest powers, came to an open understanding between 1959 and 1965; the world seemed destined to be divided between these two nuclear powers, who could "snap their fingers", as Khruschev said, "at anyone who dared to make trouble" which meant, to challenge their super-hegemony. The escalation of the war in Vietnam, while demonstrating the incapacity of the world's most powerful military machine to vanquish a resistance movement politically conscious and fighting a people's war, also demonstrated the devastation of which it was capable. It became clear after 1962, that the USA would contain and keep down the growth of China and that the USSR would not be averse to seeing the two locked in mortal combat. The only Western statesman who openly criticized this division of the world between two super-powers was Charles de Gaulle of France.

At that point, all hinged upon the decision that China would make. Would China capitulate, overawed by the apparently formidable might arrayed against her? Or would she take the (apparently) suicidal course of sticking to revolutionary principle and challenging imperialism and revisionism *together*? This, in 1963, 1964 and 1965 seemed nothing short of madness, perilous folly. And yet the decision was made, the challenge was accepted. And it was Mao Tse-tung who made it. Far from looking upon the Sino-Soviet dispute as a bad thing, Mao probably looks upon it now as a historical blessing; for the USSR's decline as leader of the socialist revolution dates from that rift. Just as the Long March, which could have been a failure and retreat, was transformed by Mao into an epic triumph, so he was now to consider the appearance of revisionism in Russia a most profitable and salutary lesson, a spur to progress, a caution that what happened there, the abandonment of principles, the betrayal of the exploited two-thirds of humanity for a "deal" with the USA, would not happen in China. But could it happen? Was there, in China too, a Khruschev, lying in wait, waiting to seize power? Was there revisionism in China? And what about the next generation? Would it truly become soft and corrupt, as the West hoped?

VI

THE THOUGHT OF MAO TSE-TUNG

The Chinese Revolution is essentially a peasant revolution . . . so the peasant problem becomes the basic problem of the Chinese Revolution and the strength of the peasants is the main strength of the Chinese Revolution.

Of all things in the world, people are the most precious.

MAO TSE-TUNG, 1893–

Man is a microcosm, or a little world, because he is an extract from all the stars and planets of the whole firmament, from the earth and the elements: so he is their quintessence.

PARACELSUS, 1493–1541

ONE facile generalization about Asians was that their traditions, customs, beliefs and "way of life" are "entirely opposed to communism", that Mao Tse-tung and communism are "un-Chinese". Today, the reverse is propounded; Mao and the Chinese brand of communism are declared "too Chinese" and therefore "unsuited" to other Asian countries.

One could point out that far from communism being opposed to Asian tradition, there are many elements in the old orthodoxies which, though opposite to Marxism in their effect, could be reinterpreted and adapted into a collective society.

Every peasant revolt in China has seen a revival of collective organization, common fields tilled in common, redistribution of land to the tiller. The Taiping revolt unbound women's feet, proclaimed their equality and formed guerrilla women battalions.

Dialectical thinking was known to China, the dualism of all things being implicit in many philosophies. The "one divides into two" of Taoism is a concept approaching Lenin's

152

unity of contradictions, as also is the Yin-Yang recognition of dualism throughout nature.

The concept of man as educable, therefore perfectible, the emphasis on thought reform by education, is basic to Chinese ethical tradition.

The word "revolution", *Ke Min*, dates back to the Han Dynasty; then, used to mean a change in the Mandate of Heaven, it was the cry of the peasantry.

The role of the intelligentsia in China's past is not one of revolt, but of conformism; its social status, as the ruling *élite*, was different from that of the bourgeois intellectual in the West. The revolts always came from the peasantry, from "the masses". Officials, who tried to alleviate the sufferings of the commoners under their care did not break with the system which engendered such suffering; the rare reformist was certainly not a revolutionary.

The breath of Western-style freedom of speech that came to China with the slogan, liberty, equality, fraternity, between the 1880s and the 1920s was an artificial plant, sustained by a very few intellectuals after the May 4th, 1919, Movement showed how illusory the Western style of democracy was when applied to China. The slogan, however, did persist among some older writers and artists whose adaptation to the realities of China were to prove as agonizing as that of any Western bourgeois.

The Communist Revolution of China has identified itself since 1927, consciously, with the tradition of peasant revolt and uprising.

The length, duration, bitterness and extent of the civil war, the continuity of Mao's policies of establishing Red bases among the peasantry, the mass support for the Communist Party in rural areas were the basic ingredients which made possible the victory of communism in China. That what happened in China can happen among the peasantry in other parts of the world is a basic premise for those who regard the Chinese Revolution as the prototype and model for World Revolution.

It behoves us, therefore, to try to understand some of the formulas derived from this application of Marxism to a world of peasants by Mao Tse-tung.

The law of contradiction, the law of the unity of opposites in all things, is the basic law in dialectical materialism. Mao's contribution to the development of this proposition is of the greatest importance: *On Contradiction* (written in August 1937), and its corollary: *On the Correct Handling of Contradictions among the People* (written in 1957). During those twenty years, Mao Tse-tung grew from the status of a revolutionary fighter, a guerrilla leader, and a military strategist of impressive talent, to the stature of a great Marxist theoretician and creator. The watershed that has made the Chinese Revolution so different from the Russian one begins with Mao's creative development of the theory of contradiction.

The word contradiction applies to every aspect of reality; it is "within the very essence of things". It is also the basic law of thought—it is "universal and absolute" (Lenin). This duality of everything Mao has adapted, with a mixture of homely proverbs and classical references, to the understanding of Chinese masses. "Failure is the mother of success", "one divides into two", "out of calamity comes good fortune". These philosophical concepts have become so much part of the Chinese language and habit of thought today, that the word *mao tun* (contradiction) is the most frequently used word in ordinary conversation. In Lenin the abstract theorizing on contradiction as a philosophical precept becomes in Mao a statement of absolute importance applicable to man himself, applicable every instant of living to every facet of life. Man, "that essential contradiction", is the focus of all Mao's thought, both as creator and destroyer,

THE THOUGHT OF MAO TSE-TUNG   155

student and teacher, man in all his myriad contradictions. With Mao, the human element is never absent in any situation; least of all in the Great Duality of the Universe: "Myself is my smaller being, the Universe my greater being."

Man is contradiction personified; not an abstract unit to Mao Tse-tung, but a concrete assemblage of subtle and differentiated concepts, his character and his thoughts a reflection of his "reality", his every emotion and judgement affected and coloured by the class outlook, which moulds his perceptions, actions, behaviour and thinking. Resolution of contradictions, therefore, can only come through *awareness*. And awareness is a conscious self-willed effort at analysing a situation, grasping the main contradiction (or achieving correct cognition) of the problem at hand, either external or applied to man by man himself, who in the process of this growing awareness comes to maturity, thus transforming himself. This transformation of man is, in Mao's view, the most essential, important and continuous process in the establishment of a new socialist system; it is called "the remaking of man" or "turning over". And the process must be voluntary. "It is painful" said Mao, speaking of himself and how he had remoulded himself from an intellectual into a peasant.

"As a student, having acquired the habits of a student, I used to feel it undignified to do any manual labour—at that time it seemed to me that the intellectuals alone were clean while the peasants and workers were rather dirty. The Revolution brought me into the ranks of the workers, peasants and soldiers, gradually I became familiar with them and they with me. It was then that a fundamental change occurred in . . . me."

As it is with man as an individual, so is it with the collective, and so with a Party, like the Communist Party, whose destiny is the leadership of the revolutionary masses. No party can take itself for granted, but must constantly strive for the correct ideology through a process of study, investigation and practice that is active performance, for "existence determines consciousness". If a party becomes complacent, believes itself above the masses and stops studying, analysing, thinking dialectically and practising what it teaches, then even after success, after the takeover of power, that party will become, like the man who stops studying, calcified, arrogant and ignorant. That way lies senescence, corruption and downfall.

The emphasis Mao places on the importance of a correct ideology, of a revolutionary theory tested and retested by the practice of revolution, has yet another development. Even after the victory of socialism, says Mao, there are still contradictions in the social system; for the new was born of the old and, in the Long March to the non-exploiting, classless society, the rooted habits, modes of thought and feelings of the past, exploiting society keep tugging us back. No socialist system can work if this is lost sight of. So long as classes exist there will be contradiction between correct and incorrect ideas, not only among people but also within the Communist Party.

Therefore the distinction between non-antagonistic and antagonistic contradictions (those which are between revolutionary and counter-revolutionary, and those which are "among the people") must be made very clear. It is here that Chinese and Russian communism differ so much, for it is precisely on the importance in remoulding man, not in killing him, the importance of analysing and studying contradictions, that Mao Tse-tung and Stalin differed most.

In *On the Correct Handling of Contradictions among the People*, Mao Tse-tung sought to refine and to extend and develop Lenin's dictum. Lenin said: "Antagonism and contradiction are

not in the least identical. Under socialism, the former will disappear, *while the latter will remain.*" But this was not apparent to
Stalin, who treated all he suspected as "enemies of the
people". With Mao, antagonistic and non-antagonistic
contradictions—those among the people and those "with
the enemy"—continue to recur, even after socialism is
established, because the new society is born of the old,
man carries within himself all kinds of relics of thought,
feeling, behaviour from the old society; feudal remnants
exist in capitalist society, feudal and capitalist remnants
exist in socialist society. Old ideas reburgeon, sometimes even disguised under Marxist labels and slogans. Even
among Party members, because many of them are of petty
bourgeois origin, because they are "surrounded by petty
bourgeois", because of their own feudal background, the
tendency to a new class, recurs; and this may continue for a
hundred years or more, perhaps longer; for class societies
have a history of 4,000 years, and it may take fifteen to twenty
generations or more to stop rebuilding new classes.[1]

These contradictions among the people *cannot and must not*
be "solved" by physical elimination (as Stalin did) because
this is the wrong way. Physical violence only applies to the
antagonist contradiction (with the counter-revolutionary
enemy). The contradictions among the people are a matter
of the soul, of the spirit. They can only disappear by remaking
the soul of man—through education, through labour,
through practice and contact with the working masses,
which are reality.

In China the methods used must be remoulding, criticism,
self-criticism and study—repeated and continuous mass
movements and mass-education campaigns, such as the

[1] Thus in the present Cultural Revolution non-antagonistic contradictions
may under certain circumstances become antagonistic ones; but they must be
treated with "reason and criticism" and not with violence until clearly proved
to be antagonistic.

present Cultural Revolution, with a maximum of exhortation, education, elucidation and a minimum of violence.

This basic difference upon a basic question makes the two revolutions entirely different in course and in outcome.

That contradictions still exist among "the people", the revolutionary masses, that class struggle continues, even in a socialist system, is good, not bad, according to Mao. The process of dealing with these is one of the motive forces of progress and consolidation; therefore they should never be dealt with harshly "as with an enemy"; they should be corrected by reasoning, by debate.

The Chinese Communist Party at all moments reflects within itself this abiding struggle between the two roads, the socialist, and the return to capitalist-feudalist, of the society in which it lives. It must, therefore, constantly be on the alert, against itself, to distinguish correct from incorrect ideas; otherwise it will "become lazy", a routine-bound bureaucracy. It must constantly learn, study, go among the masses and learn from them, summarize the experience thus acquired, derive lessons from it in the light of Marxism-Leninism, and continue to remould its thinking and revolutionary practice at all times in ideological struggles. This emphasis on conceptual man and his importance in revolution forms the outstanding feature of Mao Tse-tung's thought; it brings into focus the element of *choice*. An informed, enlightened party at all times is conscious of its responsibility and destiny as vanguard of the revolutionary masses. It must, therefore, never compromise on principles, never succumb to opportunism; victory is certain, for Marxism-Leninism is a scientific, universally applicable truth but only if "correct" ideology is maintained.

The contention that the Chinese are Chinese first, and Marxists afterwards is not valid. It is the other way round. Mao Tse-tung has repeatedly denounced the chauvinism of great powers and also Chinese chauvinism. He has time and again called upon his people to remember that they are part of the international proletariat.

To Mao philosophy is never abstract, but always logic-in-action. Philosophy is not divorced from science but is itself subject (through practice) to scientific experiment.

In an interview by the author with Marxist philosophers in January 1966, these concepts of Mao Tse-tung were discussed. For the past eighteen months a grand debate in "philosophy" (i.e. Marxist-Leninist philosophy and the works of Mao Tse-tung) had been carried out all over China: the prelude to the Cultural Revolution.

"If there is no change in thinking patterns and habits, there is no material change or progress, for spirit and matter are interlinked, spirit (thought, affects) is moulded by contact with the material world and in turn influences the material world." The philosophers deprecated mechanistic materialism, which gives no place to choice, to individual awareness, and conscious retraining; each person's motivation was important, and for this reason, each person must be willing to remould himself, to adopt the "world view" or point of view of the working masses, to stand on their side and to recognize clearly the class struggle which goes on, both in society *and within himself*. Otherwise that person cannot be a revolutionary, cannot serve the masses, and therefore, will either be a non-revolutionary, or become a counter-revolutionary.

"The masses should liberate themselves mentally, but this they must do, *nobody can do it for them*, least of all by order or command. No longer slaves, but master of their destiny, they must ask themselves: 'How can I be a master?' and must answer the question themselves." This means "aggrandizing the scope of the soul" deepening the grasp of historical knowledge, the thinking faculties. The worker, the peasant now realizes that within his grasp lies the power to decide his own motivation, his own spiritual advancement as well as his material progress, and that these two are inseparable.

In order to begin this process of learning how to think, he the worker, peasant, or soldier begins by reading the works of Mao Tse-tung, by understanding the thought of Mao Tse-tung, which means understanding how to analyse, investigate and sift facts, stick to essentials, and adopt revolutionary solutions.

This process should be done *with particular instances in mind*, rather than the other way round. When there is an immediate, concrete problem to work upon, dialectical thinking comes more easily than through merely reading theory without any practical application.

Now that literacy had increased so much, the workers were demanding access directly to material to read and to discuss; the peasants were demanding to "hear" what Mao had said; the soldiers were also demanding: "Give us a gun and a book; for man's spirit demands more than just material satisfaction."

The tradition of debate, argument, criticism in the Chinese Communist Party was very strong; this tradition was entirely due to Mao Tse-tung, and to no one else. "Only through debate can one change minds; cutting off heads does not change things."

There is no better way, says Mao, to unite than by argument, for argument and debate, criticism and self-criticism, produce their own persuasion and their own unity. This had been Mao's experience; nothing could have moulded the tremendous force which the Communist Party turned out to be if coercion had been employed; it was reason, and again reason, patience and logical debate, remoulding through the *practice* of revolution which was the fundamental alloy. And now this habit would be extended to the whole country, to the masses and to the peasantry, to the 700 million, so that 700 million peasants could become "critics of the old world, 700 million statesmen, 700 million reasoners and debaters, to carry on the tradition of the Chinese Revolution, in the way that Mao Tse-tung had forged it". "There will be 700 million Mao Tse-tungs."

The greatest problem in the world today is the problem of humanity facing itself with its burden of the past, its hopes for the future; and this humanity must be trained to think, to think objectively, scientifically, philosophically, dialectically. Truth and justice were fundamental to revolutionary masses everywhere, but the exploiting classes were afraid that once the peasants began to think they (the exploiters) would be overthrown; therefore they did all in their power to stop the people from thinking. The tradition of "keeping the people stupid" was not only pursued in feudal China; it exists today in the West (said the philosophers).[1]

Every individual has a tremendous potential of reasoning and power in him; "every man is a small base, both ideological and material". Every man must be capable of understanding, employing and developing theoretical knowledge and utilizing it; this development of man's highest faculties is essential to the realization of communism. Then only would man be able to master machines instead of serve them, to utilize abundance and wealth for the betterment of all humanity, to resist the rise of new exploiting classes. The class struggle is a supreme condition for acquiring the world outlook which would bring about this transformation of man.

It was upon the manpower reserves of the peasantry that the Chinese Revolution was based. In his speeches and statements Mao Tse-tung refers to this peasant base, to the alliance of worker-peasant (now become worker-peasant-

[1] See FELIX GREENE, *A Curtain of Ignorance*.

soldier) which formed the Red Army: the great task of the Communist Party in China in its militant expression, the Red Base era, was the solution of the peasant question and the liberation of the peasantry from oppression. In Mao's mind the educated, scientific-minded, socialist peasant who can plant and plough, write and discuss philosophical concepts, and also handle a gun or a machine is the new man which the new society must build. Mao himself embodied these aspects: peasant-student intellectual, scientific Marxist revolutionary, active military strategist.[1]

Mao's stand on the importance of the peasantry in the Chinese Revolution defined the whole subsequent course of Chinese history; and this preoccupation arose very early. His reports of peasant uprisings in Hunan are still the classics of today wherever peasant uprisings occur.

The impact of the massive Agrarian Revolution, hundreds of thousands of peasants making "revolt" on their own, this discovery of the "strength of the masses", the "inexhaustible millions" Mao would never forget; forty years later, when he called upon the young Red Guards to "revolt", he used the same word "revolt" and visualized it as a "peasant" mass uprising.

The defeat of the Revolution in 1927 by Chiang Kai-shek and Mao's subsequent actions to save the Communist Party remnants and establish the first Red base at the Chingkang mountains are inseparable from his view of the role of the Army, its organization and leadership. This preoccupation with the problem of constructing out of the peasant masses a powerful, conscious, politically advanced Army was carried out in practice first in the Chingkang mountains, and remained for over twenty years the characteristic of the Red

[1] Mao notes, with approval and joy, tension and struggle within the Communist Party as "signs of life". "If in the party there were no contradictions and no ideological struggles to solve them, the life of the Party would end."

bases wherever Mao's influence was dominant. The Red bases could only survive (though surrounded and constantly attacked by superior Kuomintang troops) precisely because of army-peasant co-operation; and this co-operation in turn was based on fulfilling the peasants' aspirations, abolishing corvée and taxes, carrying out land reform and making the Army "brother" to the peasant, no longer a feared brutal weapon of conquest, but welcome, and cherished.[1] Military tasks are political tasks, and therefore, the Army was a "propagator and organizer of revolution" among the peasantry from which the bulk of its recruits came.

It is against this background that the theories of the People's War, set forth definitely in Lin Piao's article of September 1965, were evolved. The strategy of "the countryside surrounding the cities" was first conceived at Chingkangshan in October 1927; from then on Mao carried out a debate against the "comrades ... who only think of taking the cities ... and refuse to do hard work in the countryside". Twenty years of practice in warfare, campaigns against the Japanese, and the civil war against Chiang Kai-shek, in bases, on the Long March, deepened this conviction that a people (meaning a peasant-worker alliance) highly politically aware, and fighting a just war of defence against aggression, cannot be defeated and will triumph in the end even if centuries are necessary for the process, even if the aggressor is formidably armed.

Today, the Thought of Mao is universalized and its main application to the present epoch is "The road of Chingkang mountains", use of military might to develop insurrection. "The road of the Chingkang mountains is the road of armed

---

[1] This concept of the Army was a total break with the past in China; it is this duality of interchangeable roles—peasant-soldier—which permits the success of "people's wars". It is this which exists in South Vietnam today; hence the massive destruction of peasant life and villages by the US forces.

struggle, characterized by the establishment of rural revolutionary base areas and the countryside encircling cities and ultimately taking them. In other words, it is the road of Mao Tse-tung's thought in guiding the revolution to victory."[1] This means a continuing series of people's wars. In no other way can the people truly gain their independence than by becoming ready to fight for it and take active steps to arm themselves. "It is impossible to create an independent régime, let alone one which is durable and grows daily, unless we have regular forces of adequate strength."

All of Mao's speeches and writings carry the flavour of peasant realism, direct, concrete, sticking to essentials, ignoring the transient. His metaphors and similes mix the genius of peasant proverbs with lines from the classic poets, and make us realize how the latter derived from the former. The quality of his poems is their universality, with the great sweep of exaltation which is the mark of the creator. His thinking is practical, and with him there is no gap between word and deed, thought and act. Uncluttered by abstract theorizing, he believes the function of philosophy is "not to interpret the world but to change it,"[2] and is concerned with the concrete realities of power, neither apocalyptic nor visionary. His outlook on power has a cosmic familiarity; power means the power of the masses, not of an individual; as such, it is an elemental force, the recognition of the energy potential generated by masses of humanity *in action* against exploitation and tyranny, to assert their right to be master of their own destiny. Hence the recurrent imagery of "storm centres" of the world, of the "hurricane forces" of the peasantry; the description of the Long March as a "seeding machine" and a "whirlwind". This cosmic sense of the masses as an elemental force *to be trusted* is the essential point he makes at

[1] As reported by Hsinhua News Agency 25th November, 1966.
[2] As did Marx.

all times. "Trust the masses, rely on the masses" is his repeated exhortation, and has been all through his career.

"Let the masses move; let the masses take over!" This complete assurance that, whatever the apparent chaos, the destruction produced by the oppressed and exploited in tearing down the old order, is good and healthy, for destruction must come before a new order can be constructed, induces in him the concept of revolution as a perpetual revolt; a cyclical convulsion of nature itself. This is the *esprit frondeur*, the call to revolt issued to youth in the Cultural Revolution. It is totally against the tradition of Confucian China, but in keeping with the spirit of May 4th, 1919, with the spirit of the Paris Commune (1870) and the peasant uprisings. This "revolting spirit" which he declares is the bubbling creation of the revolutionary masses, who "educate themselves in the very tumult they create", is sustained by the symbol of the Monkey, Sun Wukung, the Hanuman of China, who with his great cudgel "cleared the cosmos of dust and put demons to flight". The Monkey, a fabulous, legendary figure with supernatural powers, is known to every peasant; a rebel against the establishment, against bureaucracy; he dares to create revolt "even in Heaven". It is this "rebellious spirit" which Mao praises. "Dare to talk, to think, to act, down with pompous authority" is the recurrent theme throughout his life. "The traditions of feudalism . . . are so ingrained", he noted in 1928, "that tyrannical behaviour is not uncommon, among Party members . . ." and this can only be cured by revolt against the root of feudalism and by democracy. The repeated attempts to eradicate feudal and capitalist behaviour and thinking in the Party, as we have seen, gave rise to numerous "rectification movements", and still today the struggle goes on. To this ever-recurring evil, Mao has now opposed proletarian and revolutionary new mass organizations, such as the Peasant Associations, and the Red

Guards,[1] going back for inspiration in this once again to Chingkangshan, the peasant Red base of his youth in 1927.

In the context of world revolution, Africa, Latin America and India are the "peasant or rural countryside" providing the rich metropolises, the affluent North American and European states, with raw materials, cheap labour, dependent and subservient industries. These countries have seen no rise in their standard of living but a decline; their demands for fair trade (reflected at the UNTAD conferences) fall on deaf ears; their balance of payments is permanently at a deficit; their superstructures are unstable, sixty-six military *coups* since 1956 have occurred in these areas as misery and poverty increase and their condition is beginning to resemble that which obtained in China in the 1920s and 1930s; as in China, where the countryside surrounded the cities and finally conquered the city-based forces of Chiang Kai-shek, so (the thesis of people's war maintains) these "countrysides of the world" with their rural semi-proletariat can do the same, and finally win victory on a world scale, *provided* their peasant masses are aroused, mobilized and led by dedicated revolutionary parties.

On the question of the utilization of armed power in revolt against injustice, Mao is categorical; such violence is just and essential against the violence of counter-revolution. Imperialism will never give up unless it is militarily beaten; therefore, *armed struggle* is the task of all revolutionary parties in the national-liberation movements of today. Revisionism, talk of "peaceful transition" is a hoax.

Mao Tse-tung refers to the present epoch as that of world revolution. In this context, China has become the "strong Red base" and beacon of revolution for the whole world. She is ready, therefore, for "any national sacrifice" to fulfil

[1] The Red Guards were actually militia spontaneously formed by the peasantry in 1926 and 1927.

this great duty to humanity. This is absolutely in keeping with Mao's whole character and can be illustrated by his conduct of the Long March in the autumn of 1934.

For some six years the Red bases in south China had been under repeated attack by the Kuomintang armies; four large campaigns against them had failed; in the last and fifth, Chiang Kai-shek, helped by German military experts, employed a million men, tanks, airplanes, and scorched earth policies. The hard-pressed communists lost ground (this was to be ascribed to "left" mistakes, which lost popular support). The communist armies began what amounted to a retreat; 100,000 strong, laden with such gear as printing presses (they had been printing their own money and stamps), luggage, files, etc., they started a retreat westwards, towards the interior of China.

But Mao Tse-tung's views were different, "though there was a defeatist attitude among some comrades", Mao himself proclaimed that the armies were on the march to the north-west in order to fight the Japanese.

This to him was not make-believe. A conference of the Party at Tsunyi in January 1935, handed the leadership of the Communist Party to Mao Tse-tung. The Red Army proclaimed that it was going north to "fight the Japanese aggressors". What could have been a retreat, psychologically destructive, was converted into a triumphal progress, an epic of endurance, through the most harrowing conditions, though only 20,000 out of the 100,000 who started, survived.

All through the Long March, in spite of incessant fighting and decimated ranks, Mao insisted on carrying out ideological work among the soldiers, keeping discipline intact. Throughout there was severe "ideological struggle" within the Party. Certain leaders in strong positions advocated retreat into Tibet, Sinkiang, or even Soviet Russia, there to await "a better opportunity". Others gave way to despair. Mao resisted defeatism, maintaining the concept that, instead of moving towards safe inner areas, the Red Army must move into a *forward* position and prepare to fight Japan. Finally this was done; the result was the base at Yenan, in 1936. The end came in total victory, thirteen years later.

It is the long-term view, the unchanging goal, the inflexible principles, which govern Mao Tse-tung's and therefore China's policies. Short-term expediencies, temporary setbacks, seen in the balanced perspective of China's time scale (whose unit is the century) appear to Mao Tse-tung's cosmic sense as "flies buzzing", or challenges to yet further effort "along the correct road", which is Marxism-Leninism as today known: Mao Tse-tung's thought.

The careful study of the change in Russia, called "revisionism", only confirmed in Mao Tse-tung his tenacious belief in self-reliance, and made him decide to press on even faster to the goal—a communist society in China. The threats of containment, encirclement and bombing by the USA are to him not new but old themes; he spent twenty-two years of his life in the Red bases being contained, encircled and attacked; it is not so much the enemy without, as the enemy within China, and especially within the Chinese Communist Party that is dangerous; revisionism in China could squander all the hard won gains of the Chinese people in one short decade.

Hence the Great Cultural Socialist Revolution of 1966, after most careful preparation on the part of Mao Tse-tung himself. Hence, also, the denunciation of Russia's betrayal, the refusal to compromise or to be cajoled into subservience. The epoch is one of world revolution, and in this epoch, it is Mao Tse-tung, his thought and his writings, which are the guide,[1] and China the Red base and ideological centre of the great Revolt, "turning Heaven and Earth upside down".

---

[1] Note the word "guide". Nowhere is it claimed that the Chinese experience, as embodied in Mao's works, must be slavishly followed. *"Each country must*

The historian Barraclough, in his stimulating *An Introduction to Contemporary History* places with some degree of assurance the opening of a new period of history at the end of 1960 or the beginning of 1961. He regards this date as a breaking point between the persistence of old ways of thought and the conservative resistance to change, and the breakthrough of the new.[1] Mao Tse-tung would be inclined to agree with Barraclough's certitude that this "new world was in orbit" by the end of 1960, though he would entirely disagree with the subsequent definition that this new world rested on "co-operation" between the USA and USSR. The burden of Mao Tse-tung's pronouncements since 1962 has been that a new world era is straining for assertion, and though impeded and retarded by obsolete but tenacious "reactionary" actions (military, economic, political) *both* by imperialism *and* modern revisionism, nothing can stop its emergence. However, this can only be achieved by way of armed struggle as in Vietnam today and in other areas within the next decades.

In his view the illusion created by the USSR that co-operation with imperialist exploitation can result in a better, happier, more prosperous world is sheer nonsense and represents a deliberate choice by the Soviet leadership to side with USA imperialism against the new, emergent world to be.[2]

The USSR has abdicated from its revolutionary duty, backed away from the tasks of "international proletarianism", escaped into "selfish, greedy, self-centred national interests".

[1] *See also* G. BARRACLOUGH, *An Introduction to Contemporary History*, pp. 20–21.
[2] *See* Chapter VIII.

---

produce its own adaptation of this guide to action", just as "Revolution cannot be exported". Hence each country must fight its own way on its own soil, its own war of national-liberation; it is the international duty of others to give moral and active physical support (supplies, weapons, etc.,) but they cannot "liberate" people other than their own.

Historically speaking, the Chinese Communist Party would have to shoulder "the heaviest burden" which "others" refuse, that is the burden of being attacked and fighting a long war of attrition alone. For it is more than likely that, instead of helping her, the USSR will profit from a likely war between China and the USA by trying to occupy Sinkiang, Inner Mongolia, Manchuria.[1] The partition of China, between the USA and the USSR, is not beyond imagination. But this "mad dream", says Mao, cannot come to pass, either now or in the future. The contradictions between America and Europe are accumulating; problems of hunger and poverty increase in the Third World; even in America, richest nation on earth, the formation of a pauperized class is evident; in India, the most aid-riddled country in the world, hunger gets worse and exploitation more merciless. The war in Vietnam is an abomination, and yet only more frightful escalation lies in store.[2] Direct collision between China and the USA is now almost inevitable; the military-industrial complex of the USA wants to attack, to drop the first bomb on China. This will be the signal for "total war which knows no boundaries"; the Chinese masses must be prepared for it. They are being prepared, the Cultural Revolution today is an expression of this total preparation.

The summation of revolutionary experience in China both in war and peace is—the Thought of Mao Tse-tung, the man who, for over forty-five years, has analysed, practised, fought, theorized and led and organized the largest nation of people in the world and changed them, from a world of paupers into a world of men. Few can deny this stupendous achievement; the next decades will tell us whether Mao Tse-tung's analysis, his world view, will come to pass.

[1] *See also* Chapter VIII.

[2] Confirmed by Guam conference, intensified bombing and preparation for annihilation of North Vietnam openly stated by United States' President, March 1967.

VII

THE GREAT PROLETARIAN CULTURAL REVOLUTION

On both shores still the monkeys chatter,
Already our skiff has crossed the rapids![1]

Quoted in *Takung Pao*, Hong Kong, 14th September, 1966

Chairman Mao teaches that we should conduct the struggle by reasoning, and not by coercion or force. We must . . . act according to this instruction. The policy of adhering to reasoning and forbidding the use of coercion or force is an extremely important one in the Great Proletarian Cultural Revolution.

Hsinhua news agency, 13th December, 1966, reproducing editorial from *Red Flag*

1966 will probably become, in history, the Year of Decision for China: the decision for a material Leap Forward based upon the economic breakthrough for the achievement of an independent, modern and comprehensive national economic system; the year of a military breakthrough in nuclear weapons and delivery by guided missiles; the year of a Cultural Revolution involving a massive psychological and political campaign to reshape the motivation and socialist morality of 700 million people; also a year of total military preparedness, in which "the entire people become soldiers".

The speed of China's economic growth in the seventeen years since 1949 is already unprecedented in history; the next decade may see this speed doubled, for it is upon an

[1] These two lines are the last lines of a poem of Li Po's "Setting off from Poticheng in the Morning". It was first quoted by Chen Yi Minister of External Affairs in the context of the Cultural Revolution, September 1966.

172 CHINA IN THE YEAR 2001

economic base entirely different from and vastly more powerful than that of 1949 that the geometric progression which all such developments exhibit in all sectors of the economy will take place. It is therefore imperative that the human material, which determines how this future power will be handled, should also become totally involved in the great issue at stake. Of the two transformations, the spiritual one is the more difficult, complex, and time-consuming; in the end it is the one that is more important. Today we see, allied to the most complex technical marvels, the most appalling barbarism practised by the world's most powerful country, a backward step in humanity's evolution. The covert acquiescence of the USSR (which alone of any country in the world could stop the genocide in Vietnam in a matter of hours) and its own return to selfish national interests after attaining great power status provide a "negative lesson", according to Mao, on how a socialist State can deteriorate. Mao Tse-tung's preoccupation that the Chinese people should not become chauvinistic, abandon the cause of the exploited and the oppressed, and in turn do what Russia and the USA are doing, is basic to the whole grand debate, started a decade ago with the USSR.[1]

The Cultural Revolution is, as are all Mao Tse-tung's Long Marches, a many-levelled affair. It has been the most misunderstood phenomenon and the most misrepresented.

It is Mao who, being withdrawn from the public view since 1959, evolved the theoretical developments and the practical techniques which culminated in the Cultural Revolution.[2] It is certain that Mao personally looks upon this upheaval as his last and possibly his greatest campaign, his final contribution to make China safe for socialism, to make sure the next generation will not squander the hard-won gains of the last

[1] Polemics (concealed) actually may be said to have started in 1956.
[2] *Peking Review*, No. 34.

forty years, and to make sure that the Chinese people will never abandon the remaining peoples, almost two-thirds of the human race, who are still exploited. It is a paradox that this acceleration of an already accelerated revolutionary momentum should have been prompted by the appearance of "a return to capitalism" or revisionism, in Russia. Outspokenly, the hopes of the Western world were pinned on a similar "softening" occurring in China, or the return of self-interest, or corrupt practices, or material incentives; soft living and ignorance of the past would turn out a young generation of driftwood consistency similar to the teenage generation in Eastern European countries. The Cultural Revolution, therefore, had to be designed to make sure that the next generation, the young, would be fully revolutionary: "worthy successors of the Revolution". The psychological and physical preparation of the whole population, including the young, for a long protracted war *upon Chinese soil* had to be made. Ever since 1958 this possibility (now a conviction) has been taken into account. "We shall not build any more big plants" and "we shall not build any more large cities" were also strategic considerations, as was the commune. Increasingly, it seems, war cannot be averted, and the only reasonable course is full preparedness. The re-entry of America, as an armed power, committing herself to military occupation on the Asian mainland as well as of the Pacific island periphery round China, confirmed this conviction that China must be prepared to be invaded, "an invasion prepared since 1949".[1] Although as late as 1964 Marshal Chen Yi, in a calculated indiscretion, let out that he did not believe war was *inevitable*, yet in view of America's avowed declaration that she would "fight communism everywhere", the massiveness of her military preparations (leading even to

[1] "American involvement in Vietnam can be said to have begun in 1950". *New York Times*, 26th March, 1967. *See also* Bibliography.

withdrawal from Europe) and the outspoken debate in the USA about preventing China's industrial growth by raids to destroy her cities, key industrial sites[1] (followed by or coinciding with nuclear strikes on densely populated areas to "kill off" as many millions as possible) it would be more than ludicrous to expect China not to be prepared. By 1962 it was also clear that no help from the Soviet Union could be expected, for all the signs were that the Soviet Union would be only too happy to see America and China involved in a long-drawn-out war, to her own advantage.

Since 1962, therefore, an increasing emphasis was put on the role of the Army, the PLA, as the organizational framework for the necessary semi-militarization of the whole of China's resources, in population and production. Not as an *armée de métier*,[2] not as an aggressive force, but as the ideological as well as the military framework of a total nation, totally mobilized for defence, the PLA was retrained along the lines of "people's war" by Lin Piao, who had called for a reinforced and thorough study of Mao Tse-tung's thought throughout the ranks.[3] By 1962 Army personnel were taking part in the socialist education movement in the countryside. In terms of a people's war, every man, woman, or child, is

[1] MARQUIS CHILDS, *The Washington Post*—14th February, 1966. Mr. Childs, like many other correspondents close to the White House, has stated that the USA government's real target is China, and that Vietnam "is only one phase of the thrust . . . of American power". The USA cannot control the vast resources of the underdeveloped countries of South-East Asia, India, and Indonesia until it has destroyed China's present powerful central government and the rising industrial power of China.

[2] The history of the Chinese People's Army, not as an *armée de métier*, but as a representative of the masses, has been vindicated repeatedly throughout the period 1927-49; this meant that the ideological Party leadership at all times, and political education of the Army units were essential to its very being.

[3] LIN PIAO, *Red Flag*, 1st October, 1959. "Take Great Steps forward, hold high the Red Flag of the General Line and the Military Thought of Mao Tse-tung."

also a soldier; and the total lack of distinction between civilian and military is basic to the "fish in water" theory of people's guerrilla war.

As we examine the problems confronting China ever more clearly since 1960, the young generation and the certainty of an attack, a third problem, which I shall call the reversal phenomenon, also had to be faced. This is the problem of revisionism in the superstructure, that is in the organs of the Communist Party, at each level, and in positions of influence in the hierarchy.

Many hints and warnings, though few concrete details, of the beginning of embourgeoisement and of return to capitalism among individuals in positions of responsibility, of the "capture of certain Party branches" by "representatives of the old and new bourgeoisie" had been voiced during the past few years. The reports of the Jesuit Intelligence Service in Hong Kong and the Taipeh Kuomintang agencies presenting as "secret documents" what are actually extracts from the Chinese newspapers themselves, show the controversy very clearly. "The whole movement for the co-operatives was a bitter struggle" said Mao Tse-tung, and it is well known that increased collectivization produced the most intense debates. But so did every step in the advance towards socialism; each one was greeted, not only with injudicious slander in the Western Press, but also by opposition inside the Party itself.

After 1958-9 and the appearance of revisionism in Russia, it seems clear that the same phenomenon, though in a Chinese garb (chiefly harking back to a feudalist-reformist ideal) was present in China; among cultural, educational, propaganda leaders, as well as in industry, the Army, the trade sector, "loiterers at the cross-roads" and what Mao called "resolute shrinkers" as well as deliberate cliques and hostile factions arose. This trend in cultural circles became more evident in 1960-1, when it began to burst into print. There had been the reverses of the three bad years; temporary concessions, "the Party keeping one eye open one eye shut" emboldened not only critics but also some pro-Russian elements within the Party, and outright counter-revolutionary persons among the Party intellectuals. The influence of this tendency was particularly strong in certain universities and educational institutions because they were staffed chiefly by old-type intellectuals, and even among Party members, whose lives had been a perpetual vacillation between KMT and CCP. The young generation was too unprepared, too naïve, too inexperienced, not to succumb quickly to these theses. To them the "bitter past" was beginning to sound like an old wives' tale. Hence, in 1963-4, statues of clay, lifelike representations of heart-breaking scenes of the past had to be made and put on exhibition to remind the young of past hardships. To one like myself, to whom these representations had once been living persons, the very fact that now *statuary* had to keep the memory of the past alive was most moving and disturbing. Symbolic of the progress achieved, of the vastly better living standard, they were also symbolic of the dangers of the new ignorance among the young about what Old China was really like. For these shuffling, ragged beggars, these skeletal children, could no longer be found in China. Plays now invaded the stage, exalting feudal heroes and their greatness; in retort other plays were shown concentrating on the theme: "Do not forget the bad old days", and "never forget the class struggle", portraying lazy cadres and corrupt profiteers seducing the minds of young workers and peasants. The theme of youth was associated also with new ballets, songs, and warnings of the danger of corruption (both ideological and in the practical sense), in schools, in universities, in the communes. One power bastion, however, had been made secure already in 1959, and that was the PLA; a grand clean-up was to be carried out, by Lin Piao, who most vigorously and earliest of all managed to secure the Army and its cultural, propaganda and other organizations as "great schools of Mao Tse-tung's thought".[1]

We must remember in this context that, all through the period of the Red bases, 1928–48, there was no distinction between civil or military roles, just as there were no "ranks" in the Army. Lin Piao was President of the Resist Japan University (Kangta) at the Yenan base for many years, and as such in an educational position; Mao Tse-tung, Chou En-lai, Chen Yi, were all active militarily during those years.

In 1963 the People's Liberation Army produced a summary of the main political tasks in the Army; this marked the comparative success of Lin Piao's methods. The clean-up[2] (as part of the socialist education programme) was also carried on in the communes (where it was known as the four clean-ups campaign). The slogan: "Learn from the PLA" (not meaning learning goose-stepping, but the spirit of the PLA) sounded from 1963 to 1966. The clean-up and socialist education campaigns extended to city organizations in 1964, again with the call to "learn from the PLA". Army cadres began to send representatives to many organizations to "train young army men in various tasks as apprentices". Thus the Foreign Language Press, the Post Office, and other units all received their quota of PLA cadres. These cadres had simple mottoes: "Put political work first, ideas first, lively modern ideas first,

---

[1] "The struggle between two roads on the front of literature and art in society is bound to be reflected in the armed forces, which do not exist in a vacuum and cannot possibly be an exception to the rule ... the enemy ... will inevitably use literature and art to corrupt our armed forces."

"Since Comrade Lin Piao took charge of the affairs of the Military Commission of the Central Committee of the Party (in 1960) ... he has taken a firm grip on literary and art work." *See: The Great Socialist Cultural Revolution* Pamphlets 1, 2, 3, 4, 5.

[2] It must be made quite clear that the word "clean-up" does *not* refer to purges, but to an exhaustive sifting and investigation of *all* the problems existing in the unit of organization; personnel, bookkeeping, production, conduct, etc.

give an example of all good things, and be first to learn all good things from others." The hydroelectric power organizations throughout the land immediately announced that they would "emulate the spirit of the PLA", their example was followed by the communications network and many industrial plants. Already the Taching oil wells and plant, other sources of oil and important industrial units in the provinces, as well as State farms, were wholly or in part manned or staffed by PLA or ex-PLA men. Thus the strategic areas of power, the strategic industrial sectors, were made safe for the revolutionary wing of the Party and wrested from revisionism by Army personnel. This "takeover" was non-violent, co-operative and ostensibly welcomed by many of the cadres.

But there were other sectors which remained in doubt or in possession of firmly entrenched opponents of Mao Tsetung's views. There were high-placed officials who contended that China should "come to a compromise" with Russia; others argued for the restoration of profit incentives. In 1964 and 1965, the "philosophical debate" already referred to[1] was taking place. "Which way shall be China's way?" It was certain that a "cultural revolution", an ideological movement of immense size, was developing.

The movement for socialist education in the countryside was the concrete beginning of the Cultural Revolution. "It is a new, deeper, broader stage in the whole development of socialism in China."[2]

The socialist education movement in the countryside started on reports made of conditions in the communes, which had revealed that the standards of socialist morality had slipped in certain areas. The movement was carried out by Army propaganda cadres, teachers, university staff, university students, artists.

The four clean-ups were directed towards the abolition of

---

[1] See Chapter VI.   [2] Peking Review, 22nd July, 1966.

the return of landlord ideas, material profit motivation and conduct, embezzlement, corruption, nepotism. In some communes the leadership had actually gone into "partnership" with ex-landlord families. Reports of sexual immorality, favouritism, unjust allocation of workpoints, indicated the reversal phenomenon in the communes, a return of landlord power, of feudal bureaucracy, corruption, and abuses by cadres along the old arbitrary, feudal lines. Though only a small percentage of communes was so affected (five per cent badly, ten per cent not so badly) yet energetic action was taken. "Class struggle does not die out after the nationalization of industry, the collectivization of agriculture ... this is what Chairman Mao Tse-tung has taught us ... the education into a socialist society will cover a long historical period ... " (Chou En-lai, December 1965).

A significant development of the socialist education movement in the communes was the mass democracy process which accompanied it, the resurrection and invigoration of the poor and lower middle peasant associations which had been active during the period of the Red bases but had become dormant, a sign of the hierarchization of authority. They were reactivated to check the bureaucratic excesses of the Party leadership in the communes, as well as landlord elements and counter-revolutionaries. These associations now began the assault on the entrenched bureaucracy, and on counter-revolutionaries and others who had "infiltrated" into the command structure. And since every movement is shaped by a theory, the reading, understanding and application of Mao's thinking became the foundation and theoretical basis of conduct, intent, behaviour and action in this movement, as it had been in the PLA under the direction of Lin Piao.

It is this mass movement in the countryside, the arising of mass organizations to clean up the party leadership at grass roots level, which can be regarded as the broad-based testing ground, predecessor and preparer for the Cultural Revolution. The latter could only be successful when the first two steps, the clean-up in the PLA, and the clean-up in the communes, had been almost completed. Altogether two million people were involved in the socialist education and four clean-up movements in the countryside from 1963 to 1964, another three million in 1965.

In 1964 the movement spread to the cities. By that time the units or sectors, where authoritative leadership was actively propagating anti-Mao and revisionist ideas, had become known and clearly demarcated. Their spread in the cultural and propaganda sectors was particularly noticeable.[1] According to Mao Tse-tung, this was "the enemy without guns", the enemy within the socialist system itself. This struggle between "proletarian culture" and "bourgeois culture" had gone on since 1942.[2] In September 1962, and again in 1963, 1964 and 1965, Mao Tse-tung "gave extremely important instructions" on the question of the necessity for a Cultural Revolution, because "very little had been done" and problems abounded.

"The exploiting classes have been disarmed—but their reactionary ideas remain rooted in their minds ... we have confiscated their property—but cannot rid their minds of reactionary ideas ... they invariably try to make use of their influence surviving from the past to shape public opinion in preparation for the political and economic restoration of capitalism. ..."

"Representatives of the overthrown class try to tighten their grip on ideology and the superstructure, theoretical and academic work, literature and art, etc. ... it was a num-

[1] Many of the heads of Universities and their Departments dated from the 1930s as writers and intellectuals at that time considered left-wing.

[2] It was also present in the Party at Yenan, hence Mao's "Talks at the Yenan Forum on Art and Literature", in 1942.

ber of revisionist literary men of the Petöfi Club who acted as shock brigade in the Hungarian events . . . in the 1956 Hungarian counter-revolutionary incident, the counter-revolutionaries *prepared* public opinion before they took to the streets . . . the Soviet Union (after the establishment of socialist relations of production—i.e. a socialist base) failed to carry out a proletarian cultural revolution in earnest . . . the seizure and consolidation of political power depend on the pen as well as the gun. . . ."[1]

This required a total assault upon the ensemble of "old, feudal, capitalist, and reactionary and revisionist ideas" in a massive campaign which would involve every single person in China. And this involved a "mass line" mobilization on an unprecedented scale; a rectification within the Party, and within the superstructure of authority, also on an unprecedented scale.

This mobilization of the masses meant that the outstanding development, in the Cultural Revolution, was to be the setting up of revolutionary mass organizations, to eradicate, within Party organizations, those "persons in authority" who had been guilty of deliberately promoting a return to the past, in short, The New Class, and its ringleaders. This is, in effect, the first time in history that a communist party leadership aroused the revolutionary masses *against itself*. "We must arm ourselves against ourselves" was the way Madame Soong Ching-ling put it in an interview with me.[2] This meant, also, carrying mass democracy to the masses. "We shall give the implementation of our revolutionary policies to the revolutionary masses." In 1966, Lenin's dictum[3] was being realized in China.

---

[1] *The Great Socialist Cultural Revolution in China*, 1966 (six booklets issued in several languages).
[2] *See Eastern Horizon Magazine*, November 1966, Hong Kong.
[3] *See* LENIN, *The State and Revolution*.

The problem of the New Class, of the return of capitalism, is a very complex one, latent in any power structure. It was in the upper echelons of the Communist Party, in art and literary circles and in institutes of learning, among Party organizations and ministries, that the "leaders" of this revisionist line would be found; and they would be using Marxist phraseology to smuggle in their ideas. To investigate only the lower cadres who merely carried out orders, would have been both ineffective and harmful. A massive campaign in which every single member in the Party, every leader, everyone in position of authority, should be eligible for scrutiny, investigation and criticism by "the masses", whether he be good or bad, would therefore take place. And this meant opening wide the doors of every institution, organization, university to the people.

That this rot should begin "at the centre", that is within responsible and high-ranking cadres, is not amazing; this was the experience provided by the behaviour of the Russian hierarchy. True to the theory of contradiction, Mao reasoned that there must be, somewhere in his Party, a Khruschev-type time-server, waiting for his opportunity. The struggle between two lines in the Chinese Communist Party had always existed, as had been amply demonstrated; but after 1960 the danger was enhanced, because of the betrayal by the Soviet Union of the revolutionary cause, the appearance of revisionism in many Western communist parties, and the danger of attack upon China. The target of this cultural infiltration and embourgeoisement was, of course, the vulnerable young. In the fields of art, culture, education, the "black line"[1] was most dangerous, for it directly affected the next generation. It was also in this field that the greatest number of cadres with bourgeois or literocratic background would manoeuvre.

[1] True to the definition of "two lines of development" the revisionist line is called "black", the correct line is called "red".

Mao knew the Chinese intellectual and his ambivalent mind; he knew also how many of them had "turned coats" a few times; and he was aware of their craving for power, for "a return to their own paradise", the mandarinate of feudal days.

Investigation into the universities and higher middle schools in the cities provided a shock; after seventeen years of socialist China, over forty per cent of the students were still from bourgeois, ex-landlord and capitalist families, even if these were only five per cent of the population. In Yunnan University (Kunming), however, in 1962 I was told several times that over eighty per cent of the students came from workers' and peasants' families. But this was not true of certain universities, such as Peking University; in the Shanghai Music Institute, a friend told me that ninety per cent of the students were of bourgeois or petty bourgeois origin in early 1966.

A friend told of some ex-capitalist families in Shanghai, whose sons and daughters spent their time at the movies or in restaurants. The income of these families from their capital, invested in (now) State enterprises (which paid them a regular five to eight per cent a year[1]) was such that these young men and women could afford to do nothing. One such spent most of his time travelling around to the other cities, sightseeing, buying curios and goldfish.

Many stories of poor peasants' and workers' sons being rejected at university examinations, while bourgeois sons obtained special coaching, could not be reported in the Press, as they were suppressed by editors (related by class or even family to directors of educational institutes).

The problem of youth in China is also the problem of the future of the Revolution, a question of world importance.[2]

---

[1] The interest rate for ex-capitalists is five per cent. An eight per cent interest is paid only to overseas Chinese investments.

[2] See *Training Successors for the Revolution is the Party's Strategic Task*, 1964.

Would the next generation, say by the year 2001, be degenerate, ally itself with imperialism, return to selfishness, and become, as in so many other countries, frustrated and aimless? Would a New Class emerge, exploiting once again the Chinese peasantry? The question was not only important, it was urgent—as a whole new generation of young, over three hundred million of them, was growing up, with no direct, concrete experience of suffering and hardship, or of the past exploitation. Many of them asked ingenuously: "What is a landlord?"

The occupation of key positions, in education, administration and the arts, in the Press, propaganda, radio, universities and schools, that is in the superstructure, by people actively promoting an ideological restoration, became evident. In June 1964, already, a rectification in literary and art circles had taken place; and it had been followed by a new series of anti-revisionist plays. The old theatre had been replaced by new themes. Again in September 1965 "Chairman Mao pointed out the need to subject reactionary bourgeois ideology to criticism". But still the persistence of extraordinarily silly plays on "feudal gentlemen" went on. I remember myself at that time (1964) thinking how many better plays could be made out of the epic Long March. Finally, the magnificent ballet, The East is Red, and an excellent play Shachiapang, were produced, and from that time on, the feudal theatre was broken.

Because of the rapid accretion of members to the Communist Party after liberation (an accretion necessary for administrative purposes) and another intake in 1956 and in 1958 (for the purpose of the communes and the Leap Forward) many opportunists were recruited into "the revolutionary ranks and in various economic organizations". The author recalls a conversation in those years with a certain young person who openly said that the only way to get on was to "get into the Communist Party. I know how to do it. Shout slogans, volunteer for everything, criticize everybody; but especially shout slogans". I do not know whether this ambition has been realized, but it is certainly my opinion that a certain proportion of Communist Party members are insufferably bureaucratic, love to give orders, are avid for compliments and try to extort from visitors declarations of enthusiasm, which can then be jotted down into a report. They may be only ten per cent of the number, but as they are more "pushy" than the average modest, hard-working Party members, they manage to make a great impression, whereas the many good ones are not so easily remembered.

It was, therefore, within the superstructure that the clean-up was to be undertaken. An analysis of the root of revisionism, and how it can be checked, appears in Letter No. 14 (14th July, 1964) addressed to the CPSU.[1]

In Russia, revisionism did not begin with Khruschev; it had its roots in opportunism under Stalin in the 1930s.

In the 1930s Russia had sought to increase production. This fundamental problem, the increase of production in a socialist system, which depends on *motivation*, is one that every socialist system has to confront. It is the core of the problem of building a socialist economy *without exploitation*.

There are two ways to go about it: one is through material profit, and benefit to the individuals; whether it takes one form or another (bonuses, better housing, etc.); the other is to change the content of motivation, to provide, through continuous and painstaking socialist education, through rectification campaigns and movements, a change in behaviour, "within the soul of man". This conversion has been attempted before, in religious systems, but not with the

---

[1] Pages 64, 65 *et sqq.*, French Version *Le pseudo-communisme de Krouchtev et les leçons historiques qu'il donne au monde*. CPSU, Communist Party of the Soviet Union.

thoroughness of a science, which is Mao Tse-tung's treatment of this psychological remaking. This requires the use of the right means to the right end, and does not imply that the end justifies the means, for by using the wrong means the end goal is lost.[1]

Stalin chose the road of material incentives, Mao has chosen the second. Stalin was a man in a hurry, who believed in physical liquidation. Mao is a man who moves fast but is extremely patient, and believes in debate and re-education. The USSR, the first socialist State in the world, had to be rapidly brought to world-power status. To Stalin this meant steel, heavy industry, gigantism, and widely different levels of remuneration to different sections of the people. Mao is changing China even faster, and also believes in steel and heavy industry, but he, nevertheless, believes that principles must not be sacrificed to expediency. The changes introduced to obtain efficiency and productivity turned the Soviet Communist Party itself into an administrative bureaucracy, a class of technocrats and administrocrats, rather than thinkers and Marxist philosophers. The purges of Stalin made it possible for the type of person whose revolutionary enthusiasm is measured by the strength of his larynx and the pitch of his shouting (something which also happens in China) to assume control. The rot of opportunism, the infiltration of ideas of personal interest created cliques avid for power. The Party functionaries, the technical personnel and managerial staff in the large, heavy combines and plants in Russia became a close-knit, almost self-perpetuating *élite*. In China, agriculture came first, there was less stress on heavy industry; collectivization and entry into socialism preceded mechanization, and socialist education campaigns, adherence to the mass

[1] "The trouble with the world today is that Christian man still lives in a non-Christian society" was the way a friend in Peking put it to me. Author, 1966.

line, insistence on manual labour for administrators, insistence on three-level consultations, and equalization of salaries did away with managerial level preponderance.

"Before taking over power, history shows that the bourgeoisie always first start a cultural movement, preparing the ground, preparing public opinion, for such a takeover."

The striking lesson, derived from the gruelling experience with Russia, for Mao, was that "restoration of capitalism may be achieved peacefully, almost insidiously".

"Though the great mass of cadres are now forged and educated in rectification movements, this does not mean that our society is impeccable ... there is class struggle ... the reactionary classes are still plotting ... old and new bourgeois indulge in speculation (financial); degenerate elements exist ... and these degenerate elements *do all they can to find protectors* and agents in the higher ranks of the Communist Party organization. ..."[1]

One of the main danger signals of this phenomenon of educational revisionism was the difficulty of acquiring young volunteers for Communist Party membership at grass roots level, as well as obtaining recruits for the Army. "At present, the average leading cadre in the grass roots organizations is more than forty years old, while the number of party members over forty is very large."[2]

It was obvious, therefore, that the battle would be for the minds of the young generation. But true to the Mao thinking, the battle must not be fought on their behalf or they would never know about it. They must be totally involved. "Let the young *themselves* revolt! Let them do their own clean-up! Let the masses educate themselves through their own mass movements! On no account must anything be done for them, they must find the answers themselves."

[1] *The Great Socialist Cultural Revolution* (Nos. 1, 2, 3, 4, 5, 6) Peking 1966. Italics are the author's.   [2] ibid.

The decision to involve the young in participation is therefore neither astonishing nor unwise. On the contrary, it is far-sighted, a masterly handling of an enormous problem, the problem of passing on the revolutionary aims and spirit to posterity.

All through China's modern history, it is students, young people, who have led in revolutionary movements. In 1919 the May 4th Movement was led by young intellectuals, teachers and students, from the middle schools and the universities, and this was China's *first* great cultural revolution.

All through the 1920s and the 1930s the most prominent feature of China's seething political scene was the revolt of the young: innumerable demonstrations by students and young intellectuals, as in Latin America, India, even the USA today. In 1935, the December 9th Movement in Peking was entirely a student movement, it soon involved all the students of China: "the spirit of dissatisfaction and contempt for old restraint has been intensified. . . . Educated discontent and agitation by the young, therefore, has been a prominent feature of the revolutionary situation in China," wrote Putnam Weale in 1925. "The young renew the world", wrote Mao Tse-tung. "The whole of the Chinese revolutionary movement found its origin in the action of young students and intellectuals . . . *but they must be united with the broad masses of young workers and peasants . . . otherwise they cannot become a powerful movement.* . . . If the young wish to achieve results they must establish friendly relations with adults . . . unite with the majority of the population who are more than twenty-five years old. Old people have experience . . . [1] one cannot neglect them because they are old."

In 1926–7 the youthful Mao Tse-tung was to see the hurricane of the Peasant Revolution in Hunan. He watched

[1] Mao Tse-tung, 4th May, 1939, on the occasion of the twentieth anniversary of the May 4th, 1919, Movement. Italics are the author's.

the peasants organize their own peasant militias, overturn the established feudal landlordism, create revolutionary committees and the Red Guards. "Very good! Excellent!" he shouted then, when he saw this upheaval, "making heaven and earth change places" and praised their "spirit of revolt, of daring to revolt". Four decades later, he handed over to the next generation, the teenagers, the right to "make revolt", against the infiltrators in his own Party, against those who wanted to restore the past and hamper the future, urging them to "dare to revolt". In 1966, Mao's faith in the eternal recurrence of the young and growing forces of life to overturn the old and sterile was reasserted, as a new generation arose, to become the "successors of the Revolution" and pull down all fakes, all hierarchies, *even in the Party itself* no matter how high.

This, therefore, was no hasty impulsive action, opening the gates to "hooliganism", as reported so erroneously in the Western Press. Several editorials and articles in 1964 on the question of training successors for the revolution, calling it "the Party's strategic task, a long-term plan", laid down the guide lines for the participation and involvement of China's young into the creation of the world-to-be; making it clear that *each succeeding generation must demand and obtain its own renewal of revolutionary impetus.*

"The problem [of training successors] has been recently placed as an important item on the agenda by Party committees at all levels, in accordance with directions given by the central committee and comrade Mao Tse-tung . . . this is a vital issue . . . compared with the past the present problem has a still greater *strategic* significance . . . we must view it against a background of *opposing both imperialism and modern revisionism*, and preventing revisionism, making sure our Party and government will never change colour."[1]

---

[1] *Training Successors to the Revolution*, Peking, 1964. Italics are the author's.

"Comrade Mao Tse-tung *has studied how revisionism emerged* . . . and summed up the lessons history has taught us. He has analysed the class struggle going on *at home and abroad. He has underlined the problem of revolutionary successors.*"

The requirements the young revolutionary successors must fulfil were laid down by Mao Tse-tung in the course of 1964. They must be genuine Marxist-Leninists; serving the overwhelming majority of the Chinese people and the whole world; they must have leadership qualities as proletarian statesmen, good at uniting even with those who disagree; they must be modest in applying democratic centralism, the mass line methods of leadership, "good at listening to the masses", modest and prudent, guarding against arrogance and impetuosity, imbued with the spirit of self-criticism and with the courage to correct their own mistakes and shortcomings.

These five requirements are "the criteria (Marxist-Leninist) for choosing and bringing up revolutionary successors".

The Red Guards, the mobilization of youth, were not a sudden phenomenon, therefore, but a long-matured and well prepared strategic campaign to train revolutionary successors and a young revolutionary leadership, and at the same time to eradicate the attempts at reaction.

"The imperialists abroad, headed by the USA, pin their hope on the 'peaceful evolution' of China through the degeneration of our third and fourth generations. Who can dismiss this view as entirely groundless? So long as there are classes and class struggle, and a conflict between the socialist and capitalist roads, throughout the transitional period, there will not be one road and one prospect, but two roads and two prospects . . . if we allow the Party and government leadership to be usurped by people imbued with the ideas of the exploiting classes and revisionism, or if by neglecting to give education and training, we make revolutionary successors of young people who have been corrupted by bourgeois and revisionist ideas, then the revolution will stop half-way, socialism will 'evolve peacefully' into capitalism, and capitalism itself will be restored . . . ."[1]

"The question of training successors for the revolutionary cause . . . is a *matter of life and death* for our Party and our country."

"The training of successors is a major question for the next thousand or even ten thousand years." "The Great Cultural Revolution is therefore an issue of prime importance for the destiny, prospect and outlook of our Party and our Country. It is also an issue of prime importance for the world revolution". What China will be like in 2001 depends entirely on the Red Guards of today, on the Cultural Revolution today; what the world will be like in 2001 also depends on what happens in China today.

"The most important thing is to prevent the emergence of revisionism during the period of socialism, in order to avoid a reversal of the revolution."

Unless the successors participate actively in revolutionary movements they will not know how to deal with future crises. There will and must be further revolutionary re-beginnings, as each generation takes up where the last one left off.

In 1966 Mao Tse-tung made his reappearance, in the middle of the Cultural Revolution, not only as the leader of the Communist Party of China but also as leader of the next generation.

Because of the importance given to Lin Piao,[2] who is in command of the Army, some regard the present upheaval

[1] *The Great Socialist Cultural Revolution in China* (5).
[2] Mao Tse-tung, Chu Teh, Chou En-lai, Chen Yi, and many others have all led armies and held military command. Lin Piao's appearance does not indicate a military takeover but the continuation of the revolutionary tradition, in which it is the function of the PLA to "train cadres and successors of the Revolution". Kangta, the Resist Japan University in Yenan (1938–45) was a militarized educational institution under the command of Lin Piao.

as a "military *coup*", and speak of a military dictatorship. Such a view does not take into account the strategic significance of this enormous campaign, which is not only the culmination of the process of socialization of China over the last seventeen years, but also the taking in hand of the young generation, a concentration of effort for a material leap forward; an ideological "leap" into a higher socialist level of humanity; and, last but not least, total preparedness, the material mobilization of the whole country and its resources for the almost inevitable war that is being imposed upon China through escalation in Vietnam.

China has stated time and again that she will not shirk her proletarian international duty to bring help to Vietnam and to send troops if asked; if she is attacked, she has stated, the war will have "no boundaries". Every American base in Asia will become a battle site.

The possibility of a revisionist *coup* against Mao's leadership was removed by Lin Piao reasserting the political and ideological primacy of Mao Tse-tung's thought in the Army. The Chinese, therefore, do not regard the ascension of Lin Piao as a takeover but as the reassertion of ideological primacy over purely military ambitions.[1]

It was therefore logical in view of the overall situation, that the necessary Party political control over the Army, and the latter's tradition as an inherent part of the people should be continued and reinforced. "Learn from the PLA" launched in 1964 was not a call to become militarized; but to remain on the same basis of perpetual semi-militarization as during the hard times of Yenan and the Red base at Chingkangshan. "Boldly to nourish and select young cadres is the glorious tradition of the PLA", the *Army Liberation Daily* proclaimed on 17th January, 1966. This and other pronounce-

---

[1] Subsequently, the development of the Cultural Revolution in 1967 has confirmed this view, penned in 1966. Author.

ments, hailing the Red Guard as the PLA's strong rear, indicated
that the policy of ideological readiness, and material readiness,
is to be applied fully to the next generation.

"Revolutionary experience *comes from personal participation
in the revolutionary struggle*. If one begins working at the grass
roots, if for several years one does work that is sincere, and
not make-believe, then one will gradually accumulate valuable experience. . . ."[1] The Red Guards will be the pool from
which the future Party members will be drawn. The Young
Communist League and other youth organizations under the
previous hierarchy are at the moment under scrutiny (as is
everything in the Party in China); the emphasis now is on
"mass democracy" rather than on particular selection;
this also abolished a good deal of the aura of superiority
which surrounded Communist Party members.

"The world is yours as well as ours, but in the last analysis,
the world is yours. You young people full of vigour and
vitality are in the prime of life, like the sun at eight or nine
in the morning. All hope is placed on you."[2]

This emphasis and trust in youth implies a complete reversal of the feudal tradition of "filial duty", docility, hierarchy, status. Mao's preoccupation with the "ageing" of the
Communist Party has found an answer: new, radical blood,
unshackled by respect, daring "to revolt and to reason" will
come to the fore. Hence the great emphasis, in this revolution,
on the use of reason, criticism, debate, and not on force.[3]

Because of the assessment of the present epoch as one of
world revolution, when many areas of the globe will be
engaged in violent struggles against imperialism, and because
of the Russian abandonment of revolution, China has now
become "the strong bulwark" of revolution, she must expect,
therefore, to be attacked; must be ready "for the greatest

[1] Mao Tse-tung, 5th October, 1939.   [2] Mao Tse-tung, speech to Chinese
Students in Moscow, November 1957.   [3] *See* page 199.

national sacrifice" and therefore the greatest devastation, the ruin of all she has built. But it is the spirit of revolution which counts, for that spirit is a tremendous power, which becomes, when transmuted into concrete act, a "tremendous material force, much more powerful than the atom bomb".

Mao writes that it is ideas which change the world; it is the masses, imbued with ideas, which carry out this change, and not brute force. The Red Guards of today are the generation who, in their millions, will have to fight to defend the Revolution and its outcome.

The Problem of Education

The problem of education is inseparable from the problem of creating another revolutionary generation.[1]

By 1965 there was no illiteracy in those under forty years old[2] in China, and therefore it became all the more urgent to change the motivation of this great mass of "literates" in order to avoid white-collar class bureaucracy and the attendant brain drain into administration and into the cities. For the peasantry, to have a son "become an official" was still the peak of achievement. "What is the good of educating my children if they must remain peasants as I am?" they said. In today's Cultural Revolution, the whole purpose, and intent, of education is again being debated.

"What is meant by education?" Education is not only to teach as swiftly as possible wiping out illiteracy, to train a modern, socialist, industrial, technical, society, absorbing modern techniques and innovating and creating on its own, it must also inculcate a "greater than self" world outlook, a revolutionary and internationalist, proletarian outlook. In seventeen years enormous advances have been made in the

[1] *Training Successors for the Revolution*, Peking, 1964.
[2] *See* EDGAR SNOW, *The Other Side of the River*, for education until 1960.

field of creating a technical pool of high-grade scientists, engineers, technicians, doctors, metallurgists, geologists, but a deliberate effort to preserve the "strongholds of education" for the sons and daughters of city bourgeois families seems to have occurred. In the Communist Youth movement too, a proportion of bourgeois infiltration had very obviously taken place in idea and conduct if not class.

Since 1964 the debate on education in communes and factories, and reading and discussing the works of Mao Tse-tung increased the restiveness of the young. The complaint that the system of examination favoured "book learning", and promoted "the return of mandarins" was made time and again.[1]

In 1958 the problem was discussed extensively in connexion with the policy of labour for all intellectuals. Mao Tse-tung called for "opening wider the door of higher education to sons of workers and peasants". The economic, demographic and ideological aspects of the problem all required solution. The half-work half-study system of education was first started in that year, as an experiment; in 1966 it is certain that all education in China will, in the future, be part-work part-study; and that "book learning" will count for little; practical aptitudes and inventiveness will count a great deal.

The 1958 experiments in part-work, part-study education were started in Tientsin and Shanghai, in the factories where the workers organized their own schools. This scheme was also launched in the countryside, notably in Kiangsi province, where the leadership has had a continued record of excellence. According to Wang Ping (Minister in charge of Lower Education) inexperience in dealing with such schools led to a stoppage between 1960 and 1962, *except* in Kiangsi province.

[1] For some years a great debate on education was carried on in the Chinese Press.

In 1964 once again the scheme was promoted with greater vigour, especially in the wake of the socialist education movement in the communes.

In 1965 education was divided into higher and lower, with two ministries. The idea was possibly to cream off and to maintain, under the best conditions available, the high-grade scientific personnel required for sophisticated advance; but the situation was fraught with the danger that "higher education" might become the stronghold of the bourgeoisie, keeping down the vast upsurge from below, and not really taking in the talent that was available.

It was Marx who first wrote of half-work and half-study education and of the problem of social adaptation of the young, of vocational training, of family influence, an end to contempt for manual labour, the end of alienation and disorientation of the teenager. "Education and production must go hand in hand." This programme was put into effect in China and the system of part-work part-study designed to create a new type of proletarian intellectual. It was not spontaneously welcomed by the intellectuals; recruitment for these schools was difficult, although some were successful others could not find teachers easily. In 1966, after seven years of cogitation on the problem, the reform of education was introduced in a dramatic way during the Cultural Revolution; all examinations were abolished, and all universities and cultural institutions were closed for a year, while a thorough "sifting" of the teachers and teaching material is in progress. The new programmes for education will abolish the examination system totally. What will replace it is now being worked out.

The creation of an educated mass base has already begun to do away with the need for and reliance on bourgeois scholars and intellectuals that was evident in the first decade after liberation. No longer ignorant, but scientifically minded and aware of political and social issues, the masses now must be trusted, in other words they must have *democracy*, the *widest democracy possible*, and they must find their own creative answers to the problem of education. This alone shows the extent and totality of mass participation in this massive debate which is part of the Cultural Revolution.

From now on, it appears, senior middle school students may first be required to spend a year or two among the workers, peasants and soldiers, in the communes, factories or army; there to temper themselves in the "three revolutionary movements", the class struggle, the struggle for production and scientific experiment. These three "revolutionary movements" are the criteria by which revolutionary correctness can be gauged. Fitness for university entrance will be estimated by character and achievement, zeal and inventive spirit, and no longer by examinations "which only turns out bookworms". Selected for enrolment will be those who have shown a "firm proletarian stand". Leadership material will be chosen thus from among the Red Guards, from those who have used *reason*, not *violence* in their actions; who have shown qualities of organization, initiative, originality, daring, but also *ability to unite with the people*.

On 13th June, 1966, the State Council and the central committee of the Chinese Communist Party issued a statement that the old system of entrance examination and enrolment of students in higher educational institutions would be completely changed. Thus the examination system inaugurated in the Tang Dynasty was terminated, as a "feudal" process of discrimination, in 1966.

"The method of examination and enrolment for the higher educational institutions has failed to free itself from the set pattern of the bourgeois system of examination . . . harmful to the implementation of the guiding policy on education, and harmful to absorption into the higher educational institutions of a still greater number of revolutionary young people from among the workers, peasants and soldiers."

This radical departure from all the old concepts of scholarly "authority", both Eastern and Western, will be interesting to watch in the next decade. In the past a premium was placed on conformism, docility, the ability to memorize from books; in the future, an emphasis on spontaneity, innovation, daring and refusal to obey tradition can only be welcomed as another sign of China's entry into the Space Age.

According to the National Science Foundation there will be by 1967 a million and a half qualified specialists of all sorts in China. The next twenty years may see this number increase to ten million. A question which comes to mind is whether, in this reform of education, the future training of scientists will suffer. Evidence points to the contrary; a change of motivation can increase scientific ability. Creativeness, after all, is not stimulated by the profit motive.

In the role of intelligent discrimination between bourgeois theories and Marxist science, it is the enlightened, practical and intelligent Marshal Chen Yi who has done much to restrain those inclined to subject scientists to all kinds of idiotic pressures. Only someone who has gone through these sessions of criticism or who has watched the cadres in such a movement, knows how intellectuals can become paralysed, unable to sleep or to eat, during such a time of moral soul-searching; and too much of this sort of petty persecution is certainly not good for research. On the other hand, it is also clearly impossible to allow, under the name of academic freedom, the deliberate creation of centres of counter-revolutionary influence in educational circles, in the arts and among scientific personnel. The various movements as well as the present Cultural Revolution have sought to make ever more clear and just the distinction between outright action to sabotage the socialist programme, and "contradictions among the people"; between genuine academic differences, and politically motivated arguments. A sixteen-point memorandum laid down as guide to the present Revolution, emphasized the debating and reasoning techniques to be used at all times. In spite of exaggerated reports to the contrary, and though there have admittedly been some cases in which violence was used, yet the aim, which is a revolution by reason alone, is the dominant feature. Since the target of criticism is "those who have infiltrated the Party hierarchy and obtained positions of influence with the deliberate aim of altering the superstructure", debate, and criticism, and the castigation of acts of violence remain the dominant feature.[1]

Mao Tse-tung's ever-present concern with the practical application of democracy, in its Leninist sense, dates back to 1927 and the first Red base at Chingkangshan.

Under the motto: trust the masses, rely on the masses, functions which would devolve to security agencies, supervisory bodies, etc., inherently *not* subject to control by the population, are to be assumed by the people. The methods are outlined, "the handling of cases by the procuratorate in reliance upon the masses. The prevention of crime by the masses exercising their own surveillance and restraint."

The mass democratization process, through the opinion posters (which are such a feature of the Cultural Revolution), revolutionary committees, and other mass organizations, will further develop in the years to come.

[1] Decision of the Central Committee of the CCP concerning the Great Proletarian Cultural Revolution (adopted 8th August, 1966).

Despite an immense amount of tendentious reportage in the Western Press, the emphasis on non-violent means, and the punishment of those who "beat, or loot", is a constant feature of Chinese statements. The Red Guards are unarmed, and continue to be unarmed.

This participation by the people in the judicial and security work of the régime has worked well in the swift arrest of sabotage teams sent into the mainland by the Kuomintang. The mass-line technique, used in public health, has been successful in the eradication of venereal disease, the prevention of prostitution, the registration of births, food-rationing during the difficult years, but it is chiefly in its "education through the practice of democracy" that its development will be interesting to follow.

The Red Guards as the inheritors and successors to the Revolution must be actively apprenticed in this process, for they are tomorrow's leaders and masters, and have to "learn to swim by swimming", learn to make revolution by making it; learn democracy by applying democratic methods of reason and debate, for "coercion and force can touch skin and flesh, but not the soul". What is sought is not the physical punishment of evil-doers, but awareness, rallying and unity. This theme is the Maoist stamp on the whole of the Chinese Revolution. The very selection of leadership material among Red Guards is made conditional to their ability to "unite and rally". In recalling that "criticism should be fully reasoned, analytical and convincing", a special clause emphasizes that *the minority should not be forced to change its opinions*, "*for the minority is sometimes right*", but that "*even if wrong, it should be allowed to reserve its opinion*".[1]

This experiment bears watching; there is as yet no equivalent in the history of China for this attempt, for the long-term planning and preparation to educate a future generation for its tasks as successors, nor for educating a whole people in the exercise of democracy. The theme of revolt has opened the door wide to criticism of communist members

---

[1] But "minority" does *not* mean a pro-capitalist, counter-revolutionary minority who wants a return to the past; but only those who disagree with the methods, not the aims, of achieving socialism.

of the Party who err—a great blow to the bureaucrat. There will have to be, for each generation to come, other "revolts", "leaps in cognition", accompanied by "clean-ups" of the Party itself, until communist society is achieved—*and that may take one thousand years*. Will Mao's successors be as wise or far-sighted as he? Will they allow dissent against their own ever-recurring small foci of corruption, resurgent from the past millennia of exploitation? The answer may well be in the twenty-first century.

In his book *The State and Revolution*, Lenin describes some steps leading to the communist society as: "abolition of the standing army; all officials to be elected and subject to recall; the great majority of the functions of State powers performed by every literate person for ordinary workers' wages; all functions stripped of every shadow of privilege; no special military or bureaucratic apparatus; no special apparatus of suppression, this to be done by the armed people (the masses themselves . . .)".[1]

Already the abolition of all rank in the PLA has taken place; the peasant-worker-soldier interchangeability is happening (referred to several times in August–September 1966). The possibility of all officials being elected and subject to recall is being actively discussed;[2] the example of the Paris Commune is quoted; the functions of the State are being taken over by the masses. Education itself may be based on the election system; the wages of high officials have already been lowered (they were never very high anyway). Is China really approaching communist society swiftly? Only the outcome of the Cultural Revolution of today can provide us with a definite answer.

In terms of practical economics the Cultural Revolution

---

[1] LENIN, *The State and Revolution*.

[2] In December 1966 it began to be applied to "organs connected with the Cultural Revolution" that is propaganda and cultural sectors.

produces and provides the revolutionary impetus necessary
for the accomplishment of the economic breakthrough during
the period of the Third Five-year Plan (1966–70).[1] It means a
shake-up in all departments, factories, plants, industrial
concerns as well as communes; an upsurge in production has
been reported in the first months of its inception. This
second leap envisages the consolidation of all the gains
acquired during the last seventeen years plus another speeding
up of development, to promote an even greater economic
growth rate and this is, of course, linked to the ideological
remoulding of motivations now taking place.

The Cultural Revolution will probably continue for another decade, with periods of upsurge and subsidence, with
gradual sifting and refining of concepts, with the development
of young leadership and replacement of old cadres by enthusiastic young ones. The teaching of mass democracy
goes hand in hand with dictatorship of the proletariat. While,
on the one hand, there is a call for more active unification
under "the banner of the thought of Mao Tse-tung"; on the
other, there are also, but *within the framework of the guiding
principles embodied in Mao Tse-tung's thought*, appeals for wide
and all-embracing critical outspokenness from the masses.

"China is a great socialist State of the dictatorship of the
proletariat and has a population of 700 million. It needs
unified thinking, revolutionary thinking, correct thinking.
That is Mao Tse-tung's thinking. With it, and in no other
way, we can maintain vigorous revolutionary enthusiasm
and a firm and correct political orientation."[2]

The theme of "unified thinking" is the one most repugnant to the West, and is pointed at as "military dictatorship".
On the other hand, we have the statement in the authori-

[1] Speech of Chou En-lai, 15th September, 1966.
[2] *On Living Study and Application of Chairman Mao's Works*, LIN PIAO,
reprinted by Hsinhua 26th September, 1966.

tative *Red Flag* magazine, voice of the Central Committee of the Communist Party:[1]

"The masses have the right to criticize and raise suggestions on Party and State policies and links in the State apparatus. The masses have the right to criticize leading cadres at all levels no matter how meritorious their service, how high their position or how senior their qualifications. It is necessary to institute a system of general elections, like that of the Paris Commune, for all organs of power leading the cultural revolution without exceptions. The masses have the power to replace through election or recall any elected member at any time. Extensive democracy should also be carried out among the masses themselves and between mass organizations in order, by arguing things out, big-character posters[2] and great debates, to unify understanding and thinking, to heighten political consciousness, and to master Marxism-Leninism, Mao Tse-tung's thought. Such extensive democracy is the best method for the masses to educate themselves."

"Without such extensive democracy, without hundreds of millions of people's attention to State affairs, supervising the organs of the party and the State, and supervising leading cadres at all levels, it is impossible to prevent the usurpation of leadership of the Party and the State by counter-revolutionary revisionists, and impossible to prevent the changing of the dictatorship of the proletariat into the dictatorship of the bourgeoisie."

The situation at the close of 1966 during the full blossoming

[1] As in *Hsinhua News Agency Bulletin*, 13th–14th December, 1966.

[2] Big-character posters are those large handwritten posters put up by any individual in any street or on any wall in cities, factories, schools, or elsewhere in China, giving his individual opinion on any aspect of the government, and any minister, or high personality. It is these posters which have given rise to so much astonishment in the West, yet they are merely the free expression of public opinion, and as such the most obvious feature of the practice of democracy being taught today.

of the great Proletarian Cultural Revolution was described as follows: "A vigorous and lively political situation initiated by comrade Mao Tse-tung is taking shape throughout our country, in which there are both centralism and democracy, both discipline and freedom, both unity of will and *personal ease of mind.*"

However bewildering this may appear, all one can say about this unprecedented and massive experiment is that it is China's way of preparing herself for the future, both in war and in peace. If war should come, China's peoples will be prepared to fight a people's war; and if there is peace, to go on building, as fast as possible, a socialist system which will provide both material security for the millions, and a freedom of spirit which also has never existed in the past millennia.

Although it is quite true that errors and extremes have been noted during the course of this upheaval, a more objective view will probably, in a few years' time, reassess the Cultural Revolution as a most significant step in the achievement of socialism in China, and indispensable in her Long March to the future. It will also recur, and may evolve a model of government organization and of Communist Party organization likely to affect all the revolutionary movements in the world.

The denunciation of "The Chinese Khruschev" in the person of Liu Shao-chi and his followers, the clique representing the return to bourgeois capitalism, marks the end of the first phase of the Cultural Revolution. However, recurrences of the struggle throughout the whole period of the transition to communism are expected; but the awakening of 700 million people to an acute political consciousness is the best guarantee and the main bulwark for advance, both in socialist construction at the base, and in the superstructure, till the desired end is reached.

VIII

WAR AND PEACE—WORLD RELATIONS
AND THE BALANCE OF TERROR

We are advocates of the abolition of war, we do not want war, but war can only be abolished through war, and in order to get rid of the gun it is necessary to take up the gun.

MAO TSE-TUNG, 6th November, 1938
(in the midst of the Sino-Japanese War)

IF one must quote from Mao Tse-tung, it is because Chinese policies have been formed and guided by his viewpoint (or world-outlook) to an extent in which we can identify, almost, the main lines of China's development and policies with the ideas of Mao Tse-tung and his own development. Almost, but not always, as the previous chapters illustrate. At every moment of crisis, Mao Tse-tung has formulated the precise choice and wrenched a result out of the jaws of controversy, carrying the Chinese people towards the envisaged goal. But after seventeen years, and with the evidence of the upheaval going on in China today, it is clear that the preconceived notions that a dictatorial Mao Tse-tung has had it all his own way all the time is in-correct. Duality rather than single-mindedness attended many issues, and even officials' pronouncements; this was the recurrent feature of the very life of the CCP since its beginning.[1]

No secret of this fact is made, indeed, the Grand Debate going on in China today is a continuation of the "two

[1] *Resolutions on Questions in Party History*, 20th April, 1945.

roads, two lines, two destinies for China". But today it has become a life-and-death struggle, for never was the choice so decisive, so acute, or of such immense scope. It is not only China's future, but the future of the whole world, which is at stake.

In discussion of foreign policies, therefore, it is just as imperative as in our previous discussion of internal policies not to lose sight of this dualism. Essential issues have been obscured rather than made clear by experts wont to study Chinese policies *in vacuo*, or as a monolithic structure, or—as in earlier years—a devilish scheme to conquer the world. The basic postulates of any sovereign State, the geographical location of the country, its size and potential strength and the behaviour and relations of other sovereign States towards it have been lost sight of in the process of condemnation rather than impartial observation. No study of Chinese policies which does not investigate the attitudes of other countries can be valid; in an able speech at the Toronto University Teach-in, John Gittings pointed out that certain policies had been imposed upon China rather than initiated by her.

We might for clarity's sake divide the subject of China's foreign policies into recognizable periods: the first from 1949 to the Geneva Conference of 1954; the second from 1954 to the autumn of 1959; the third from autumn 1959 until the end of October 1962; the fourth from 1962 till today.

In each period, we might determine which chief events or situations, not necessarily brought about by the actions of China, but by the actions of others as well, conditioned and determined Chinese attitudes and responses; for every foreign policy has both its active[1] and passive sides.

In the first period, 1949 to 1954, the Korean War remains

[1] The "passivity" of China's foreign policy was suggested by John Gittings, who opined (Toronto Teach-in 14th–16th October, 1966) that China did not have a definite foreign policy. I do not agree with this—Author.

the single factor which made it impossible for China to initiate any other foreign policy than the "lean to one side" policy proclaimed by Mao in 1949. This attitude was itself determined by the role played by USA in its determined aid to Chiang Kai-shek, against the communist Red Army, during the post-World War II Civil War 1946-9 in China, and was logical and obvious; for the United States had helped Chiang to the limit, everything short of becoming physically involved itself in an Americanization of the war in China. Soon after the Communists came to power, in 1949, the Korean War broke out in 1951. There had been no time for China to evolve a foreign policy other than lean to one side and hostility to USA in view of its continued support of Chiang.[1]

Had the Korean War not taken place, things might have gradually worked out differently; but in the next three years, China's policies were necessarily dictated by her primary needs, both for self-defence, and for the rebuilding of her devastated economy and the setting up of an industrial base. Moreover, a UN embargo had been placed upon her by the USA. She was, therefore, almost compelled to continue "leaning to one side", that is to Soviet Russia.

In his lucid and expert book *America's Failure in China*[2] Dr. Tang Tsou marshals some evidence for the hypothesis that had the Korean War not taken place, or rather, had the Chinese not been forced by MacArthur's avowed intentions towards the Chinese border, to enter Korea with volunteers (on the request and with the formal assent of a recognized sovereign socialist State, that is the North Korean government), then things might have been very different. But evidence to the contrary is possibly just as convincing, and though it is valuable to have a precise delineation of the ambivalence which reigned in Washington for a brief while,

[1] *See* the US White Paper on Foreign Policy; also Mao Tse-tung's *Works*, Statement on the US White Paper *et al.*   [2] *See* Bibliography.

over whether to "stick with Chiang" or recognize Peking, there is some doubt whether events would not, in any case, have brought us to the point reached today.

In June 1951, war broke out between North and South Korea. Who attacked whom? There are two theories: one that it was a deliberate incident instigated by Russia, in order to "test American firmness" (in her commitment to Syngman Rhee's American-backed South Korean government). The other is that the USA incited the South Korean troops to attack the North; this view was substantiated by Rhee's own warlike explosiveness, but the withdrawal of some USA troops from South Korea a few weeks before, together with a singularly conciliatory speech by Truman on 5th January, 1951, is always cited against this hypothesis.

Whatever the truth of the matter, the fact remains that *China had had nothing to do with the Korean* outbreak. In fact it took Peking Radio almost two days (recovering from surprise, and probably from some top level conferences) to come out with the North Korean version, which, as a "brother socialist State" is not surprising.

Hypothesis one has another fascinating by-product, developed to me by an eminent American expert,[1] that Stalin deliberately instigated the Korean incident in order to embroil China and USA in war with each other, for the last thing that Russia wanted was a potential *modus vivendi* between the two.

Whatever the cause China was dragged into a war in Korea. It was the last thing she wanted. But MacArthur's threatening gestures towards the Chinese border could not be ignored. The entry of Chinese volunteers marked a turn in the tide of war; the United Nations troops, consisting chiefly of Americans, were rolled back, and a stalemate ensued; China was branded as an "aggressor" by the UN in a

---

[1] Mr. Harrison Salisbury, Assistant Editor, the *New York Times*, at the Chicago University Conference on China, February 1966.

grotesque miscarriage of justice; the prodigious emotional resentment in the United States against China swept out all rationality on this topic for some years.

The event which, for the Chinese, confirmed their judgement that American ambitions in Asia were permanent, and not temporary, was that, the day after the Korean Civil War broke out, the decision was taken to dispatch the Seventh Fleet to "neutralize the Formosa Straits".[1] In a public statement on 27th June, 1951, President Truman declared that the fleet would "repel any attack" on Taiwan and though Chiang was kept "leashed", that is not allowed to attack China, this to the Chinese merely indicated that America was not yet prepared to fight a massive land war in China for him. At the same time Truman announced increased aid to the French in Indochina and strengthened American forces in the Philippines. It is possible that the State Department experts saw the whole picture as a massive combined Russian-Chinese assault upon American possessions (present and future) in Asia; but to link Taiwan, Vietnam and the Philippines with a civil war in Korea was either a hysterical reaction or an open statement of the extent of American ambitions in Asia. The dragging in of the issue of Formosa, Vietnam and the Philippines confirmed Mao's thesis that US imperialism had never changed its policy, which was to dominate the mainland of Asia; and that the disengagement from China was only temporary.[2] The patrolling of the Formosa

[1] TANG TSOU, *America's Failure in China*, p. 558.

[2] In January 1944, already, Roosevelt had explicitly stated in a memorandum to Cordell Hull that the US would administer the Indochina peninsula as a trust territory; this was made public by the State Department on 28th June, 1965, after the US issued on 8th June, 1965 an order to the American forces in South Vietnam to take part in the fighting, thus leading to the Americanization of the Vietnam War. *See also* Princeton University John Foster Dulles Oral History project, reported in *New York Times*, 26th March, 1967. The USA altogether contributed US $2 billion to aid the French to "restore stability" to Indochina.

straits by the Seventh Fleet was a flagrant and direct provocation to China, and the announced accelerated military assistance to Indochina, viewed in the light of China's own national interests and her geographical position, was also another beachhead for American war against China; for China's interests require that the marginal lands that surround her should not be used as bases by an enemy power, in order to launch or mount an attack upon her.

The American occupation of Taiwan, "which is part of China, affirmed by the Cairo declaration, the Potsdam declaration, and the existing conditions after Japan's surrender, constitute armed aggression against the territory of China and total violation of the UN Charter."[1]

The re-entry of America into military activity *directed against the mainland of Asia* negated, therefore, the hesitant period which had immediately preceded it; America had never given up her ambitions in China; only events in Europe, and especially lack of manpower, had forced a temporary withdrawal from the Chinese theatre of operations; now the USA was back, and moreover dragging the UN at her heels. This is how the Chinese saw it.

Chou En-lai charged that the Korean Civil War was a "pretext for the USA to invade Taiwan, Korea and Vietnam and the Philippines".

From that date America's preoccupations with the other side of the Pacific, her rebuilding of Japan (again in the traditional sense of utilizing her against China), her occupation of South Korea, Taiwan and now of Thailand, part of Laos and the South Zone of Vietnam, are hard to explain away, except as a confirmation of the Chinese statement.

At the winding up of the Korean War, and at the Geneva Conference of 1954, China for the first time was able to seize an initiative in policies and her performance there was both

[1] Chou En-lai statement.

impressive and moderate; in fact, of outstanding moderation. It was the beginning of China's role as a world power
in world politics, opening a period in which active initiatives
were taken, and yet this epoch of goodwill and moderation
has been one of the most distorted of present history, for at
no time between 1954 and 1965 were China's moderate
statements, or active peace initiatives, given any notice,
credence or publicity in the Western Press. At no time, as
John Gittings says, did America take advantage of this
"moderate phase", nor of China's many appeals for understanding and relief of tension. In those years, time and again,
at international conferences, in statements, in interviews, the
essentially realistic postulates upon which China wished to
construct her foreign relations with other countries were
repeated, only to fall on deaf ears. American opposition to
China's admission to the UN, and her support of Chiang were
not modified. Throughout that period, from the Geneva
agreement of 1954, right up to the Laos Conference in
1961–2, the Chinese did seek, by all possible means, an "un-
tying of knots" as Chen Yi put it,[1] or in other words, a *détente*
in the situation created by the Korean War. Bandung and
the Panchshila statement were part of the assertion of China's
independent line in foreign relations; it coincided with the
search for a Chinese model in industry and in the national
economy, the opening of China to visitors, the setting up of
the Canton trade fairs, the offer to give fifteen American
correspondents visas to visit China in 1956 (turned down by
the American State Department), and the obvious interest in
achieving State relations with as many countries as possible
on the basis of co-existence.

Ambassadorial talks between the USA and China at Warsaw
were started with the assent of Chou En-lai. We cannot

---

[1] Interview notes by the author who interviewed Marshal Chen Yi,
External Affairs Minister in 1961 at Geneva, and in Peking in 1962.

find, on the USA side, any similar moves or steps towards relief of tension. On the contrary in 1953 the "unleashing" of the Chiang régime by Eisenhower nullified the "neutralization" of Taiwan; in September 1954, as soon as the Geneva accords had been passed, the formation of SEATO, a joint defence system for South-East Asia against China, was initiated by the USA. In December 1954, the USA concluded a bilateral alliance with Chiang Kai-shek. The ANZUS pact, the establishment of an American strategy of "massive retaliation" all formed part of a policy of rearmament, which started to boom after 1958.[1] Sixty per cent of post-war gross investment in the USA became military spending; most of it in highly strategic economic sectors.

The Chinese initiatives for peace were interpreted as a "grand strategy" to win the world for communism. China was struggling to assert her independence from Russia, she was not interested in establishing communism in South-East Asia or in any other country. Not communism, but a genuine neutralism was what China sought, and that was made repeatedly clear, especially at the Laos Conference of 1961–2. When in 1962 the Brunei outbreak began the confrontation between Malaysia and Indonesia, Peking radio at first interpreted the Brunei rising as an American CIA plot! But a desire for an end to hostility, an acceptable *modus vivendi*, did not mean the relinquishment of basic principles of national sovereignty. Taiwan was an integral part of China. There could not be two Chinas but only one (and neither one China one Taiwan).

Several times, in these years, the Chinese were to call for

[1] Documentation on the increasing size and power of the military-industrial complex in the USA is available in the *Wall Street Journal, U.S. News and World Report*, and also in books such as FRED COOK, *The Warfare State* (London, Cape, 1963). PAUL SWEEZEY, ALVIN HAUSER, in *The Postwar American Economy*, assert that "the only new feature (in the American economy) is the increased arms budget. All other government spending is about the same percentage of GNP as in 1929."

pan-Pacific meetings or summit meetings of leaders from all States or States bordering the Pacific, for agreements not to use nuclear weapons in countries bordering the Pacific. The anxiety of the Chinese not to provoke any increase of tension, but to seek a loosening of it was evident.[1]

But the American build-up of Chiang Kai-shek continued, though Peking continued to try to engage Chiang in talks. Quemoy and Matsu which had been only lightly garrisoned in 1955 were strengthened substantially from then onwards with troops and military supplies concentrated on Quemoy, and American military advisers were stationed there in 1958 where none had been present in 1957.

The island was now openly declared to have become "a stepping stone to the mainland" for the Chiang forces. Commando attacks against China, and the landing of subversive agents, were intensified.

"At that time (1958), the governing American desideratum was the restoration of Chiang Kai-shek's control of the mainland; at minimum, the containment of communist China, and the retention of Formosa as base."[2]

In August 1958, the offensive preparations on Quemoy were counteracted by the communist shelling of Quemoy island and this brought on American intervention; by planes, ships, and US marines. Chiang Kai-shek was happy at the prospect that American military forces would at last come to grips with the Communists; for only in such an American war on China would a return be possible for him ... but the moment passed. Another gesture of conciliation was made in September 1958; Premier Chou En-lai broadcast a statement charging the Chiang régime with use of the

---

[1] 28th February and 18th April, 1959; 10th April, 25th July and 1st August, 1960; 2nd September, 1961; 31st July, 1963; 16th October and 17th October, 1964. *See Jen Min Jih Pao* and Hsinhua News Release of dates as above.

[2] *Twentieth Century China*, CLUBB, p. 369 *et seq.*

offshore islands to harass China but proposing at the same time resumption of talks "for the defence of peace".

In the years from 1958 onwards, the power situation becomes a triangle: China–USA–USSR. A very rapid shift in the USSR policies towards the USA and China became evident. Kennedy's New Frontiers speech was the first harbinger of this triangular power play.

Barraclough and Walter Lippmann[1] both point out that the "new frontiers" policies enunciated were not new; that the myth of American isolationism and the Monroe doctrine in the nineteenth and early twentieth centuries served to build an image of disinterested benefaction abroad and preoccupation chiefly with internal affairs but that the reality was different. From the foundation of the United States (says Lippmann), US foreign policy has been isolationist (non-interventionist) *only as regards Europe*; but America has always been moving westward, expanding and intervening across the continent of America, on to Alaska, Hawaii and the Philippines[1] (and he might have added: Taiwan–Japan–Indochina–China). It was only on Europe that she turned her back. Her influence in the Commonwealth (Australia, New Zealand, Canada) has increased, to be followed in time by greater influence in erstwhile colonial possessions in Asia—Vietnam, Malaysia, Indonesia.

This preoccupation with extending the westward-ho frontier across to Asia has gripped American policy makers ever since the 1850s.[2]

The first treaty between Great Britain and China, the treaty of Nanking (1843), was followed by the Wanghsia

[1] *See* WALTER LIPPMANN, "Today and Tomorrow", *Hong Kong Standard*, 16th November, 1966, *also* G. BARRACLOUGH, *An Introduction to Contemporary History*, p. 96 *et seq.*

[2] "Imperialist traditions and coupled with them a determination to play an active part in international politics reach back to the beginning of history of United States", writes BARRACLOUGH, *see* Bibliography.

treaty of 1844 between China and the USA in which extra-
territorial privileges more extensive and precise than the
British had fought for were obtained by threat alone. "The
British do the fighting, we cash in" exulted Caleb Cushing.[1]

US diplomats put these extraterritorial and other privileges
into practice, and maintained them for a solid century.[2]

American history has represented the "open-door policy"
as a manifestation of unselfishness and humanitarian concern
for the Chinese people. It is upon this interpretation, as well
as "missionarism", that the myth of benefaction in China,
leading to the post 1949 traumas is rooted. A China parti-
tioned between the then powerful European nations would
have denied markets to the USA, unless an open-door policy
of equal opportunities within a nominally independent China
was achieved. The "open-door policy" again was referred
to by the USA when Japan occupied Manchuria in 1931–2;
her chief concern then was that her markets would
not be disturbed. Japan's reassurances on this subject led to
the stance of neutrality towards Japanese aggression, and
active supply of seventy per cent of Japanese iron requirements
for the war on China, until Pearl Harbor in 1941.

After the Second World War, the weakness of European
powers became manifest; the rise of Asian nationalism could
not be ignored; political independence was achieved by many
ex-colonial territories. America was involved in the Civil
War in China, and when all-out aid for Chiang failed, her
preoccupation became to disengage, for her scattered forces
and resources did not allow her to pursue a land war in Asia.[3]
Her greater commitment to European capitalism whose
arsenal, reserve, and treasury she had become and the Marshall

[1] C. Cushing's report to Department of State, 4th May, 1848, No. 596.
[2] DR. TONG TE-KONG, *U.S. Diplomacy in China 1844–1860*.
[3] The US White Paper, also TANG TSOU, *America's Failure in China: Disengagement*.

Plan in Europe kept America busy there for almost a decade, but already by 1954, the signs of an "imperialist return" to South-East Asia were evident.

Today's policy of "containment" of China is a continuation, with more formidable military means, of the policy which was not abandoned after 1949 but only temporarily stalled. Not content with an island periphery, America is advancing to enclaves upon the mainland, from which to keep China in subjection. This means in Pentagon terms bases for the bombing of China's industries, for the destruction, with chemical and bacteriological warfare of her population, sabotage and subversion, the "killing" of the revolution in China, the replacement of today's strong, independent communist government by one soft, corrupt, and willing to sell national interests. The tacit acquiescence of Russia after 1959, the knowledge that she would abandon China, encouraged American militarism to consider it had "a free hand" in Asia.

America reinforced the building up of Okinawa and bases in Japan and Taiwan. Her activities increased in Indonesia, in the Indian Ocean, and the infiltration in Laos, Thailand and Vietnam also multiplied. Thus began the 1960s in which Russian behaviour, abandonment of socialist solidarity and the interests of the countries of the Third World in favour of alliance with America, plays a decisive role.

The story of Russia's relations with China from the 1850s to 1917, the Russian Revolution, is that of any other European colonial power. The occupation of the Amur region of China and participation in all privileges of other powers in subsequent decades only stopped when the 1917 Revolution occurred, with the abrogation of all unequal treaties. The year 1919 marked the beginning of China's turning left, confirmed in 1921 by the foundation of the Communist Party of China. The failure of the Peasant Revolution in 1927, and

Chiang's massacres, marked a rupture of relations till 1934, not only with the official government, but also the decline of Comintern influence over the policies of the Chinese Communist Party; there were, however, sporadic returns of such influence through the years until 1944. Russia retained the territories of the Amur basin and also the railways in Manchuria which she later sold to Japan.

Whatever Stalin's merits as a builder of Russia, it is certain that in foreign policy matters, he always underestimated Mao Tse-tung and the CCP; his "partiality" to Chiang Kai-shek has been erected into hostility to Mao. Actually it was not so. It is known that, in 1948, he suggested to Mao Tse-tung that the Red Armies should stop at the Yangtze river, Mao was to keep North China, and leave South China to Chiang Kai-shek, "otherwise the USA would go into all-out war to save Chiang". Mao did not agree; he asserted that America would not fight then, and gave the order to cross. Mao was right.

Relations between the USA and Russia from 1917 to 1943 were ambivalent. Although frightened of Bolshevism, and actively encouraging attacks upon Russia, it was yet physically impossible for the USA to wage war upon the Soviet Union. By 1940 the Russian metallurgical industry was second in the world, and so were her oil and coal industries. For a short period from 1945 to 1949, the USA had a supremacy of power in the atom bomb; uprisings, some say Russian-fostered, then occurred in many areas of South-East Asia, Brunei, Malaya, the Philippines—by 1949 the USSR too had the bomb. By 1957 the Sputnik into space asserted Russian primacy in space research. After 1958, the open acceptance of a two-power control of the world was explicit.

But the implicit acceptance of a two-power hegemony began at Yalta in February 1945. The main effects of the

Yalta agreement were to the disadvantage of China, who was treated in the Yalta agreement as "object to be disposed of"; no representative of China's Red Armies attended, nor was Chiang consulted or invited, and yet it was the fate of the Far East and China which was being decided.

On the American side, the Yalta agreement was based on the belief that to shorten what Roosevelt envisaged as a long land war in Asia, for which America did not have the manpower, it was necessary to bring the Russians into direct conflict with Japan.

Patrick Hurley, US Ambassador to China, had told Roosevelt that the Red Armies of Mao relied on Soviet support (which was incorrect). If Stalin could be manoeuvred into "openly supporting Chiang Kai-shek", the Chinese Communists would be forced to agree to a "coalition" government with Chiang. Such a coalition government, in America's view, would produce a stable "reformist" régime in China. Chiang Kai-shek would remain in power, the Communists would be suitably diluted, but their programme and popular support could be utilized to rally support to Chiang. Thus China would remain within the expanding American orbit in Asia and later, another massacre could get rid of the Reds when Chiang was suitably strengthened.

The Yalta agreement was in itself evidence to Mao Tse-tung that the US government's aim, through "coalition government" was the consolidation of its hold on China.[1] On 24th April, 1945, Mao made a political report, setting forth the guide lines and conditions upon which coalition government could be instituted; and even gave a favourable view of Roosevelt's "refraining from adopting a policy of helping the KMT to undertake armed attacks on the CCP". But Roosevelt died,

[1] MAO TSE-TUNG, On Coalition Government, 24th April, 1945; On the danger of the Hurley Policy—12th July, 1945.

Chiang was rearmed,[1] he was helped to undertake armed attacks on the CCP and Mao did the obvious: he denounced American help to the Kuomintang.

Yalta confirmed Outer Mongolia as "independent", a satellite State under Russian domination. It admitted Russian entry into Manchuria and occupation of Port Arthur, which the Russians left six years after the CCP came to power, entry into Sinkiang province, and a free hand there to detach it from China. The Russians left Sinkiang in 1955, but border trouble is now active there and in Manchuria since 1962.

Stalin wanted to prevent the entry of US troops into these sensitive areas bordering Russia's own territory. While giving ostensible support to Chiang, he was making sure that the disarming of Japanese troops in Manchuria would be left to the Russian Red Army and not to the US or Kuomintang troops. Whether through Great Power chauvinism, Stalin was returning to a Czarist foreign policy, an account of the 1950 meeting between Stalin and Mao alone can tell us.

The advent of "Khruschevism" was the continuation of a withering away of socialist principles in the Russian socialist State, already started with the development of a technocratic managerial class, under Stalin.

The foreign policy of the Russian State, to preserve the interests of the new class would be a big-power, self-centred, one. It did not intend to imperil itself in the defence of any other socialist country; it would on the contrary, utilize the others in a deal with the United States.

By 1956–7 China's emergence as a potential power, her independence of mind, were considered not only a threat to American imperialism in Asia, but also to the USSR leadership.

Since then the USSR has abandoned the revolutionary cause

[1] Hurley Report to State Department, 2nd April, 1945.

of the militant two-thirds of humanity to ally herself with the USA in a division of the earth, and of space.

In 1954 the USA did enter Indochina. The Ngo Dinh Diem régime was set up by the United States *fifteen days before* the signing of the Geneva accords, which demarcated Vietnam temporarily into two zones, North and South, and ended French colonial domination.[1]

The SEATO organization, a military alliance to "contain" China, was set up in 1954.

The nation-wide elections in the southern and northern zones of Vietnam (as laid down in the Geneva agreements) to take place two years after the cessation of hostilities were sabotaged by the USA in 1956, with President Eisenhower frankly stating that "had elections been held . . . possibly eighty per cent of the population [in South Vietnam and North Vietnam] would have voted for Ho Chih Minh".

In 1956 Khruschev's anti-Stalin speech at the Twentieth Congress of the USSR Communist Party led Dulles to assert that considerable liberal forces existed within the Soviet government; should the Soviet Union be interested *in giving up world revolution*, and taking *united action, through the UN*, then "co-operation with Russia" was possible.

In March 1958, Khruschev showed that he was anxious for co-operation by agreeing with the Western proposal for dealing with a *coup* in Iraq within the confines of the UN and sabotaging the Communist Party there (later many militant communists were to be turned over to the CIA[2] by Russian communists in Latin America, Africa and the Middle East).

The polemical and theoretical arguments between China and Russia have overshadowed these understated step-by-

---

[1] BERNARD FALL, *The Two Vietnams.*

[2] Central Intelligence Agency. *See Ramparts Magazine,* February 1967; also March and April 1967.

step approaches to collusion with the USA which the Russian leadership under Khruschev has performed. The long silence kept by the Chinese on these matters also tended to leave propaganda adverse to them a clear field. The notion that "China wants war, Russia wants peace" became a firmly implanted emotional rather than an intellectually rational assessment. And emotional attitudes are almost impervious to reason.

In autumn 1957, during Mao's second visit to Moscow, an apparent agreement occurred, ratified by an accord in which the USSR leadership undertook to help the Chinese with nuclear weapons and to continue helping with the industrialization process. (It was probably on the strength of this accord that the First Leap Forward was planned.)

In 1958, in an interview between Mao and Khruschev the latter made demands which were tantamount to China's becoming a Russian colony: garrisoning Russian troops in strategic regions of China and handing over the army, navy, and air force to Russian command, as the "price" for nuclear know-how.[1] This was rejected by the Chinese. Khruschev then objected to the Chinese counter-offensive against the Quemoy military build-up. It is possible that this build-up, the unleashing of Chiang Kai-shek by the USA was a feint to put pressure upon the Chinese while Khruschev tried to get from them a satellite compliance; for if the Russians objected to the Chinese riposte, it meant that Russia was not ready to back China in what she considered her vital national interest, the eventual recovery of Taiwan, her national territory. It would also lead the USA to assume Khruschev's eagerness to maintain a climate of immobility in which Russia and the United States could proceed with a closer *entente*.

In January 1959, the communes, the general line, and the First Leap Forward were denounced by Khruschev at the

[1] *See* JEAN BABY, *La Grande Controverse Sino-soviétique*, Paris, Grasset, 1966; also THEJA GUNAWARDHANA, *Kruschevism*, private printing, Colombo, 1962.

Twenty-first Congress; on 20th June, 1959, the agreement on nuclear know-how signed in autumn 1957 was unilaterally abrogated by Khruschev; this was followed by his visit to the USA, and the "camp David spirit"; in October 1959, Khruschev arrived in Peking to try to convince the Chinese of the "threat to world peace" unless China gave in on the subject of Taiwan, agreed to the formula of "peaceful evolution" and "listened to Big Brother".[1] It is said that Mao pointed then to the enormous increase, in 1958 and 1959, in the militarization of the United States; 1959 was an absolute boom year for military expenditure, with billions of dollars being poured into obtaining a lead for strategic weapons. If this was peaceful intent why was all this money being poured into nuclear stockpiling? To what purpose?

In July 1960, 1,390 Soviet experts were withdrawn from China, and 343 contracts and supplementary agreements as well as 257 technical contracts were unilaterally cancelled.

In December 1960, a meeting in Moscow of eighty-one parties occurred, and a declaration was drawn up, which tried to paper over the deep, still apparently only ideological split between Russia and China. But the concrete issues at stake were the totality of Russia's foreign policy, anxious for accommodation with the USA in a two-super-power hegemony over the world, a reflection of the abandonment of all socialist ideology, a return to the real-politik of an acquisitive State.

In 1960–1 the Laos conference took place in Geneva; the Laotian forces were backed by Soviet equipment and arms, Khruschev consented to a "neutralizing action", in return for *détente* in Europe, thus clearly indicating to Kennedy that a "free hand" in return for *détente* on the European front would be acceptable to him.

The Staley-Taylor plan was then drawn up by the USA to pacify South Vietnam within eighteen months.

[1] The author was in Peking in October–November 1959.

On 12th November, 1961, the first batch of US troops, four hundred of them, landed in South Vietnam.

On 9th February, 1962, a US military command, South Vietnam, under General Harkins, was set up with a military strength of 12,000 men.

In an article in *Eastern World*, London, July 1963, Kennedy's policy towards China is analysed by F. Joss. "Just as Roosevelt, resolved to lead his nation to maximum commitment, had to follow a tortuous and often misleading path . . . so Kennedy prepares for the day when he can and must openly unroll his strategic map with a momentous New Frontier in China."

The New Frontier means the application of the Monroe doctrine to South-East Asia; that is the non-intervention of *other* powers save American power, in that area. US influence over Australia and New Zealand is already considerable. The participation of their troops in the Vietnam aggression marks their role as the new bases of imperialism in Asia.

The policies devised by Kennedy after 1960 were based on the assumption that the ideological differences between Peking and Moscow were now beyond questions of revolutionary tactics and ideology and even the rectification of frontiers. The basic attitudes of the two great communist powers were irreconcilable.

A policy of further probing of intent by a cautious series of military advances in proxy regions, each designed to enlarge the conflict between Moscow and Peking, but at the same time aimed at preventing the definite victory of one or the other, now governed State Department policy. It initiated conciliation and *rapprochement* towards *both* but without really giving in on concrete points. In 1963 a "hot line" was instituted between Moscow and Washington. The rumour that Kennedy was a "liberal president" and might even recognize China was current.

If what appeared to be conciliatory measures were extended towards China the onus of refusal would be China's.

Nowhere was there an indication that the Taiwan question would be settled, nor that the USA would stop supporting Chiang Kai-shek's régime or a two-China policy, or a one-China-one-Taiwan policy. Meanwhile military strategies of "special warfare," counter-guerrilla warfare together with research in chemical gases, defoliants, death rays, bacteriological warfare and other forms of genocide were openly discussed.[1]

On 25th November, 1961, collusion between Russia and USA came the nearer with the visit of Adzhubei, Khruschev's son-in-law, to President Kennedy; the visit was to offer the USA a divide-the-world set-up on a twenty-year-peace basis. Kennedy put forward his demands: the unification of Germany on his own terms; the Western powers to occupy Berlin, opposition to Cuba; Laos to become a US protectorate (the Laos conference was then going on). Peace for twenty years in Asia, Africa and Latin America, meant cessation of help to militant national liberation movements. Khruschev was anxious to confirm this pact except for Cuba where he could not give in without losing face, and German reunification.

The installation of Russian missiles in Cuba was known to American intelligence; it was either an act of rash folly, indicating that Russia was ready to use Cuba for an attack on the USA, or else a direct provocation to the USA to invade Cuba.

The withdrawal of the missiles *in return for a guarantee that Cuba would not be attacked by the USA* has since then been much played up as an example of Soviet Russia's amazing success in maintaining peace and arresting the US invasion of Cuba.

The "dramatic confrontation" was to convince the

---

[1] *Wall Street Journal*, 27th February, 1967: "Shape of the Future: US Builds Capability for both Nuclear War, Vietnam-size Conflicts"; also report by California Technological Institute biologist, J. BONNER, 8th March, 1967, Industrial Associates Conference.

peoples of the world that the slightest "wrong move", that is any revolt anywhere, would face humanity with a crisis (like the Cuban crisis) in which "humanity would be destroyed".

Further to impress the world that it must keep quiet, and submit to the two Big Ones, "who need only wag a little finger" to keep "all troublemakers quiet" (Khruschev's words), came the theory of escalation of Herman Kahn,[1] in which the precise play on the ladder of nuclear/non-nuclear blackmail was set out, together with its psycho-propaganda accompaniment.

Then came the test ban in 1963. The real aim of the test ban, as set forth by Stewart Alsop on 28th September, 1965, was to stop China from becoming a nuclear power by whatever possible means. "The test ban is the *first* essential step— but only the first . . . to that end." But *total nuclear disarmament* which China advocated was never mentioned in the test ban; and Chou En-lai's letter of 2nd August, 1963, to all Government Heads, proposing a conference to discuss the complete, thorough, total and resolute prohibition and destruction of all nuclear weapons was not circulated in the more important newspapers of the Western Press.

It was the fallout, not the *use* of nuclear weapons, which the test ban condemned. The US and USSR now proceeded to underground testing. The next step in the collusion of the two "super states" would be a recrudescence of the blackmail of terror, and active moves for stopping "nuclear proliferation". But nothing was done about nuclear disarmament or the disposal of the huge nuclear stockpiles in both countries.

In 1963 (ending in 1964) China began the publication of her polemics with the USSR giving her side of the argument.[2]

---

[1] See HERMAN KAHN, *De l'Escalade.*

[2] JEAN BABY, *La Grande Controverse Sino-soviétique.* Also *see* Foreign Language Press publications. Khruschev first denounced Albania in 1961; China was then denounced in 1962 both by Khruschev and other European communist parties at Congress Sessions.

These articles were ignored even by many communists. Could it be that the *Chinese* now dared to become theoretical Marxist-Leninists, to develop their own contribution to the scientific principles of communism? For a long time the assumption that Soviet Russia was the fountain head of all wisdom and all knowledge would continue to stop many communists from even taking the trouble to read the Chinese arguments.

In the years 1963 and 1964 the engagement of the United States in Vietnam became complete; the determination to set up the southern zone of Vietnam as an American base, and also bases in Thailand, and eventually to dominate Singapore (the best and largest port in Asia for both the Seventh and the Indian Ocean fleets) was then made. Great Britain in great financial difficulties would not be able to resist pressures; her "policies" in South-East Asia would be as a satellite and help to America; the ANZUS pact had already transferred the New Zealand and Australian power complex to a more direct linkage with the US than with the "mother country". It was in those years that US determination to finish off China one way or another was taken and this became more evident as the Cultural Revolution did not bring about a "collapse" of China.[1] The idea still nurtured abroad that Kennedy was moving "towards recognition of China", was a "man of peace", and that Johnson is "warlike", is incorrect. Johnson's policies are a more brutal, overt continuation of the policies initiated by Kennedy; just as today's Russian leadership continues Khruschev's line.

In November 1963 Ngo Dinh Diem, who suspected that America wanted South Vietnam as a permanent base for itself, and had begun to make approaches to North Vietnam,

---

[1] A collapse or fragmentation of China, civil war and return to warlordism were predictions made by many "China experts" in the months of October 1966 to April 1967.

was liquidated, if not at American instigation, at least without any regret on their part.

This was followed, nineteen days later, by the assassination of Kennedy. Elected on a peace-in-Vietnam ticket, Johnson was to carry out Pentagon shaped, warlike policies in another escalation of military domination in South-East Asia.

In January 1964 long-range naval exercises were held between Hawaii and Okinawa; in June 1964 the Honolulu conference decided on escalation in Vietnam and a pretext was found in the "Tonkin gulf" incident. In October, 1964, Khruschev was displaced by a palace *coup* but the policies did not change since they represented the policies of the ruling group in Russia. The day after Khruschev's fall, China became a nuclear power by exploding her first nuclear device.

The day she detonated her first atomic device, China called again for the total destruction of atomic weapons, including her own.

Early in 1965 Kosygin went to Vietnam; the day after his arrival the South Vietnam National Liberation Forces made an attack on the Pleiku military base. The US forces in Saigon began the bombing of North Vietnam.[1]

Kosygin was going to Hanoi to warn Hanoi that the USA intended to use nuclear and atomic bombs (atomic weapons were landed at the Da Nang American base in March). He asked Hanoi to hand over to Russia the command of their land, sea and air forces in return for protection in the form of missiles. The North Vietnamese refused politely to "hand over" their sovereignty.

It was impossible in these circumstances to carry on the farce. Had it been successful, the Big Two, after a little byplay designed to frighten the world that a "nuclear showdown" was forthcoming, would "avert such a disaster" by "negotiating"

[1] February 1965. *See* files of *New York Times*, *Ta Kung Pao*, Hong Kong.

and deciding how to deal with the situation in Vietnam, *without* letting either the Hanoi government or the National Liberation Front in the South make their own decisions.

This would be evidence that only by recourse to the Big Two could any problem in the world be solved; every country would have become subject to their interference.

In 1966 the tragedy continued. The "reckless course pursued by the United States in South Vietnam bids well to bring the US into direct military confrontation with China" says Gittings.[1] "Russia has gone eighty-five per cent of the way to meet the US demands" said an English diplomat to me.[2]

The active help given by Russia in damping the fires of revolutionary militancy, is the result of this total collusion, no longer secret, but openly avowed by both. What personal motives or interests is the Russian leadership pursuing? A war involving America and China in mutual destruction might leave Russia sole master of the world.

The present military destruction of North Vietnam by US bombing[3] is to force a "suing for peace" which will—

1. Diminish the prestige of China, and prove to the restive peoples of the Third World that armed insurrection and national liberation movements cannot succeed.

2. Assure and consolidate a base in South-East Asia in order to keep the whole of South-East Asia in subjection, and its resources assured for American exploitation.

3. Assure an enormous base (with Cam Ranh bay port and others the largest ports in Asia) for men and materials in order to mount the projected grand offensive against China.

[1] Toronto Teach-in, October 1966, John Gittings.
[2] December 1966.
[3] In March 1967, a policy of "more bombing" and destruction of North Vietnam was openly proclaimed by President Johnson; *see New York Times* files, 10th February to 29th March, 1967.

4. Provide a breathing space and a time for reorganization and consolidation for the USA, whose finances are beginning to run into trouble and whose balance of payments has been at a deficit for a long period.

Can the US government, the Pentagon, trust the USSR leadership and the Russian military structure to take concerted action with her against China? Will the ever-growing talk of the partitioning of China between Russia and the USA succeed in making world opinion accept this move? Or will the USSR move its divisions into the northern areas of China under the pretext of coming to China's help?

Manpower shortage has all along been a prime American consideration in any war, and has now become urgent with the garrisoning of so many bases scattered round the world and the war in Vietnam. It is primarily because of this lack that some American experts fear over-extension and over-development of American forces over the globe, and therefore, recommend disengagement from ever more extensive enclaves on the Asian mainland, deeming it possible to pursue the containment of China from an island periphery; long-range missiles and bombers, they argue, would make swift attack on China, should she "move", ever more possible.[1]

But this hypothesis does not take into consideration the facts underlying the internal system of capitalist monopolies which want to assure themselves the resources of South-East Asia, nor the essence of the military-industrial complex, which is not reason or logic, but a drive towards war. The invocation of reason and logic ignores the compulsion to expansion and profits, which dictates the policies already

[1] The "containment" of China actually means stopping her industrial growth by a constant pressure and threat maintained upon her. The "partition" of China between the USA and the USSR is not phantasy; it has been openly discussed in many responsible journals and newspapers; the authors of such speculation being professors of history and political science.

responsible for two vast holocausts. It is this ever-increasing imperialism which *cannot* allow the nations of Asia, be it China today or India tomorrow, with their large manpower and their great resources to develop.

The consequences of nuclear weapon development upon political thinking and foreign policy in the West has been a devaluation of the human factor, an almost blind faith in the lethal machine and its genocidal capacities, and this has rendered the USA increasingly unable to evolve any new policies, or to generate ideas capable of restructuring the world. It seems very much simpler to use carpet bombing to liquidate resistance than to use reason or debate.

"As a result", says John Mendelsohn,[1] "every political problem has been immediately looked at as a strategic problem." No more inapposite hoax could be played on the people of the world than talking of "peaceful transition to socialism" when it was increasingly evident that even reform will now meet with suppressive violence. The finger is for ever on the trigger, and the bombers in perpetual motion above one's head.

Nuclear weapons have had another effect: they have brought into being a new class of adviser on foreign policy, the nuclear scientist, whose views outweigh those of the diplomat and the politician. The whole art of "policy" in the United States has become the imposition of might through terrorism, and Herman Kahn's nuclear rungs in this escalation of terror illustrated the kind of "bomb-think" which has taken the place of "human-think".

No country is accounted worth while, unless it has nuclear lethal capacity which alone guarantees national sovereignty and respect. Being feared is the passport to being heard. And this return to the most primitive barbarism has happened so

[1] John Mendelsohn M.P., Toronto University Teach-in, 14th–16th October, 1966.

quickly that few have had time to realize how much international relations have become nuclear terrorization.

The psychosis of racism, the hysteria of anticommunism, the "yellow peril" complex, derive their power to eliminate reason from the deep racial antagonism fostered by two centuries of Western domination. German Nazism was only an acute form of this disease.

Neither "ideology" nor the evolution which has happened to Russian communism makes for "peaceful" coexistence between the USA and the USSR, but the parity of nuclear power which makes absolute domination by one impossible *unless* a third emerges, who must either be eliminated, or wooed to become an ally of *one* or the *other*, in an endeavour to achieve supremacy. Within the impossibility of a war between the Big Two, the ever-growing production of America's military industrial complex, that is arms and weapons of all kinds, would lead to an effusion of strictly limited wars, almost everywhere, by tacit *entente*, in which the opportunity to waste arms and ammunition to a massive degree out of proportion to the targets aimed for is the *sine qua non* of increasing profits. This set of proxy wars, like gladiatorial combats in imperial Roman circuses would be quite "safe" provided the final settlement is left to the Big Two.

The fact that without help from Western powers, China has developed thermonuclear devices and also delivery by guided missiles poses an enormous challenge to the bipolar hegemony and its exploitation of fear to induce submission.

So much was the world conditioned to accept that *only two* super powers could have nuclear weapons that the test ban of 1963 was signed with enthusiasm; yet it never condemned *using* nuclear weapons, only *testing* them, and this should have been obvious to every head of State, but it was not.[1]

[1] Except to Charles de Gaulle of France, Norodom Sihanouk of Cambodia, and, of course, the Chinese.

China's strides to nuclear power represent today the most important political and military development of our time. The building of an operational intermediate ballistic missile, with a nuclear warhead, means that China has now surpassed both England and France in the field of nuclear missiles and must be regarded as the third nuclear power in the world.

China can now build H-bombs of an advanced type and use of enriched uranium 235 which implies stock-piling can progress much faster than expected. There is now talk of an intercontinental ballistic missile from China possibly within two years.

Though there is as yet no parity in the amount of stockpiling "unacceptable damage"[1] can be done to one or two cities of the USA should a nuclear attack be made on China. Talk of "denuclearizing" China by the nuclear bombing of her nuclear installations has now faded away; it is now realized that nuclear bombing is outplayed and outdated.

The logic of China's nuclear capacity is the same as the French *force de frappe*; if enough nuclear strength can be built up to neutralize, or render the possibility of nuclear damage to even one or two cities in America more than likely, then only conventional war can be waged against China, and a "threat" of nuclear war becomes ineffective. This means the end of "atomic diplomacy" and a "balance of terror".

In a conventional war, of course, the advantages to China are manifold, given the huge manpower and also the strategy of people's wars which now becomes a multi-dimensional and potent means of self-defence. Though undervalued by Western strategists, *because a people's war can only be defensive*, this is precisely what is required to break at last the cycle of aggression.

"Now is the time" says I. F. Stone, "to recall those occasions in the late fifties and sixties when China appealed to us

[1] *I. F. Stone's Weekly*, 7th November, 1966.

in vain for a nuclear-free Pacific, for a pledge that nuclear weapons would not be used against non-nuclear powers. . . ."[1] It is scarcely necessary to repeat that today, in the wake of China's missile, forty non-nuclear powers, at the UN, are asking precisely what China asked before, an assurance that nuclear weapons will not be used against countries with no nuclear weapons. This assurance was not given and the non-proliferation treaty is doomed before it has been even put into writing. India's suggestion that nuclear renunciation must be mutual, bespeaks a new courage arising out of frustration; and the bipolar hegemony dating from Yalta will be now the target of increasing challenge.

[1] *I. F. Stone's Weekly*, 7th and 14th November, 1966.

IX

CHINA AND THE WORLD—ONE
FAMILY UNDER HEAVEN

It is only forty-five years since the revolution of 1911, but the face of China today is completely changed. In another forty-five years, that is in the year 2001, China will have undergone even greater changes. She will have become a powerful, socialist, industrial country. And that is as it should be.

China . . . ought to have made a great contribution to humanity. Her contribution over a long period has been far too small. For this we are regretful. But we must be modest. Not only now, but forty-five years hence as well. In our international relations we Chinese people should get rid of great-power chauvinism, resolutely, thoroughly, wholly and completely.

We must never adopt an arrogant attitude of great-power chauvinism. Every nation, big or small, has its strong and weak points.

MAO TSE-TUNG, extracts,
September and November, 1956.

IN the ten years from 1955 to 1965, the conspicuous features of the non-affluent world, the two-thirds of humanity who emerged out of colonial bondage in 1945, are the disintegration of non-alignment, the disappearance of bourgeois democratic copies of parliamentary type left in place by European colonial powers in their withdrawal, the withering of many illusions nurtured and entertained about the intentions of the affluent towards the needy, the emergence of arbitrary right-wing repressive and dictatorial military warlords' régimes. Besides these political failures of "democracy", Western style, there is an even more tangible and more crucial economic deterioration, and a rising quota of upheavals, rioting and discontent. The steps of this swift and irrevocable disintegration, have been fully documented both by international organizations and many other economic studies—growing deficits in balances of payments, growing poverty, increasing hostility to imperialist (mostly American) financial penetration and military manifestations, even in the Philippines and Thailand. In very many of these countries, financial neo-colonialism has preceded or accompanied deliberately provoked *coups*, bringing to power rulers "favourable" to the United States. The backing of retrograde and repressive military rulers[1] has made a mock of pretensions to democracy and duplicates the state of China in the early twentieth century, when the West backed the most feudal and reactionary warlords, in the end destroying any chance of Western type of democracy implanting itself. The situation is paradoxical; the West is its own worst enemy; for it is not because of China's emergence that the unrest, upheavals and economic deterioration occur, but because of imperialism's continued policies of domination under the forms of financial stranglehold and military suppression practised in the name of "anti-communism". The disappearance of all forms of democratic structure, the loss of non-alignment, the growing ascendancy of extreme right-wing military satrapism, necessarily reliant upon USA subsidies for suppressive forces to quell the risings of their own peoples, the Balkanization of many countries, and the resurgence of tribalism, dismember and tear the Third World into a chaos which shakes and confuses. This fragmentation is greeted with joy by the "democracies", for the attendant weakness and disunity bring hopes for another "vampire gorging", as in China in the 1890s. The subservience and servility of many Western-oriented ruling *élites* in the Third World help this new colonial domination. In fact, the "comprador middleman" class, which Western capitalism established in China, is reproduced on a global scale.

[1] There have been sixty-eight *coups d'état*, mostly military, in the years since 1959.

In the decade since the Bandung Conference of 1955, hopes of an Afro-Asian solidarity of the poor against the rich have seemingly evaporated. The state of the Third World, in 1965, is much worse economically, than in 1945. Famine stalks the millions, but instead of putting the blame where it lies, on ever more oppressive exploitation, increase in population is blamed for all evils. Termed "population explosion", it is another in a long list of hypocrisies; for neither Africa nor Latin America are over-populated. Though population increase does mitigate against a swiftly rising standard of living, population control by itself will neither arrest, nor retard, nor indeed solve any of the economic problems of exploitation. Obsession with "the demographic factor" indicates the disquiet[1] at the power of world-wide people's wars against imperialism. As Fritz Baade points out, the world could sustain twenty times its present population were its resources well used.[2] In the "wealthiest" countries, such as South Africa, a vast majority live at substandard level, because the mineral wealth of the country is in the hands of a small racialist minority.

The so-called "failures" of Chinese foreign policies towards the Third World in the last five years have been a feature of the Western Press. In Indonesia, in Africa, the hostility of extreme right-wing ruling cliques, brought in by military *coups*, is held up as an example. Why does China no longer woo the "non-aligned" is the question asked. At one time China's "wooing of the non-aligned" was seen as a sinister move to be countered by the break-up of neutralism. This break-up has been accomplished; sixty-eight military *coups*, many openly engineered by Western agencies,[3] have

---

[1] Already present in 1898, with the "yellow peril" propaganda.
[2] FRITZ BAADE, *The Race to the Year 2000.*
[3] For the CIA's role in these *coups see* D. WISE and T. B. ROSS, *The Invisible Government.*

contributed to it; the failure is not China's; but of the Western type of democracy, and a vindication of Mao Tse-tung's thesis that "bourgeois-democratic rule" can no longer exist and is doomed, especially in the two-thirds of the needy world. That this destruction was accomplished by imperialism itself is not surprising. So it was in China. Therefore the way of armed struggle, with a two-stage national revolutionary process remains the only way which eventually all nations demanding true independence (both political and economic) will have to follow: the "road of Chingkang mountain". And it is being brought about by the very actions undertaken by the USA to "stamp out communism".

The only small country which can still afford neutralism is Cambodia, where the enlightened and intelligent ruler, Norodom Sihanouk, has maintained it by refusing US aid. The worst failure of non-alignment is India, where the words have become a sham, with two-thirds of India's currency in US hands and rising tides of militancy marking the onset of a pre-revolutionary decade. India, the most "aid"-prone country today (apart from Vietnam) demonstrates that there exists, at the moment, *no visible alternative to* the Chinese model.

The theme of "peaceful transition to socialism" is not only outdated but, to many Asians, suspect. For the question is not whether the people wish a peaceful transition to take place; but a transition is not acceptable to the ruling *élite*, nor to monopoly imperialism; as witness the *coups* and other efforts at manhandling situations and displacing governments who want to accomplish reforms—as in San Domingo. The apparatus of *armed* violent suppression used even against mild reformism, is the most convincing evidence that the Chinese thesis, "Imperialism will never lay down . . . its knife", may be valid. The self-given right which the US President enjoys to interfere *anywhere* in the world where necessary "for American interests" and "the defence of the free world", this is the picture of which the "small nations" are becoming uneasily aware. The growing restiveness and discontent, even of American-dependent régimes, at the detrimental effects of American financial monopoly upon national economies, is evident even in the Philippines. US demands for political and financial compliance from ruling groups in the Third World grow heavier as the pressures of the armaments race grows. With the new programme for anti-missile missiles begins a new spiral of military costs;[1] but this will in no way obviate the danger of long, protracted guerrilla wars on a global scale, for which manpower is the chief requirement. Hence the search for manpower (USA's greatest shortage) to prosecute wars will lead to the "purchase" of this commodity on an increasingly larger scale from subservient satellites. Loans to the needy countries[2] will be conditioned by these strategic viewpoints and plans and blueprints for economic rehabilitation or help in industrial or agricultural self-reliance will remain ineffective.

The word "aid", already defined by Kennedy as "the defence of the frontiers of the free world", has had its meaning exploded as it becomes increasingly obvious to the "free world" that it is subsidy to American business, that its primary function is to guarantee export monopoly capital against loss by nationalization or other untoward events in the restive needy nations. The channelling and orientation of expenditure into the military budget in the USA (at present US $70 billion out of a total of US $140 billion) is out of proportion to the total expansion of the economy; another US $30 billion at least will be costed for the nation-wide anti-missile missile system, and this expense is "but the

[1] JOSEPH ALSOP, "A Matter of Fact" *Hong Kong Standard*, 1st January, 1967.
[2] The international aspect of such loans does not change their essential nature, which is to protect Big Business against loss.

bare beginning of the problem".[1] The rapid attrition of resources in the USA itself forces the search for resources elsewhere, *increases* the pressure for increasing militarization to make other areas "safe for democracy", and produces a pattern of the harshest military colonialism; with bases and garrisons to be manned all over the world *and also in space*.

Because of the growing "instability" in the Third World, in spite of suppressive actions, there is an increasing tendency for the movement of private capital between the industrialized countries themselves, especially for manufactures. The amounts going to the needy two-thirds therefore concentrate mainly on obtaining monopoly of extractive industries (minerals, copper, uranium, gold, and oil). The countries which pursue "aid" or "foreign investment" as a source of foreign exchange for their development, find the going increasingly harder and will be obliged to offer more and more "favourable terms" directly and obviously detrimental to their own national interests.

The deterioration of the internal markets and trade outlets of needy countries is also evident in the increasing export of commodities by the affluent to the non-affluent, whose native industries cannot be protected by barriers without being black-listed as "unfriendly" and "pro-communist" and who find it difficult to obtain loans or credits from "international" organizations unless their policies become "more liberal". The imports of food from the USA to such "agricultural countries" as India testifies to the serious stagnation of agriculture which has occurred in the last twenty years; the needy are waking up to this fact, only to find that a monopoly of chemical fertilizer industries, essential for increased yields, is also in foreign hands.

The result of war abroad, in this case the war in Vietnam, has resulted in a cutting down in welfare and benefit

[1] J. ALSOP, op. cit.

plans within America itself; a sharpening of division between rich and poor, with the poor, in this instance, also belonging to a particular ethnic group, the Negro. The problems of American cities, which in the next twenty years will become vast ghettoes for the Negro, are alarming. But the war in Vietnam takes precedence over urgent internal needs. The resulting serious financial problems have been amply discussed in a wide range of American publications.

The focus and catalyst, single example of this acute and rising tide of revolt, precursor of changes to come, is, therefore, the war in Vietnam. The spectacle of the largest country in the world, the richest, and the most formidably armed, bogged down in an endless war by a poor, "undeveloped", non-industrialized but valiant people living in a sliver of territory one-twenty-sixth the size of the USA is a profound lesson to Asians and Africans. The massive tonnage of bombs dropped upon the northern part of Vietnam without effect (90,000 tons per month) and the overall insanity of a policy which pretends to pursue "peace" by bombing is having its effect in every country. Americans themselves, such as Walter Lippmann, see the folly of this war. "The US for all its wealth and military power, and all its ideological pretensions is unable to conduct a global crusade for its way of life and its favourite doctrines.... The weak and poor people of the earth have found a response to our wealth and our weapons ... they can subsist when the rich would starve, fight with simple weapons against the great and sophisticated weapons, and they are hard to conquer because so many of them are ready to die. The old military superiority of the Western world does not find it easy to cope with the guerrilla.... This great country now has problems of its own which it cannot ... except at grave risk, merely tinker with any longer...."[1]

[1] WALTER LIPPMANN, Newsweek, 1st August, 1966.

As a once needy, impoverished, chaotic nation, emergent from the world of the exploited into great-power status, China has been a success in the eyes of the Asians and Africans who have waited, very long, for "machines to drop from heaven" and instead find themselves returning rapidly to colonial dependence and submission.

No matter how unpalatable the hard, tough road that China has taken, however strange and disturbing the long, gruelling work and the ideological demands China appeals to the two-thirds of humanity who see no hope in the West, and who today echo the Chinese students of 1919; "No sun will rise in the West for us." In spite of setbacks, in spite of errors and shortcomings, and the fabrications and distortions of the Western Press, it is China's drive, her stubborn achievement and the amazing pace of her progress, which fill every Asian and African with emotion and pride. "The Chinese people have stood up." Even if it arouses fear among the Western-orientated *élites*, whose education in the West often alienates them from the true interests of their own people, it is China's success which is exalting and convincing many millions of other Asians, disgusted with servility and subordination, corruption and inadequacy.

The most impressive feature of the Chinese way, because the most dramatic, is the development of nuclear power, although the synthesis of insulin is actually a better indicator of the advanced international standards reached and on the point of being surpassed by Chinese science. The manufacture of atomic devices entirely indigenous to China and the obvious disarray of both the USA and USSR confronted with China's new power is not lost upon the rest of the world; a host of new relations of strength have already sprung into being, and the next decade will see an ever-accelerated change in the emergence of these new line-ups. China's interpretation of world trends is already vindicated, for it is almost impossible to visualize, on the part of the USA, the drastic and thorough revolution in thinking and behaviour necessary to halt the Pentagon and the military-industrial complex in their conviction that they can bomb and slaughter their way to power and dominion in Asia.

Should, however, an ever-increasing scale of bombing be successful in bringing North Vietnam to its knees (which is doubtful), it will be because of the pressures exerted by the USSR and will constitute a permanent partition of Vietnam, the South as an American base, the North as a Russian one. A period of uneasy cold war will ensue, but the categorical imperatives of military power will again make themselves felt in a renewed drive, for the world will not stay still. At the present moment the prospects are not towards a lull but towards an extension of the escalation, with ever more deployment of forces. Both in Thailand and in Laos other active military fronts, already sucking up their quota of manpower, are contriving the spread-eagling of American power into a meaningless quagmire of guerrilla war. In either case, hot war or cold, and whether China is attacked and fights the "war without boundaries" announced by Chou En-lai, it is quite impossible for America to win a war in Asia. Will the USSR then actively help imperialism in making war on China? But this, too, is highly dangerous; for in East Europe things are moving: Germany's renewed and nuclear-armed Nazism, will, sooner or later, demand reunification under a Nazi hyper-nationalist government. In Europe de Gaulle stands as leader of a new "neutralism" appealing to many Europeans. The breakup of NATO is a reflection of this new pattern. In the perspectives of the next decades, the retrogression of ideas that has occurred in the USA and the USSR has had the effect of resurrecting latent petty-national and chauvinist demeanours and demands in European states not least in the East European ones.

The Chinese thesis that the present situation is fraught with "revolutionary prospects" bears serious thought. China's challenge and defiance of the super-power complex and her attainment of nuclear status has broken the atomic blackmail. Militant struggles stalled by the "peaceful transition" placebos are in the ascendancy. The prospects before us are, therefore, violent ones.

The United Front

The period 1955 to 1962 can also be seen as that in which China actually sought a medium and a means of solving the problem of Taiwan—obstacle to any solution of the Sino-American situation—as peacefully as possible.

Between 1958 and 1962 she became aware that not one, but two enemies confronted her and were opposed to her emergence as a great modern socialist State.

From 1962 (the Cuba farce) to 1965, the increasing conviction that America's military escalation in South-East Asia would eventually lead to war with China made her adopt a policy which some have qualified of "verbally inflammatory, though actually restrained and prudent."

The Vietnam War, on her doorstep, coming so soon after Laos Conference agreements of 1961-2 was a direct provocation to China as well as a violation of the accords concluded at Geneva in 1954 and 1962. Yet the Chinese were prudent and cautious, and, as Chou pointed out, "would in no way provoke or attack the USA". The onus of aggression would be very clearly upon the USA alone.

Some time at the end of 1965 (September 1965—January 1966) in the series of top-level debates in Peking, which led to the great Proletarian Cultural Revolution, there must also have been a thorough summarization of foreign relations and the evolving of a more militant, internationalist line. Robert

Guillain, the distinguished and perceptive French correspondent of *Le Monde*, also reported this in his articles: "La Chine accepte le combat".[1]

It was then that China decided to challenge the USA and the USSR to do their worst and to support Vietnam to the fullest extent. In September 1965, Lin Piao's article on revolutionary people's war appeared; in November the Cultural Revolution was already beginning. Since then China has done more: she has declared herself ready "for the greatest national sacrifice", declared the thought of Mao Tse-tung the guide to world revolutionary action "the crystallization of experience" of revolution and the "acme of Marxism-Leninism" in the period of world revolution; declared there is no other way out for the exploited than China's way, the way of armed struggle, "the road of Chingkang mountain". She has prepared the entire Chinese population for long, protracted war, of any kind, to last for decades if necessary; she has refused any underhand deals or bargains at the expense of the exploited and denounced the USSR revisionist leadership and its collusion with US imperialism. The Cultural Revolution is designed to *obviate the possibility that any sell-out of* the cause of revolution should happen. She has called for the largest possible united front of all those who oppose US imperialism.

It is again paradoxical that, far from "turning in" and being "isolated" as Western propaganda strenuously avers, never has China been *less* nationalist and *more* internationalist than today, less preoccupied with what Mao Tse-tung calls "pots and pans", that is with her material achievements and more with the revolutionary duty of becoming "the staunch, reliable Red base" of a world revolutionary movement. "If any country in Asia, Africa or elsewhere meets with aggression by the United States, China will give support and help, and

[1] Robert Guillain, *Le Monde*, 2nd and 3rd August, 1966.

should such action bring on aggression against China, we shall rise in resistance and fight to the finish." "China is prepared. Once the war breaks out it will have no boundaries."[1]

In this preparation for fulfilling "international proletarianism", Mao has called upon the Chinese people to "carry the heaviest burden", and to be prepared for the worst. The "triple alliance" of Red Guards, workers and peasants, which is being evolved through the Cultural Revolution, is part of this preparation for a war to last "generation after generation".

One thing we may be sure of: China's way will not be Russia's way. There will be no compromise, no deals. The course set by Mao today will be the course followed for the twenty years to come.

[1] Chou En-lai, as reported by A. L. Strong in Letter—No. 39, 4th June, 1966.

X

CONCLUSION

IN the time from now to 2001, a great revolt looms; there is no neutralism, no middle of the road left; all humanity will be involved to varying degrees, on one side or the other.

The touchstone, dividing line, watershed between the new epoch and the old has begun in Vietnam.

Historians of the future may write that the Third World War began in February 1965 with the bombing of North Vietnam by the USA.

China is *already* a great power, and whether the next three decades will be a cold or a hot war, nothing can stop her now. By the year 2001 she will be a powerful industrial socialist State.

But what kind of a State will she be? What kind of morality will she practise?

This question is being resolved now, strenuously, painfully, through the Great Cultural Revolution. The remaking of man is being attempted for one-quarter of the world.

It will be impossible for man to fulfil himself, to become more human, if in fear and servility he accepts that Might decides his fate; if he does not challenge brute power; if he does not put his own *personal* or *national* considerations aside and work for the good of the whole. It is Mao Tse-tung who has seen the problem in its universal terms, the Remaking of Man.

Those who see in Mao a "return to Confucius..." and in Chinese aims a "return to imperial China" usually point to the theme of China as the fount of wisdom, the great teacher of mankind and the "centre of the world" as if these themes were in essence a return to the past. And in a way it is true that the emphasis on moral education is in the Chinese tradition.

But it is the lapse of others, which has propelled China today into shouldering the responsibility of revolution. China has also emphasized that the other nations of the world must themselves liberate themselves; this can only come through their own armed struggle, for freedom is only won by those who are ready to fight for it, it cannot be bestowed by anyone as a favour. Nor can any other nation, however great and powerful, do it for them.

Here we also touch upon the problem of the evolution of mankind itself. For, in the final analysis, it is the drama of man upon earth which we see enacted today in China, in the world of the needy; it is mankind's maturing, across and through the cultures he builds, the systems he evolves, the classes he generates, and the ideas and actions engendered by his social being, the machines with which he builds and destroys himself; it is man trying to break the slaveries of the past and to build a better future, who today, painfully, must make his choice.

The process of the humanization of man is the one which resists brutality and animality, depersonalization and the return to barbarism.

It is this process which Mao refers to when he says (with those who have been most deeply conscious of the humanization of man): "Humanity is still in its infancy . . ." and when he refers to the destiny of the Chinese people as "bringing a much greater contribution to humanity . . . than they have so far".

This contribution, today, means accepting the challenge that a supremacy of weapons cannot decide Man's fate but that Ideas and Man are more important than the Nuclear Bomb.

The decades before us are momentous. The empires of yesterday have gone, and those of today are bringing about their own downfall. For some time yet, what is already evident will be strenuously denied; but already the future has entered our present. The year 2001 has begun, in China, today.

SELECT BIBLIOGRAPHY

ABEND, HALLETT, *Pacific Charter. Our Destiny in Asia* (New York, 1943).

ADAMS, RUTH (Ed.), *Contemporary China* (1966).

ADLER, SOL, *The Chinese Economy* (N.Y. Monthly Review Press, 1957).

ALLEN and DONNITHORNE, *Western Enterprise in Far Eastern Economic Development* (London, Allen & Unwin, 1954).

ALLEY, REWI, Complete Works.

ALPEROVITZ, GAR, *Atomic Diplomacy—Hiroshima and Potsdam* (London, Secker & Warburg, 1965).

BAADE, FRITZ, *The Race to the Year 2000* (1961).

BABY, JEAN, *La grande controverse sino-soviétique* (Grasset, 1965).

BARNETT, A. DOAK, *China on the Eve of Communist Takeover* (Thames & Hudson, 1964).

BARRACLOUGH, G., *An Introduction to Contemporary History* (London, The New Thinker's Library, Watts, 1964, 1966).

BELFRAGE, CEDRIC, *The Man at the Door with the Gun* (Monthly Review Press, 1964).

BETTELHEIM, CHARLES, *La Construction du Socialisme en Chine* (Edited by F. Maspero) (1962).

BLUM, ROBERT, *The United States and China in World Affairs* (Edited by A. Doak Barnett).

BOORMAN, HOWARD L. and ECKSTEIN, ALEXANDER, *et al.*, *Moscow-Peking Axis. Strength and Strains* (N.Y., 1957).

BOTTOMORE, T. B., *Elites and Society* (London, The New Thinker's Library, Watts, 1964).

BOWIE, ROBERT R., and FAIRBANK, J. K., *Communist China 1955–59 Policy Documents* (Cambridge, Mass., Harvard U.P., 1962).

BRANDT, C., SCHWARTZ, B. and FAIRBANK, J. K., *A Documentary History of Chinese Communism* (Cambridge, Mass., Harvard U.P., 1952, 1966).

BUCHANAN, K., *The Chinese People and the Chinese Earth*.

BUCHANAN, K., "The Changing Face of Rural China", *Pacific Viewpoint*, March 1960.

BUCHANAN, K., "West Wind, East Wind", *New Zealand Geographer*, October 1961.

CHAO, KUO-CHUN, *Economic Planning and Organization in Mainland China—A Documentary Study (1949–1957)* (Cambridge, Mass., Harvard U.P., 1959).

CHEN, JEROME, *Mao Tse-tung and the Chinese Revolution* (London and N.Y., 1965).

CHEN, PO-TA, *Notes on Ten Years of Civil War* (Chinese version, Peking).

CHEN, PO-TA, *Mao Tse-tung on the Chinese Revolution* (Chinese version, Peking).

CHEN, PO-TA, *Notes on Mao Tse-tung's "Report on an Investigation of the Peasant Movement in Hunan"* (Chinese and English version, Peking).

CHEN, PO-TA, *A Study of Land Rent in Preliberation China—Socialist Industrialization and Agricultural Collectivization in China* (Chinese edition, 1955).

CHENG, YEN-SHIH, *Lenin's Fight against Revisionism and Opportunism* (1965).

CHEVENY, JULIAN, *Éloge du colonialisme* (Juillard 1961).

CHI CHAO-TING, *Key Economic Areas in Chinese History* (Paragon Book Reprint Corporation, 1963).

CHOU EN-LAI, *Political Report*, 30th January, 1956.

CHOW TSE-TUNG, *The May 4th Movement* (Cambridge, Mass., 1960).

CLUBB, O. EDMUND, *Twentieth Century China* (Columbia U.P. N.Y., 1964).

COMPTON, BOYD, *Mao's China—Party Reform Documents 1942–44* (University of Washington Paperback, Seattle, 1966).

COOK, FRED. *The Warfare State* (Cape, 1963).

CROOK, DAVID, and ISABEL, *The First Years of Yangyi Commune* (Routledge & Kegan Paul, 1965).

CROOK, DAVID and ISABEL, *Revolution in a Chinese Village: Ten Mile Inn* (Routledge & Kegan Paul, 1959).

DEUTSCHER, ISAAC, *Stalin* (O.U.P., 1949).

DJILAS, M., *The New Class* (London, Thames & Hudson, 1967).

DUMONT, RENÉ, *La Chine surpeuplée, tiers monde affamé* (1966).

DUMONT, RENÉ, *Révolution dans les campagnes chinoises* (Paris, 1957).

ECKSTEIN, ALEXANDER, *Communist China's Economic Growth and Foreign Trade* (N.Y., McGraw Hill, 1966).

ECKSTEIN, ALEXANDER, *The National Income of Communist China* (N.Y., Free Press of Glencoe, 1961).

ECKSTEIN, ALEXANDER, *Communist China's Economic Development*.

EPSTEIN, I., *The Unfinished Revolution in China* (Boston, Little Brown, 1947).

ÉTIENNE, GILBERT, *La voie chinoise* (Presses Universitaires de France, 1962).

FAIRBANK, J. K., *The U.S. and China* (Cambridge, Mass., Harvard U.P., 1962).

FAN HSIU-CHU, *A Struggle between two Lines over the Question of How to deal with U.S. Imperialism* (1965).

FEIS, HERBERT, *The China Tangle* (Princeton, 1953).

FITZGERALD, C. P., *The Chinese View of their Place in the World* (O.U.P., 1964).

FITZGERALD, C. P., *The Birth of Communist China*.

FORMAN, HARRISON, *Report from Red China* (London, 1946).

FULBRIGHT, J. WILLIAM, *Old Myths and New Realities* (Cape, 1965).

GALBRAITH, JOHN KENNETH, *The Affluent Society* (Hamish Hamilton, 1958).

GRANET, MARCEL, *La pensée chinoise* (Paris, 1934).

GREENE, FELIX, *A Curtain of Ignorance* (London, Cape, 1965).

GREENE, FELIX, *The Wall has Two Sides* (London, Cape, 1963).

GUILLAIN, ROBERT, *Dans trente ans la Chine* (1965).

GUNAWARDHANA, THEJA, *Krushchevism* (private printing, 1963).

HALPERIN, MORTON, *Is China Turning In?* (Harvard University Center for International Affairs).

HALPERN, A. M. (Ed.), *Policies Towards China: Views from Six Continents* (McGraw Hill, 1966).

HAMM, HARRY, *China. The Empire of the 700 Million* (1965).

252   CHINA IN THE YEAR 2001

HARVARD UNIVERSITY CENTER FOR INTERNATIONAL AFFAIRS AND EAST ASIAN RESEARCH CENTER, *Communist China 1955-1959—Policy Documents with Analysis* (Harvard U.P.).

HAUSER, ALVIN, and PAUL SWEEZEY, *The Postwar American Economy* (1964).

HINTON, HAROLD, C., *Communist China in World Politics.*

HINTON, WILLIAM, *Fanshen* (Monthly Review Press, 1966).

HINTON, WILLIAM, Forum on the Great Proletarian Cultural Revolution (New York, March 1967).

HO, PING-TI, *Studies on the Population of China 1368-1953* (Cambridge, Mass., 1959).

HOBSBAWM, E. H., *The Age of Revolution 1789-1848* (London, Weidenfeld & Nicolson, 1962).

HSIEH, A. L., *Communist China's Strategy in the Nuclear Era* (Santa Monica, Rand Corporation, 1962).

HU, HWA, *History of China's New Democratic Revolution* (in Chinese) (Peking, 1953).

HU, SHENG, *Imperialism and Chinese Politics* (Peking, 1955).

HUGHES, T. J. and LUARD, D. B. T., *Economic Development of Communist China, 1949-1958* (London, O.U.P., 1959).

HUNT, CAREW, R. N., *The Theory and Practice of Communism.*

ISRAEL, JOHN, *Student Nationalism in China (1927-1937)* (Stanford U.P., 1966).

JELLINEK, F., *The Paris Commune of 1871* (N.Y., Universal Library, 1965).

JEN, YU-TI, *Géographie de la Chine.*

KAROL, K. S., *La Chine de Mao* (Paris, Robert Laffont, 1966).

KUAN, TA-TUNG, *The Socialist Transformation of Capitalist Industry and Commerce in China* (1964).

KUO, MO-JO, *Culture and Education in New China* (Chinese version, 1950).

KUO, PING-CHIA, *China: New Age and New Outlook* (Penguin, 1964).

LATOURETTE, K., *History of China* (London, Macmillan, 1934).

LATOURETTE, K., *The History of Early Relations between the United States and China, 1784-1844* (N.Y., 1964).

LATTIMORE, OWEN, *Collected Papers 1928-1958* (London, 1962).

LEWIS, JOHN W., *Major Doctrines of Communist China* (N.Y., 1964).

LEWIS, JOHN W., "Leadership in Communist China", in *Policies Towards China—Views from Six Continents* (Edited by A. M. Halpern) (McGraw Hill, 1966).

LIANG, FANG-CHUNG, *The Single-Whip Method of Taxation in China* (Harvard U.P., 1956).

LIAO, YU YEN, *Collectivization in China* (1964).

LI, CHIEH-JEN, *The Works of* (in Chinese). Historical novels on modern China.

LI CHOH-MING, *Economic Development of Communist China—An Appraisal of the First Five Years of Industrialization* (University of California Press, 1959).

LIN, PIAO, *Long Live the Victory of People's War* (September 1965) (Chinese, English and French versions).

LIU, CHUN, *The National Question and Class Struggle* (1966).

MAGDOFF, HARRY, "Economic aspects of U.S. Imperialism", *Monthly Review*, November 1966.

MAO, TSE-TUNG, *Selected Works* (4 Vols.; Chinese and English versions, 1962, 63, 64).

MAO, TSE-TUNG, *Selected Military Writings* (Peking, Foreign Language Press, 1963).

MAO, TSE-TUNG, *The Chinese Revolution and the Chinese Communist Party* (Chinese Edition).

MAO, TSE-TUNG, *Socialist Upsurge in Chinese Countryside* (Chinese original, 1955).

MAO, TSE-TUNG, *On the Correct Handling of Contradictions among the People* (Chinese and English versions 1957, 62, 64).

MAO TSE-TUNG, *Statement Opposing Aggression against Southern Vietnam and Slaughter of its People by the U.S. Ngo Dinh Diem Clique* (Foreign Language Press, 1963).

MAO, TSE-TUNG, *Statement Calling on the People of the World to Unite, to oppose racial discrimination by US Imperialism and Support the American Negroes in their Struggle against Racial Discrimination* (Foreign Language Press, 1964).

MAO, TSE-TUNG, *Statement Expressing the Chinese People's Firm Support for the Panamanian People's Just, Patriotic Struggle* (Foreign Language Press, 1964).

MAO, TSE-TUNG, *Talks at the Yenan Forum on Literature and Art* (1950, 1956, 1962 and other editions in Chinese, French and English versions).

MAO-TSE-TUNG, *Statements by Mao Tse-tung Calling on the People of the World to Unite to Oppose the Aggressive and Bellicose Policies of U.S. Imperialism and Defend World Peace* (1964).

MASPERO, FRANÇOIS, *Le pillage du tiers monde* (Cahiers Libres 68).

MEHNERT, KLAUS, *Peking and Moscow* (Putnam).

MENDE, TIBOR, *Regards sur l'histoire de demain* (1954).

MONNEROT, JULES, *Sociology and Communism*.

MYRDAL, JAN, *Report from a Chinese Village* (Heinemann, 1965).

NEEDHAM, J., *Science and Civilization in China* (C.U.P., Vols. I, II, III, IV (1 and 2)).

NOVE, ALEC, *Collectivization of Agriculture in Russia and China* (1961).

PA, CHING, *The Works of* (in Chinese).

PO, I-PO, *Socialist Industrialization and Agricultural Collectivization in China* (1964).

PRESSES UNIVERSITAIRES DE FRANCE, *Économique appliquée* (1963).

PRIESTLEY, J. B., *Literature and Western Man* (London, Heinemann, 1960).

ROBINSON, JOAN, *Notes from China* (Oxford, 1964).

ROSINGER, LAWRENCE, K., *China's Crisis* (N.Y., Knopf, 1945).

ROSTOW, W. W., *The Prospects for Communist China* (M. I. T. Technological Press, 1955).

ROWE, DAVID NELSON, *Modern China. A Brief History* (Princeton, 1959).

RUEFF, JACQUES, *Le lancinant problème de la balance des paiements* (Payot, Paris).

RUEFF, JACQUES, *L'age de l'inflation* (Payot, Paris).

RUSSELL, BERTRAND, *Power—A New Social Analysis* (London, Allen & Unwin, 1938).

RUSSELL, BERTRAND, *Freedom and Organization 1814–1914* (London, Allen & Unwin, 1949).

RUSSELL, BERTRAND, *The Problem of China* (London, Allen & Unwin, 1965).

SAWYER, C. A., *Communist Trade with Developing Countries 1955–1965.*

SCHEER, ROBERT, *How the United States got involved in Vietnam* (1965).

SCHRAM, S., *The Political Thought of Mao Tse-tung* (London, Pall Mall Press, 1964).

SCHURMANN, FRANZ, *Ideology and Organization in Communist China* (Berkeley, 1966).

SCHURMANN, FRANZ, *The Politics of Escalation in Vietnam* (Fawcett Press, 1966).

SCHWARTZ, HARRY, *Tsars, Mandarins and Commissars* (London, Gollancz, 1964).

SEWELL, WILLIAM, G., *I Stayed in China* (London, Allen & Unwin Ltd., 1966).

SMITH, CORDELL A., *The Marshall Mission to China.*

SNOW, C. P., *The Two Cultures* (C.U.P., 1959).

SNOW, EDGAR, *The Other Side of the River* (London, Gollancz, 1963).

SNOW, EDGAR, *Journey to the Beginning* (London, Gollancz, 1959).

SNOW, EDGAR, *People on our Side* (N.Y., 1944).

SNOW, EDGAR, *Battle for Asia* (Cleveland, 1942).

SNOW, EDGAR, *Red Star over China* (French ed. reprint, 1964, London, 1938).

SNOW, EDGAR, *Scorched Earth* (Vols. I and II).

SOROKIN, P. A., *Russia and the United States* (Steven & Sons Ltd., London, 1950).

STEELE, A. T., *The American People and China* (McGraw-Hill, 1965).

STRONG, ANNA LOUISE, *China's Millions* (N.Y., 1928).

STRONG, ANNA LOUISE, *The Rise of the Chinese People's Communes— and Six Years After* (New World Press, Peking, 1964).

STRONG, ANNA LOUISE, *Revolution in China* (1928).

STRONG, ANNA LOUISE, *Letters from Peking* (Complete collection).

STRONG, ANNA LOUISE, *The Chinese Conquer China* (New York).

TAYLOR, CHARLES, *Reporter in Red China* (1966).

TENG, SSU-YU and FAIRBANK, J. K., *China's Response to the West* (Harvard U.P., 1954).

TONG, TE-KONG, *United States Diplomacy in China, 1844–60* (University of Washington Press, Seattle, 1964).

TRAVERT, ANDRÉ, *The Attitude of the Communist Party towards China's Cultural Legacy* (Reprint Chapter 13(b)).

TREGEAR, T. R., *A Geography of China* (London, U.L.P., 1965).

TSOU, TANG, *America's Failure in China (1941–50)* (Chicago U.P., 1963).

TUNG, TA-LIN, *Agricultural Co-operation in China* (1965).

WALKER, KENNETH, R., *Planning in Chinese Agriculture, Socialization and the Private Sector, 1952–1962* (London, 1965).

WALTON, LORD, *Agriculture under Communism*.

WARD, MARION W., "Recent Population Growth and Economic Development in Asia", *Pacific Viewpoint* (1964).

WEALE, PUTNAM, *Why China sees Red* (1927).

WEALE, PUTNAM, *Japan and China* (1927).

WHITE, T. H. and JACOBY, A. L., *Thunder out of China*.

WILSON, DICK, *A Quarter of Mankind—Anatomy of China Today* (London, Weidenfeld & Nicolson, 1966).

WILSON, J. TUZO, *One Chinese Moon* (Hill & Wang, 1959, New York).

WISE, DAVID and ROSS, THOMAS B., *The Invisible Government* (London, Cape, 1965).

YANG, C. K., *A Chinese Village in Early Communist Transition* (Cambridge, Mass., Harvard U.P., 1965).

YIN, HELEN and YI, CHANG-YIN, *Economic Statistics of Mainland China (1949–1957)* (Harvard U.P.).

YUAN, LI-WU, *The Economy of Communist China. An Introduction* (Praeger, 1965).

PEKING PUBLICATIONS

A Struggle between two Lines over the Question of How to Deal with U.S. Imperialism (1965), FAN HSIU-CHU.

Long Live the Victory of People's War! (1965), LIN PIAO.

Vive la victorieuse guerre de peuple! (1965), LIN PIAO.

The Socialist Transformation of Capitalist Industry and Commerce In China, KUAN TA-TUNG.

The National Question and Class Struggle (1966), LIU CHUN.

Political work: The lifeline of all work (Foreign Language Press, 1966).

Agrarian Reform Law—1950 (Chinese original).

Agrarian Reform Law of People's Republic, 1950, 1953, 1959 editions.

The First Five-year Plan (published 1956).

Critical History of New Democratic Stage (Chinese Original, 1955).

Land Reform in North-western Region of China (Chinese original, January 1951).

The origin and development of the differences between the leadership of the CPSU and ourselves (1963).

Confessions Concerning the Line of Soviet-U.S. Collaboration Pursued by the New Leaders of the CPSU ("Red Flag" Policy Review No. 8, 1966).

The Leaders of the CPSU are Betrayers of the Declaration and the Statement ("Peoples Daily" and other publications).

Carry the struggle against Khruschev revisionism through to the end ("Peoples Daily", "Red Flag", 1965).

The Great Socialist Cultural Revolution in China Nos. 1, 2, 3, 4, 5 and 6 (1966).

The Historical Experience of the War against Fascism (1965).

On the Question of Stalin (1963).

Co-operative Farming in China.

Decisions on Agricultural Co-operation.

Some Questions concerning Modern Revisionist Literature in the Soviet Union.

Vice Premier Chen Yi answers Questions put by Correspondents (1965).

The Brilliance of Mao Tse-tung's Thought Illuminates the Whole World (1965).

Report on Adjusting Major Targets of the 1959 National Economic Plan and Further Developing the Campaign for Increasing Production and Practising Economy (1959).

Main Documents of the First Session of the Third National People's Congress of the Peoples Republic of China (1965).

On the Question of Stalin, Comment on the Open Letter of the Central Committee of the CSPU (1963).

Training Successors for the Revolution is the Party's Strategic Task (1965).

Le pseudo communisme de Krouchtchev et les leçons historiques qu'il donne au monde (1964).

La Yougoslavie est-elle un pays socialiste? ("Peoples Daily" and "Red Flag", 1963).

Des défenseurs du néo-colonialisme (1963).

Deux lignes différents dans la question de la guerre et de la paix (1963).

Deux politiques de coexistence pacifique diametralément opposées (1963).

L'aveu par la nouvelle direction du PCUS de sa politique de cooperation soviéto-américaine ("Red Flag", 1966).

La révolution prolétarienne et le révisionisme de Krouchtchev (1964).

Pour la fin du monopole nucléaire, pour la destruction des armes nucléaires! (1965) "Peoples Daily" editorial.

Les dirigeants de PCUS—les plus grands scissionistes de notre temps (1964).

Dix-sept médecins belges en Chine, mémoires de l'institut de recherches et de documentation No. 3.

Proposals of Eighth National Congress of CPC for Second Five Year Plan, HSINHUA, 1956.

Second Session of the Eighth National Congress of the Communist Party of China.

Sixth Plenary Session of the Eighth Central Committee of the Communist Party of China.

University of Hong Kong, Golden Jubilee Congress, Sept. 11th–16th, 1961.

Speeches by Chen Yi at Afro-Asian Writers' Emergency Meeting, 1966.

PERIODICALS

Asian Survey.

Asian International Trade Fair (*Supplement*) *of FEER*, 10th November, 1966.

China Quarterly.

The Far Eastern Economic Review, Hong Kong.

Far East Trade and Development (London).

Minority of One, New Jersey.

Monthly Review, New York.

Red Flag, Peking.

U.S. News and World Report.
Wall Street Journal.
Ta Kung Pao, Hong Kong.
Jen Min Jih Pao, Peking.
Peking Review, Peking.
Kwang ming Daily, Peking.

INTERVIEWS, LETTERS, PRIVATE PAPERS, ETC.

INDEX